ISLAND MILITIA WOMEN

Island Militia Women

Li Ju-ching

FOREIGN LANGUAGES PRESS PEKING

1975

First edition   1975

Illustrations by

TSAI JUNG

Printed in the People's Republic of China

CONTENTS

Chapter 1
ON THE TRAIN   1

Chapter 2
FATHER AND I   9

Chapter 3
THE SECRET OF THE STEELYARD   14

Chapter 4
WHY SEA-GULLS' WINGS ARE WHITE   26

Chapter 5
FISHERMEN'S FAMILIES   33

Chapter 6
A TUB OF RICE, A BUCKET OF WATER   43

Chapter 7
PLATOON LEADER FANG'S STORY   54

Chapter 8
STORM IN A RICE BOWL   64

Chapter 9
A CLEAR HEAD FOR SEEING CLEARLY   76

Chapter 10
THE WRITTEN MESSAGE   90

Chapter 11
THE RIBBON OF ROAD ROUND THE ISLAND   102

Chapter 12
AFTER THE GUNS WERE DISTRIBUTED   110

Chapter 13
SELF-CRITICISM   120

Chapter 14
MOTHERLAND AND MOTHER   128

Chapter 15
SINGING ON THE SLOPE
135

Chapter 16
A MAN AND WIFE
142

Chapter 17
SPRING FESTIVAL
149

Chapter 18
CONFLICTING VIEWS
155

Chapter 19
THE ONE-LEGGED VISITOR
168

Chapter 20
THE ACCIDENT
174

Chapter 21
A STORM IS COMING
184

Chapter 22
A TEAR IN THE MESH
191

Chapter 23
A WIDER VISION
200

Chapter 24
SURPRISE ATTACK
208

Chapter 25
GOOD NEWS FROM THE SEA
215

Chapter 26
TWO GENERATIONS
225

Chapter 27
RIDING ON THE CREST OF THE WAVES
238

Chapter 28
THE ENCOUNTER
245

Chapter 29
STRANGE SIGNALS
257

Chapter 30
AT CLOSE QUARTERS
262

Chapter 31
THE END OF BLACK WIND
269

Chapter 32
CAUGHT IN THE NET
274

Chapter 33
READY IN BATTLE ARRAY
286

Chapter 34
THE END OF THE STORY
294

Chapter 1

ON THE TRAIN

S PRING, 1960. The south-bound Express No. 13 from Peking thundered through the early morning.

The green window curtains ruffled by the warm east wind gently fanned the passengers.

All of us in Coach No. 10 were returning from the National People's Militia Conference, each in possession of a shiny new semi-automatic rifle, handed to us personally by leaders of the central authorities on behalf of the motherland and the people. I mused, the rifle in my lap will protect all that is dear to me — our island, our motherland, our happiness.

My fellow travellers were a lively lot. They included veteran Red Guards from southern and northern Fukien, and former fighters of the South Chekiang Guerrilla Column, militia men and women from the plains, the mountains and the islands. Many militant friendships had been formed in the short course of the conference, and now we would very soon be saying good-bye to each other. There was still much to talk about! Some talked of past battles, others about their present work. Some of the younger militia members suddenly burst into the song *March of the Militia*.

> *We're the people's militia,*
> *Red of heart and mind.*

1

Defend the motherland!
Build up the motherland!
Hai! Let us show what we can do.

We're good at production,
And no laggards at fighting.
As handy with pen as with rifle,
Everyone a soldier!
Hai! We have immense strength.

The hills and valleys, wood and plain, the whole world outside seemed to be in tune with us.

The rising sun was bathing the land in a golden red light. How vast is the motherland, her boundaries stretching far beyond to the horizon! See the tender green of the rice seedlings, the darker green of wheat, the purple of the distant mountains, the pellucid blue of the streams, the cattle and sheep browsing on the slopes, the tractors ploughing the land.

I pressed my face against the window pane. There was so much to see! My neck grew stiff and my back ached, but still my eyes couldn't drink in all the flow of life rushing by the window. Ten pairs of eyes would not suffice me.

Neighbours had told me much about our beautiful land before I left for the conference, and how I had often tried to picture the motherland to myself. But how much lovelier, a thousand times lovelier, was she as she streamed past me.

How wonderful it would be to have all the militia on our island here with me to witness all this! If the motherland asks it of me, her daughter, I will give my life without a qualm. I must take in everything. I must remember everything so that I can tell everyone in our company about it and everyone on our island, too, so that they could share my happiness.

My eyes followed the moving beauty of the land. How dear the motherland is! For a moment my eyes misted over. . . .

Seated opposite to me was Comrade Liu Hsiu-chen, a sturdy if older woman. She had a kindly, understanding smile. This comrade had once fought in the ranks of the South Chekiang Guerrilla Column and was now the Party secretary at the East Wind People's Commune in Pingyang County. We had been in the same discussion group at the conference, so I had got to know her well, learned much from her, and had come to love her.

While feasting my eyes on the passing scenes outside, I had the feeling she was watching me with those motherly eyes of hers.

Suddenly she reached out and plucked one of my braids over the table. She murmured, "You are a sly little puss, Hai-hsia! At the conference you were always listening to what others said and begging them to tell you more. You were all ears, took everything in, but never said a word yourself."

"I really didn't have much to say," I defended. "Compared with the others, we've done very little on our island."

"But, Hai-hsia, what you have done isn't your affair alone. It was made possible by good Party leadership and Chairman Mao's great military thinking. You've learned from others and others can learn from you. Telling others what the people on your island have done is not boasting."

The listening delegates supported her and turned expectantly towards me. I did not know what to say.

Hsiu-chen came to my aid. "Do you love your little island, Hai-hsia?" she queried.

"You know I do."

"And your comrades in the militia?"

"Of course, I do. I've dreamt about them half a dozen times in the fortnight I've been away."

"Why do you love them?"

"Why? That's rather hard to explain right off." I fingered my braids nervously.

"Look at it this way. You defend the country's coast, right out on the front. People want to know how the militia there lives and fights."

The others' eyes were all on me, eagerly urging me to speak.

Yes, I thought, there is much to tell. I felt a surging in my breast and wished everyone could come and visit our island.

3

As soon as you set foot there you would see the militia, armed men and women, on guard high up on the cliffs keeping an ever watchful eye on the sea approaches of our motherland. The waves below them batter on the rocks and send up spumes of spray. Sea gulls wheel and swoop about them as they stand guard, martial and stern.

The Amity Reservoir is a little beyond the wharf. The soldiers and militia of the island built it. Every rock of it has been firmly placed in position by the hands of our People's Liberation Army men and militia women. There too is our sea wall enclosing several hundred *mu** of paddy-rice. The crop looks even greener than the sea. On the slopes are the stands of young trees. At low tide emerge a myriad oysters encrusting the rocks. We gather hundreds of baskets of rock oysters from them every year. A visit to our net factory is well worth while too. Our young women's hands are very nimble!

From the island comes the cheerful singing of sea chanties. In the old days, the songs were sad and accompanied by much weeping. But today our songs are full of joy and happiness. They urge us on to greater victories. Tide-Watcher's Point is only a couple of hundred metres above the sea, but from below it looks very high and lofty. It is the highest spot on our Concord Island. Take the path winding upwards and if you search carefully among the sisal hemp you will make out the zigzags of trenches and shelters constructed by our militia.

Nestling in the cove below Tide-Watcher's Point are the two halves of the fishing hamlet of Yungchiao. The walls are whitewashed and the roofs of the new houses and fishing sheds are of grey tile.

This charming, tidy little village is divided into an East Yungchiao and a West Yungchiao which lie on slopes of the hollow, with Tide-Watcher's Point rising above and behind them like the back of a chair, and the two halves forming its two arm-rests. Down below, in front of the settlement, is Gourd Bay, its narrow mouth opening out to sea and its big

---

* One *mu* = 1/15 hectare, or 1/6 acre.

belly making up the bay itself. It is shaped like a gourd, hence its name. Six or seven hundred metres outside the mouth of the bay is Tiger-Head Isle. It shelters the bay from raging winds and high waves. At night the ships' lights show up a forest of spars.

Astride the gully dividing the hamlet stands a gnarled old banyan tree. Its luxuriant dark green foliage provides cool shelter in summer and its massive matted roots form a natural bridge across the gully, giving our hamlet the name Yungchiao, meaning Banyan Bridge.

We patrol the beach at night and stand sentinel at the Point. As the sun rises out of the sea, first a pale glimmer far to the east, then slowly spreading silver like the underside of a fish, comes the dawn, and the sky changes from silver to a rosy pink like the bloom of a girl's cheeks, and on rapidly to orange. Clouds streaking the sky reveal a tip of golden light, growing slowly into a huge orb colouring the eastern half of the sky a fiery red. A golden sea ripples below. As the sun rises over the sea, a rosy glow bathes the whole island. Smoke begins to curl upwards from the village chimneys. Fishing boats unfurl their sails like birds taking wing, to head for the open sea and the sun.

At such moments our little island seems the loveliest place one could ever wish to see. Every stone, every blade of grass glistens as the sun drives the night away. At such times I think how our great leader Chairman Mao and the glorious Communist Party of China have brought light to our motherland and into our lives. Thoughts like this link us very close to Peking, and we tighten the grip on our guns. Every hill and stream, every blade of grass and tree is precious to us. We will never let an enemy touch any of it! Never!

I would like to tell everyone about our island's militia. At the first blast of the alarm-sounding conch weaving shuttles are stopped, babies are gently taken from the breast and carrying poles are dropped from stalwart shoulders. Cartridge belts are slung and rifles are at the ready. Like a tornado, girls and young women rush to muster by the old banyan tree. Our blouses are of many colours and our rifles are of various kinds. Our under-age trainees come armed with fishing spears.

Meet our militia members! There is that robust militia woman who puts our neat ranks awry by carrying a baby on her back. She is Sister Ah-hung, one of our platoon leaders. This mother of three children is known for her tough fighting spirit.

That little chit of a girl with brownish hair standing behind Sister Ah-hung is short and slight but she is full of fight. Her name is Chen Yu-hsiu. It was once said that she would never make a good militia woman because she clapped her hands to her ears when a firecracker exploded, but she is now one of our best shots. After a shooting tournament a military sub-area commander said of her, "Well, I never! That girl is accurate and no mistake!" Chen Yu-hsiu is now afraid of only one thing — reporters with cameras asking permission to take a shot of her.

That slender, winsome Huang Yun-hsiang is patient and meticulous, modest, quiet-spoken and well known for her fine singing of fisherfolk's songs. She is married but seldom stays at home with her parents-in-law, for she doesn't like to be away from our militia women's company. On the eve of her wedding day she suddenly flung herself into my arms, sobbing, "I'm afraid, Hai-hsia!"

"Afraid of what?"

"Leaving our militia unit. I hope that will never happen!"

We would not like to lose her, either, so I told her I would leave her name on the company roll, as her new home wasn't far away.

I can't talk about our militia without mentioning Comrade Fang, our tall, strong Party secretary, without whose guidance we could not have made progress.

We also owe much to our elders like thoughtful even-tempered Granddad Teh-shun, and to gruff, straight-speaking Granddad Wang-fa. Both men, who had their fill of suffering in the past, are today full of revolutionary vigour.

6

But there are too many people to tell about them all, though I would dearly love to.

Once on our island, you can't fail to feel the martial atmosphere there. You'll see rifles stacked at the edge of the field where the militia are planting rice, and on the beach where they are making fishing nets. You cannot fail to see the guns mounted on the boats. Even the youngsters parade spears with red tassels. Every man, woman and child on our island understands Chairman Mao's great strategic concept of people's war. Bearing profound hatred for the enemy, everyone on our fighting little island cherishes his rifle and keeps it close at hand, rain or shine, summer or winter. Chairman Mao's great directives: **The army and the people are the foundation of victory** and **Political power grows out of the barrel of a gun** are deep in our consciousness.

All the while I mused, Hsiu-chen was sitting opposite me. Like the other militia delegates she was waiting for my story about our island and about our women's militia company, for I was the leader of the company.

But what was I to tell them?

I thought of how our militia company started and of how we grew up. We'd had our ups and downs and taken many tumbles. Our company grew up like a child learning to walk under a loving mother's care — a few hesitant, stumbling steps forward, a tumble, tears, but up on its feet again. In the old society I was useless and ineffectual. I had eyes but saw nothing, a tongue but could say nothing. Then the Party opened my eyes for me and I took heart, for I could see our island as part of the motherland and the whole wide world.

I've tasted the sweetness of victory that comes through struggle, and I have tasted too the bitterness of failure. I have had discouraging moments and I have shed tears, but with Chairman Mao and the Party to encourage, help and guide me, I have conquered difficulties, faced the storm and stress of the times and gone forward.

"Very well," I said addressing Hsiu-chen and the others, "if you really want to hear about the suffering of the people on our island in the old society and how our militia company grew up in struggle, then I will tell you."

CHAPTER 2

FATHER AND I

IN the old days there were two tyrant families on our island who rode on the backs of the fishermen, plus three families that monopolized the fish market. We fisherfolk called them "Twin Axes and Three Knives," and made up a song about them:

> Don't go to Concord Island if there's anywhere else to go,
> A fisherman's lot there is nothing but suffering and woe.
> Twin Axes dangle over your head
> And Three Knives are pressed against your chests.

Such was the world I was born into. My first recollections are of hunger, cold and bitter hatred for the "Twin Axes and Three Knives."

Our family name is Li, and my father was known by the unusual name of Li Eighty-Four. I learned his story of grief and pain from my mother after I grew up.

For generations our family lived off the sea. Grandfather, and grandmother too, went out to sea in fine weather and foul the year round, but there was never enough food and clothing for the family. The year father was twelve grandfather fell sick. As he could not go to sea the family had nothing to eat.

Grandmother told my father to go out and gather wild plants. Father, who was sitting by the door, only shook his head and burst into tears.

Grandmother fled into a rage and scolded father, telling him that he was a lazy good-for-nothing who did not care what was worrying his elders. She flung a battered basket at father's feet, crying, "You're twelve this year, you young scamp! Get along!"

Father made no move to go out. Big tears rolled down his cheeks, and as grandmother was about to take a stick to beat him, she heard someone singing in the street.

> *With no more bitter greens on the hill,*
> *We eat grass roots which do not fill.*
> *Even Mercy Clay* is found no more,*
> *We chew up wild herbs, leaves, stem and core.*

Grandmother realized then she had wronged father. No more edible herbs were to be found. What was she to do? She couldn't let a sick man starve to death, so she steeled her heart and bonded her young son to work for fish merchant Chen Feng-shih, father of Chen Chan-ao, one of the two despots who owned the fishing boats. In return, grandmother was to be given a hundred *jin*** of dried sweet potato chips. When she got them home and weighed them she found there were only eighty-four *jin*. Grandmother could do nothing but rage and weep. She cursed the heartless Chen Feng-shih.

As the boy was about to leave her, she embraced him, saying, "Son, don't blame your mother. Father is very sick."

My father consoled her, "Don't blame yourself, mother! I understand. I shall not be the only one forced to work for that despot."

"You mustn't ever forget what they've done to us, son," grandmother replied through her tears.

"I'll remember it all right. I'll remember it as long as I remember my name is Li!" And he walked away, not once turning round, for he did not want his mother to see his tears.

---

* A white clayish substance often used for food by people during famine in the old days.

** One *jin* = 0.5 kilogramme or 1.1 lbs.

When father walked up to the counter in Chen's shop, Chen Feng-shih tapped his head with a walking stick and said, "So you've come, eh? You little turtle's spawn! Why! You're as skinny as a monkey. You look like one who wolfs down food and never does any work! I know your type. What do they call you?"

"I'm called Eighty-Four *Jin*," father burst out.

"What? What did you say? Eighty-four *jin*?" shrieked Chen.

"Eighty-four *jin* of dried sweet potato chips!" replied father defiantly.

"Ha, ha, ha!" Chen cackled, realizing what father meant. "So you're not satisfied, eh? You beggars aren't worth half a cent! Eighty-four *jin* of chips is over-payment for you!"

This cruel joke was soon being repeated all over the island and the name Eighty-Four stuck, a name compounded of grief and hatred. Eighty-four *jin* of dried sweet potato chips! That was all a fisherman's life was worth!

Grandfather and grandmother had passed away long before I was born. My parents were already in their forties, and my arrival did not bring joy and gladness to them. In fact, I was not wanted. In those days female infanticide was common on the island, centuries of class oppression and feudal prejudice having made people value the male child only. Everything possible was done to rear a child only if it was a boy. Most baby girls were drowned in a tub of water before their lungs drew in the first breath of air. The whole family regarded the birth of a girl as a tragedy and the enraged grandmother would immediately get rid of her. My parents, however, did not have the heart to drown me.

"Let her live no matter what happens," my mother pleaded softly. "What does it matter if it is a girl-child? She's flesh of our flesh."

Mother had no milk. Living only on wild herbs and sweet potato leaves, how could she? I sucked at her breast till I drew blood.

Father said, "The child is starving and we have nothing to feed her." Then, in a reluctant but firm voice, he said, "Let's give her away. We can't keep her."

Mother thought the same and began bundling me up, weeping the while. She begged father to find a family living nearby so she might see me frequently.

Father gave a bitter laugh. He stood for a long moment by the door with me in his arms. Then with a deep sigh he picked up a tub, put me in it and walked towards the beach.

The tide was coming in. He placed the wooden tub on the beach, saying softly, "Go, child. Lucky for you if you live. If you die, you can't blame your parents."

I was bawling at the top of my lungs, and my father shouted, "What are you howling for? Don't you want to leave this hateful world? Go your way. There's nothing in this life for you but pain, grief and suffering!"

He left the beach with heavy steps, turning to look back from time to time. The sea crept further up the beach, nearer and nearer to the tub. Father ran back once, wanting to pick me up and take me home, for my wailing clutched at his heart. But he forced himself to return without me.

Reaching home, father sat on the stone before the door, his head in his hands, motionless as a statue. He could not bear to go in and face mother, nor did he notice Uncle Liu standing near.

Uncle Liu was another fisherman working for Chen Chan-ao, the elder Chen having died. Uncle Liu was an honest, short-tempered man. He was one of those whom people describe as "preferring to die standing on his feet rather than run away; starve rather than bow his head in servitude." He knew everything a man could know about sea. He was a good swimmer and knew the ways of the fish. He was also weather-wise, and was held in high esteem by all the fishermen. Even Despot Chen had to respect him. My father and he were firm friends.

Waving a bottle of wine he said, "I've come to celebrate your happiness, brother."

Only then did father notice Uncle Liu. "What's there to celebrate, Brother Liu, when a child is born to a poor family? And besides, I've sent it on its way to the Dragon King of the Sea."

"What did you say? You didn't!" exclaimed Uncle Liu, flinging the bottle down and running to the beach.

The tub was already bobbing in the water. Uncle Liu dashed into the sea and brought the tub ashore with me in it. He took me home and rebuked my father, saying, "A child is a human being, even if it's a poor man's child. You must let it live."

"Do you think I don't want it to live?" retorted father. "But what are we to feed her on? Her mother has no milk!"

After a long pause Uncle Liu looked up and said, "I know. We'll get Rock's mother to wean him and feed your girl." Without waiting for a reply he turned and hurried with me to his house.

Rock was Uncle Liu's only child, a year-old boy. He was immediately weaned and Aunt Liu nursed me. She became more of a mother to me than my own mother could be.

When mother came to visit me Aunt Liu said, "Give the child a name. You're her real mother."

"Why bother to name her?" said mother, remembering with a pang of bitterness how father had got his name. "She's just a child of poor fisherfolk. Anything will do — Girl, Drudge, or something like that. I won't have people making a mockery of us as they do when they call the girl's father."

"No, such names won't do. We are poor, but we are not lacking in spirit," cried Uncle Liu. "We'll give her a name as fine as anyone's."

"You name her," said mother. "It was you who took her out of the sea and gave her back her life."

Uncle Liu puffed thoughtfully at his pipe. "The sky was all a rosy red over the sea the morning I took her up out of the water. It was a good sign. Suppose we call her Hai-hsia*?"

---

* Sunrise over the Sea.

13

CHAPTER 3

THE SECRET OF THE STEELYARD

MY early childhood was tragic, but I knew much love and did not worry. I had many moments of happiness — the quilted jacket of old, wadded cotton that mother made out of her worn-out gown, too tight for comfort and too threadbare to keep a body warm. To me it was lovely and a comfort. A meal of thin, sweet potato gruel was marvellously appetizing and fragrant. And where other children had only one mother's love I had two, and I had a big brother, too, in Rock. He was always close at hand if anyone tried to bully me.

When Rock was thirteen he seemed to be grown up. He was only a year older than I but I accepted everything he said without questioning. We were inseparable. We scooped oysters together, harvested seaweed together, caught shrimps and climbed Tide-Watcher's Point together to collect firewood.

Rock had a strong will and was very brave. Once little Hai-hua accidentally dropped her chopper over the cliff and started to bawl. None of the others cutting firewood could do anything to help her.

Rock said to her, "Stop crying and go down and get it."

Some of the youngsters peered over the cliff and drew back in alarm. It was a twenty-foot drop.

One of them flung at Rock, "You talk big. Let's see you go and get it. I dare you to!"

"Taken!" replied Rock, and he leapt. A minute or two later he threw up Hai-hua's chopper but found he couldn't climb back up. His leg was hurt. Luckily Granddad Teh-shun was gathering firewood not far away. He had a rope and pulled Rock up.

"You headstrong little devil," scolded Granddad Teh-shun as he bound up Rock's leg. "Don't let me catch you doing such a thing again."

"I'll time my jump better next time," Rock promised.

"You're like your old man. Headstrong and rock-hard," said Granddad Teh-shun with a throaty chuckle.

I liked Rock for it.

One day Rock and I went gathering sweet potato leaves. We collected a huge pile in no time at all and were very happy. It takes so very little to fill young hearts with joy. When we found a tiny tuber the diggers had missed, we would crow with pleasure as if we had found something wonderful. Quickly filling our baskets, we started for home in great spirits. And then we ran smack into Despot Chen. He sidled up to us like a fat loathsome pig, his round melon of a head set squat on his shoulders, a thick roll of fat where his neck should have been. His shifty eyes squinted right and left as if he was searching for something. At his heels was his steward, Yu Erh, whom we all called Yu the No. 2 Dog.

Chen prodded our baskets with his walking stick, then rapped Rock's head as he muttered, "You got those from my land, didn't you, you turtle's spawn? Now, run and take them to feed my pigs!"

Rock looked at him sullenly, said nothing but began walking away.

This made the despot furious. He went up to Rock and struck him on the head with his stick. "What have you got for ears on that nut of yours?" he shrieked. "You dirty little turtle's spawn!"

Rock never uttered a sound. Tossing his basket aside, with one swift pull he wrenched the stick out of Chen's grasp. Holding it with one hand he stamped hard, breaking the stick in two.

"Mr. Yu! Tie him up for me! The dirty little turtle's spawn! A garter snake would be a dragon, eh!" Chen, livid with rage, kicked the basket over and stamped it to pieces.

Rock fought like a tiger but they soon had him trussed up, bleeding from a cut on his head. I was so frightened I just stood there blubbering. Rock stared accusingly at me. "You only know how to cry," he seemed to say. "Haven't you the sense to give me a hand!"

That winter, when the fishing season was coming to an end and we were preparing for the Spring Festival (lunar New Year), something important happened.

For some time Uncle Liu, Uncle Li Shuang-ho and my father had been meeting frequently and quietly in our house. At first I thought they were discussing fishing prospects following the Spring Festival. Then I found that that was not so, and I was bursting with curiosity. When I poured tea for them I kept my ears open hoping to find out what they were talking about.

"This year we're not going to let them cheat us as they have done before," father said quietly but firmly. "If Chen Chan-ao won't meet our demands we won't go to sea. Our wages must be paid and the money he owes us for the catch, too; otherwise how will our families live while we're away?"

"What if Chen won't?" asked Uncle Shuang-ho doubtfully.

"We must get all the poor fishermen and hands together and refuse to sail!" exclaimed Uncle Liu. "This time we must settle accounts with Chen."

I was very pleased to hear this, and as I continued to pour tea I said, "And don't forget to make him pay for our basket and that load of potato leaves, too."

"He owes a lot more than that," Uncle Liu said with a chuckle. "A hell of a lot more!"

"Owes us a lot?" I echoed.

"Yes. He owes us a lot more than money," said Uncle Liu taking the tea I poured him. "Hai-hsia," he said suddenly, "can you sing us a song?"

"Of course, I can! Many!"

"Then sing one for us."

I was overjoyed. A grown-up asking me to sing! I sang in a very loud voice:

> What fish sports a pair of whiskers?
> Which is without a pair of eyes?
> What fish is born dolt silly?
> And which is wet and slippery?
> A cuttlefish shows its whiskers,
> A jellyfish is blind. . . .

"Hold it, Hai-hsia. There's no sense at all in that song," broke in Uncle Liu. "Let me teach you one."

"Oh, good!" I clapped my hands and giggled. Here is the song Uncle Liu taught me:

> A ten-thousand-jin catch,
> Won by muscle and sweat,
> Shrinks to seven thousand on his scales.
> Cut the price — five thousand jin,
> Payment deferred brings it down to two thousand,
> We're diddled and driven into debt.
> So swallow back your salty tears. . . .

"I won't sing it," I teased, " 'cause it doesn't sound very nice."

"Haven't you any idea how we fisherfolk suffer, Hai-hsia?" Uncle Liu demanded as if he was talking to an adult.

"Those 'Four-by-Sixers' bleed us white and they gang up with the fishmongers to take another bite out of us. They weigh our catch at sea and give us a piece of paper for it instead of cash. And then they settle for less at the end of the season. They load the scales, lower the price and hold back payment. There's no end to their tricks, robbing us at every turn. . . ."

"Why do you call the fishing firms 'Four-by-Sixers'?" I asked.

Uncle Liu explained, "It's like this. If we bring in ten fish, well, Chen takes six and leaves us with four. We get paid for only four fish and even then Chen doesn't pay up until weeks and months later when all the time the prices of commodities are getting higher and higher. What would buy us a hundred *jin* of rice in the morning buys only eighty in the afternoon. Money buys less and less and by the time we're paid our four fish are only worth the price of two. That's how Chen has got so filthy rich! He grows fat on our blood and sweat!"

"Why don't we make him pay for it?"

"Why? Chen has money and influence. A handful of us are no match for him. We have to get together, all of us, and then we can fix him. It's like building a bonfire on the beach. When everyone puts his share of the firewood on it, the fire burns strong and fierce."

"But what has that song you were teaching me got to do with all this?"

"When the fishermen hear you singing it, they'll understand. They'll know who's the one that's exploiting them and they'll come together. You can teach your friends to sing it, too. The more people who sing it the more useful it'll be."

It didn't seem possible that a simple song like that could do so much. Liking action, I put the teapot down and ran to my friends playing by the sea. I soon had them all singing the song after me, tall, skinny Yun-hsiang, roly-poly Hai-hua, brown-haired Yu-hsiu, and the rest.

We all sang, but Yun-hsiang was by far the best singer. She had the right voice for it and knew how to put feeling into it. Her singing sometimes moved even grown-ups to tears. She could improvise as she sang, too.

The way she sang Uncle Liu's song and altered it made the song catchier and more appealing.

> *A ten-thousand-*jin *catch of fish — ah,*
> *Harvested by sweat and toil — ah hai,*
> *Grows lighter and lighter — ah,*

When they hold back payment — ah hai,
Juggle the scales and prices — ah,
We're diddled and driven into debt — ah hai,
So swallow your salty tears — ah!

Wherever we went we sang the song and soon had the boys singing it with us.

One day as we were singing our song on a street corner Granddads Teh-shun and Wang-fa, who were smoking their pipes in the sun, called to us. "That's a fine song you're singing. It's exactly what we're thinking. Who taught it to you?"

"We made it up ourselves," I answered warily.

"Don't give us that, Hai-hsia. You know us." Of course they were not taken in by me. They knew very well that we couldn't have made it up ourselves. But what was I to do? I didn't like telling my elders another fib. "Uncle Liu told me not to tell," I blurted.

Granddad Wang-fa smiled and said, "All right, Hai-hsia. You didn't tell us a thing."

That evening when Uncles Liu and Shuang-ho and my father were absorbed in talk the two old men dropped into our house. Once inside the door they said, "We've got scores to settle with that Chen Chan-ao, too."

"Who told you that we are talking about such things?" asked Uncle Liu, surprised.

"Hai-hsia did," Granddad Wang-fa said, nodding at me.

"I did not!" I said indignantly. "I just said that Uncle Liu told me not to tell, that's all!"

Everyone laughed and I suddenly realized what a slip of the tongue I had made. Grown-ups are so wily!

"It's a real good song, Hai-hsia. The only thing the matter with it is that you don't name that son-of-a-bitch Chen Chan-ao. He's the devil who cracks our bones and sucks our marrow dry!" Granddad Teh-shun said vehemently. "Let me add the name to the song." And he began:

Chen Chan-ao is a slimy old leech,
Drinking dry our fishermen's blood.
If we're not paid, no boat shall leave the beach.
Come, one and all, together we'll settle the score.

Mother, who was mending a net, asked anxiously, "Do you think we can win against Chen Chan-ao? He's rich and powerful, and I've heard people say he's sworn brother to Black Wind."

Black Wind was a villainous pirate, cruel and fiendish, whom the fishermen regarded with almost superstitious awe. The very mention of this ruthless desperado's name made men quake and hushed crying babes. Superstitious fishermen uttering a quick prayer before setting out to sea never forgot to add, "And may I not meet Black Wind." Some took the oath: "If I go back on my word, may Black Wind come for me at sea!"

Black Wind was not only ruthless; he was also very sly. No one had ever seen him, for he sent his thugs to murder and rob. If he did appear, he always wore a black mask. He and his gang came and went mysteriously, leaving no trace. Their hideout was never in one place long.

Mother's words, which made Uncle Shuang-ho lower his head, sent a shiver through me.

"If you want live fish you've got to go and get them out of the sea," exclaimed Uncle Liu. "And if you really want to have it out with Chen, you mustn't look for imaginary wolves ahead and tigers in the rear!"

"Anyway, it's Chen Chan-ao who has driven us to it," father pointed out. "It's better to die fighting than to sit and starve to death! We've got to be firm."

"I'm afraid our people won't stick together," Uncle Shuang-ho said doubtingly.

Father said slowly, "That Chen Chan-ao who has plenty of money and pull also has the heart of a wolf. It won't be an easy matter to take him on. But once we have him where we want him he'll have to give in. Everybody will stand together when they see how the Chens have been rooking us for generations with that loaded steelyard of theirs! Everyone will be fighting mad when they see!"

"Are you sure about that trick steelyard?" asked Uncle Liu.

"Dead sure of it," father assured him. "I've worked half my life for that family and never once would they let me so much as touch that steelyard. I've had my suspicions for a long time. Then on the eve of the Spring Festival when they were guzzling and having a good time over at their house, I got hold of it, took it to the warehouse and tried it several times. My suspicions were confirmed."

"That's fine," Uncle Liu said, looking relieved. "But don't be in a hurry to bring it out. We've got to wait for the right moment."

One day Chen's steward, Yu the No. 2 Dog, heard me singing our song in the street. He came up to me with a mirthless grin on his face and said, "Um, you sing fine, Hai-hsia. Um . . . um. . . . Will you sing it again, for me?" That skinny old rat with his "ums" made me want to vomit, but I sang.

> *A flowing tide and billowing sails,*
> *My brother is fishing at sea.*
> *I'll lend him a hand*
> *To bring in full nets with every fling. . . .*

"Not that one! The one you were singing a moment ago. Who taught you that song?"

"You did!" I threw at him.

He questioned and questioned but I wouldn't tell him. Then he tried a different tack. "Um . . . I'll give you . . . um . . . a silver dollar to buy a pretty dress if you tell me."

He took out the coin and held it before me on the palm of his hand. I slapped it away. "Who wants your dirty money!"

He cursed as he bent to pick up his dollar. "Ungrateful bitch! I forbid you to sing that song again!" He was fit to burst and forgot his usual "ums."

"What I sing is none of your business. I'll sing what I like!" said I, and sing I did, much louder.

He suddenly gripped and twisted my arm, angrily shouting, "Getting uppity, eh! Want to rebel, eh! I'll teach you!"

I yelled at the top of my voice, "No. 2 Dog is beating me! Help!"

The fishermen out sunning themselves quickly came and grouped about us. Granddad Teh-shun said, "Mr. Yu, you mustn't do that. She's only a child. You're the very venerable steward of the esteemed Yufeng Fishing Firm. It doesn't befit a man in your position to beat her!"

No. 2 Dog gave me a murderous glare and slunk away amid guffaws of laughter.

March was the season for yellow croakers, but the fishermen and fishing crew stayed ashore. Chen Chan-ao fumed and raged. One day when everyone was gathered on the beach, Uncle Liu announced, "If Chen doesn't pay us, we won't go to sea. If there's no grain for our families, we won't go to sea. If there's going to be any more monkeying with the scales or cutting down the price of fish or forcing up the price of grain, we won't go to sea!"

People crowded round the big banyan tree. We youngsters who sang that song were also there. Chen came swaggering up brandishing a new walking stick. It was thicker and shinier than the one Rock had broken.

"Fellow villagers," croaked Chen. "As sure as I'm surnamed Chen, I have never been unfair to any one of you. It was not my fault the price of fish fell. It was those fishmongers. They refuse our catches if the prices aren't low enough to please them. You know what happens when they refuse to buy — your catch rots in the hulls!"

Father shouted from the crowd, "You and the buyers are hand in glove! You split fifty-fifty with them!"

"Wait a moment, Li Eighty-Four," Chen said. "You can't throw accusations around without very firm proof of what you say!" Chen glared at my father and, without waiting for a reply, went on, "How can I pay you when those fishmongers don't pay me? I don't make the money myself, you know. Do you think I'm not as anxious as you to get the money? Look here! These are the letters and telegrams I've sent asking them to pay up. Read them yourselves." He waved a sheaf of coloured papers in the air.

There was a sudden silence. A stillness like when a ladle of cold water is poured into a boiling pot settled over the gathering.

Chen saw his ruse had taken effect. He took out his cigarette lighter. He clicked it so that everyone could hear, and then nonchalantly lit a cigarette.

"Fellow villagers, I, Chen Chan-ao, have always been fair and square in all my dealings. I have never resorted to such things as loaded steelyards and swapping pans to cheat anyone of his due. I use the same steelyard for fish and rice. I've treated you all fair! I never thought I'd meet with such ingratitude. Why do you do this to me?"

The crowd stirred, and there were loud murmurings. Someone ventured, "That's it. It was probably those fishmongers who held the money back so that Mr. Chen can't pay us."

"If that's so, then we'd better get back to our fishing."

Granddad Teh-shun look worried as he elbowed his way through the crowd to Uncle Liu. "Some of them are wavering. What shall we do?" he asked.

"Take it easy. Chen is as bloodthirsty and sly as an old fox. But in another few minutes we'll have him by the tail and skin him!" Uncle Liu turned and whispered something to father, then father turned and pushed his way out. Others made a move to leave.

Uncle Liu cried, "Don't leave yet! Since Mr. Chen wants proof, we'll give it to him! Li Eighty-Four has gone to fetch it."

"I'd like to see what proof you have!" Chen sneered.

Father returned in a twinkling with the huge steelyard. It was fashioned of redwood and six feet long. Chen flinched as if struck by a whip. All the colour drained from his face.

Uncle Liu took the steelyard and weighed it in his hands. "Here it is! This is how Chen has been cheating us! Watch!"

He broke the arm across his knee. Quicksilver ran out like beads from the hollow beam. Everyone gasped. Then there was an angry roar as the people rushed forward. . . .

It was no steelyard! It was a bloodsucker's tool! This was the syphon which the Chens had used to drain us fishermen dry generation after generation. When fish was being weighed, a quick shake would send the mercury sliding down to the long graduated end of the hollow arm so that even when the arm slanted upwards, giving the fishermen the impression they were getting a fair deal, they were actually being cheated. A hundred and twenty *jin* of fish were weighed in as one hundred *jin*. When grain was being measured out to the fishermen, another shake and the quicksilver ran into the short end of the arm. Now I saw how that one hundred *jin* of dried sweet potato chips the Chens had got my father bonded for came to only eighty-four *jin*!

The broken steelyard was like a fresh breeze fanning the fishermen's smouldering anger into a roaring fire. Every family had been gouged by that trick weighing device! While the people's attention was on the broken steelyard, Chen sneaked away.

Aunt Ta-cheng shouted, "Those Chens have the hearts of ravenous wolves!"

"We should put a torch to their lair!" urged Sister Ah-hung pointing to the Chens' grey-tiled buildings.

"Fellow villagers," Granddad Teh-shun cried, "that steelyard alone has robbed us of a lot, not to mention Chen's other cheating ways. We must settle scores with him!"

"Come on. Let's settle scores with the Chens!" cried Uncle Liu waving aloft a broken half of the steelyard. The people flocked after him and surged up to the front door of the Chens' house.

"Open up or we'll break down the door!" people shouted.

The door opened a crack and No. 2 Dog squeezed himself out sideways, made a low bow and said with a jerky smile, "Um. . . . Fellow villagers, let's talk this matter over calmly, eh? That steelyard was an heirloom his ancestors left him.

Um . . . um . . . Mr. Chen didn't know there was anything wrong with it. Mr. Chen takes into consideration your difficulties, and agrees to all your demands. First, um . . . um . . . you're all going to get paid. Second, every family will be given a hundred *jin* of dried sweet potato chips as a start. Third, um . . . a new steelyard will be used. All will be entirely aboveboard. And as time and tide wait for no man, how about starting fishing tomorrow?"

He hemmed and hawed again, then slipped back behind the door.

All the fishermen's demands were met. They had won, and on the way home I heard grown-ups humming our song. For the first time in my young life I tasted the sweet fruits of victory born of struggle.

I said to Uncle Liu as I skipped merrily by his side, "Chen is scared of you."

"No. It's not me," he said with a chuckle. He pointed to the people walking happily home. "It's them Chen is afraid of. He's scared of all of us when we're together. Remember that saying about 'many faggots build big bonfires'?"

Granddad Teh-shun caught up with us and said to Uncle Liu in a low voice, "Chen has bowed before the masses today. He's bending before the wind. You must be careful. He'll try and get you and the others who spoke out. He's an ugly customer to cross and stops at no evil, so watch your step."

"You're right," Uncle Liu replied. "We'll all have to be careful."

CHAPTER 4

WHY SEA GULLS' WINGS ARE WHITE

THE people were elated and happy the first few days after we had got the better of Chen. But later, thinking things over more calmly, they began bit by bit to nurse all sorts of doubts and anxieties. There was a deceptive quiet on the surface which masked gnawing uneasiness.

"Why was Chen humbled so easily? Surely he's not going to leave it at that."

"Chen is wolf-cruel. He gave in only to get everyone out to sea. He's sure to get his own back on us!"

After the fishing boats had put out, it rained without let-up day or night. Day was like dusk. It was damp indoors and wet and muddy outside, and the atmosphere was growing more and more oppressive. Disquieting talk could be heard on all sides. People were wavering. I kept indoors. Mother sat on the bed mending clothes while I repaired nets, each of us engrossed in her own thoughts.

The dim oil lamp cast a gloom about the room as if the oppressive darkness were too heavy and thick for its light to penetrate. I made five mistakes in a row with the mesh. I felt anxious and dismal as I thought of our people out at sea.

I crept into bed but sleep would not come.

"Mother," I said, "tell me a story or something."

"Aren't you asleep yet? It's very late."

"I can't sleep. I feel restless all over."

Mother was silent for a while, then asked, "Do you know why sea gulls have white wings?"

"No. They're white because they're white, I suppose."

"There's a reason," mother went on, "and I'll tell you what it is."

Mother began to tell me the sad story about a young fisherwoman.

"Once, long ago, there was a poor fishergirl called Yu-ku. She was a lovely young woman, clever and industrious, and very strong-willed. She could weave nets faster and sing better than anyone else. Her sweetheart was a young fisherman named Yu-lang.

"A local tyrant who rode roughshod over the fisherfolk had long had his eyes on the young woman. He was determined to take her for his concubine! Then one day, when Yu-lang was away at sea, this evil man sent his steward to entice Yu-ku to his home.

" 'If you make the old gentleman happy, you'll have everything you could wish for,' he said. 'All the silks and brocades you can dream of, the choicest delicacies of sea and land, and gold, silver and precious gems. You'll be rich and respected. . . .'

"Yu-ku went on weaving her net without even looking up. Then she gave her reply, singing:

> *In the tyrant's house*
> *Lie silks and satins in chests piled high,*
> *Caskets of gold and fabulous jewels.*
> *Each and every treasure there*
> *Is stained with the blood and tears of the poor.*
> *The tyrant's heart is black and beats with hate,*
> *He's more savage than a tiger or a wolf*
> *And as evil as the devil.*

"When the steward went back and told his master, the tyrant flew into a rage. He sent his thugs to seize the girl's nets, her tiny store of clothing and furniture, and ordered them to throw her out of her home. They sealed up the door of

27

the empty house, so Yu-ku sat by the sea, singing this song as she waited for the return of her Yu-lang.

The tyrant has seized my nets,
Stolen my blouse and skirt —
Deprived me of house and home.
We fisherfolk's misery is deeper than the sea.

"When Yu-lang returned with his boat laden with fish, Yu-ku said to him, 'Let us marry now and save ourselves more trouble from that tyrant.'

"Yu-lang agreed. 'I'll sell the fish first; then we'll have money to marry,' he said to Yu-ku.

"Later that day they were married and that evening the whole village went to their wedding to make merry. But in the midst of the rejoicing, the tyrant appeared with his thugs. They fought their way in and seized the bride and groom. The tyrant ordered his thugs to carry the bride to his house and bind and throw the groom into the sea.

"Yu-lang knew they intended to kill him and steal his bride. He shouted, 'Yu-ku! Avenge my death!'

"They tied stones to Yu-lang's bound hands and waist and threw him into the sea.

"The tyrant shut Yu-ku up in a room in his courtyard and tried by force to make her his concubine. Yu-ku firmly rejected him. She refused food and drink and never stopped reviling her abductor. The tyrant was furious, but he could do nothing. Finally, he called in his smooth-tongued sisters to help. They came and spent days and nights trying with honeyed words to talk Yu-ku into marriage, but she would not change her mind. Yu-ku expressed her hatred and disgust in song.

Though you're skilled with fancy words and fine promises,
And your glib tongues have done their worst,
Know you the poor have wills of iron,
And neither sharp knives nor fire brands can bend my will!

"Seeing that Yu-ku was still expecting Yu-lang to come and rescue her, they said, 'You can forget about your Yu-lang. The fish have been feeding off him for the past three days, so you can stop your pining.'

"Yu-ku set up a loud lament for Yu-lang when she heard this. Then she fainted. When she came round she wept bitterly and loudly."

"Oh, what a sad story!" I could not help crying, for my heart went out to Yu-ku.

"But the saddest part is still to come," mother said, and went on with the story. "The tyrant's sisters scolded and threatened Yu-ku. They said, 'What are you howling like that for? Yu-lang's dead and gone. Stop your bawling and do what our brother asks, otherwise you'll come to grief yourself.'

" 'I've something to ask of you,' said Yu-ku suddenly.

"The sisters were delighted at this, thinking that Yu-ku was weakening. 'Oh, anything, anything at all,' they exclaimed in one voice."

"That Yu-ku is acting like a spineless creature," I interrupted angrily. "She's given in!"

"Let me continue," mother said, and went on with her story. "Yu-ku asked them for a pair of scissors and a length of white silk. The sisters didn't know what to do, as their brother had told them never to let anyone take a knife or other sharp instruments into Yu-ku's room lest she attempt suicide. They asked Yu-ku what she wanted these things for.

" 'To make myself a dress to mourn Yu-lang. How can I do that without white silk and a pair of scissors?'

"The sisters talked it over with their wicked brother and they decided to let Yu-ku have the things. On the third day that Yu-ku had worn mourning the tyrant was no longer able to restrain his impatience and told his sisters to ask Yu-ku when she would marry him.

"Yu-ku's reply was: 'When the seas run dry and the rocks turn to dust. When I've killed that goat-fiend brother of yours!'

"The tyrant was exasperated when he heard this and decided to force himself on Yu-ku. That night he drank himself tipsy and broke into Yu-ku's room.

"Yu-ku was prepared for this. She pulled out the scissors from beneath her pillow and ran at the tyrant, aiming for his throat. He raised his arm to ward off the thrust and the scissors pierced his right eye. Screaming with pain he ran out of the room. . . ."

"What happened to Yu-ku?" I asked, my heart pounding.

Mother heaved a heavy sigh. "What could she do? The tyrant's mansion has many courtyards and very high walls. The one-eyed tyrant, gnashing his teeth and spitting venomously, had Yu-ku trussed up in the yard and dried faggots piled high around her. Then the faggots were set alight.

"The whole village saw the flames and smoke of the fire, but what could they do? Only cry out in anger and vexation. Then suddenly they saw a girl in white mourning clothes fly out of the roaring inferno. . . ."

"How could she fly?" I demanded.

"It was not Yu-ku who flew out. Yu-ku had changed into a sea gull with long, graceful white wings. They were the garment she wore in mourning for her Yu-lang.

"The sea gull uttered a heart-rending cry. People tried to comfort her, telling her that her Yu-lang was not dead but had been rescued by passing fisherfolk.

"Grief-stricken, Yu-ku flew to every fishing boat, wailing in anguish, 'Yu-lang! Yu-lang!' and has been doing so ever since. She is still searching for her sweetheart to this day. . . ."

I could not held weeping, it was so sad. I couldn't believe it, either, and I didn't want to! "Mother, you made that up, didn't you?"

"Why do you say that?"

"Because there was only one Yu-ku but there are very many sea gulls!"

Mother sighed. "There are many, many poor fishergirls like Yu-ku in this world. A great many."

I wept silently. I had always thought that the sea gulls' cries were lovely to listen to, but not now. As I lay in the darkness, I thought I could hear their plaintive mewing: "Yu-lang! Yu-lang!"

Mother must have thought I had fallen asleep. She quietly folded up the garment she had mended and crept into bed beside me. My body shook with sobbing, and she exclaimed, "Aiyah! Hai-hsia! You're crying!"

Yes. I was crying, crying for all those unhappy, unfortunate, suffering Yu-kus.

Bang . . . bang . . . bang. . . .

My sobbing was suddenly interrupted by a knocking at the door. I shook mother.

"Mother, there's someone at the door!"

"Who is it?" mother called, slipping into her clothes.

"It's me, Shuang-ho!"

"But aren't you at sea? Have the others returned?" mother asked, lighting the lamp.

"Quick! Open the door! Hurry!"

As soon as mother opened the door, Uncle Shuang-ho, soaking wet, fell inside.

"Heavens! What has happened? Hai-hsia, help me! Come quickly!" mother called.

I helped put Uncle Shuang-ho on the bed. What has happened? I asked myself. I felt as if I had been doused with cold water, stiff and numb.

When he came round, Uncle Shuang-ho said in a weak voice, "Oh, it was terrible!"

Mother quickly poured him out a bowl of hot soup, which he gulped down hungrily. He handed me the empty bowl. His speech and looks told us something dreadful had happened.

"Chen Chan-ao ganged up with Black Wind and killed Big Brother Liu and Big Brother Li!" he said with great effort.

"What! What did you say?" mother asked, unable to believe her ears. After a moment which seemed like hours she realized what he had said, and fainted. I was too scared to cry. The bowl dropped from my hand and broke into pieces, shattered like my hopes.

Uncle Shuang-ho was breathing heavily. When mother came round, she said, "Go and fetch Granddad Teh-shun. Hurry!"

Granddad Teh-shun was too old to go to sea so he stayed ashore manning the ferry out to East Beach Island. When he heard the tragic news, he struggled into his clothes and came hurrying to my house with me.

What had happened was that after their victory over Chen Chan-ao the fishermen had gone contentedly out to sea. The shoals were large and numerous and the boat was soon loaded. As they sailed home with their big catches they were suddenly assailed by Black Wind just off Tiger-Head Isle. The pirates, in black masks and dressed entirely in black, swarmed onto the fishing smack like a horde of demons, demanding Uncle Liu, father and Uncle Shuang-ho.

Not a fisherman responded.

"If you don't give them up we'll shoot the whole lot of you!" they threatened, training their guns on the crew.

Uncle Liu and father stepped forward, unwilling to let the others come to grief.

"I'm the one who led the people to fight Chen!" declared Uncle Liu. "And I'm proud to say so. The others had nothing at all to do with it!"

Uncle Shuang-ho was stunned. He stood rooted to the spot, not knowing what to do. Father had just shouted, "Jump, Shuang-ho!" when the pirates shot him and Uncle Liu. The shout broke Uncle Shuang-ho's trance and he leapt headlong into the sea. The murderers fired after him but missed and he swam home.

This was the story Uncle Shuang-ho told us in a shaky voice.

"Uncle Teh-shun, will you ferry me over to the mainland? I can't stay on this island any longer. The black-hearted Chen will not let me off easily, you know." He turned to my mother and asked, "And what are you going to do?"

"Don't you worry about us," mother said through her tears. "You go your way. Quickly. Curses on Chen Chan-ao! May the devil come for him, and soon!"

CHAPTER 5

FISHERMEN'S FAMILIES

THE death of father and Uncle Liu was a catastrophe for our two families. If the sky had fallen in, things couldn't have been worse for us. Mother and Aunt Liu were grief-stricken, crying and refusing food for days.

Chen Chan-ao made no attempt to hide the fact that it was he who was responsible for the foul deed. He even gave out a warning that if anyone else wanted trouble they would meet the same fate.

Some people hung their heads like young grass blighted by frost. Some avoided us in daytime. Granddads Teh-shun and Wang-fa, however, visited us frequently. They were two solitary old men without a tie in the world. They came and spoke a few words of comfort to mother or just squatted by the stove brooding as they sucked at their pipes.

One day Granddad Wang-fa, no longer able to contain himself, suddenly exclaimed, "I won't have it! Why can't we deal with him?"

Granddad Teh-shun knocked the dottle from his pipe and said with a sigh, "What's the use of huffing and puffing with rage when the knife is in someone else's hand?"

"Can't we seize the knife from him?"

"Tell me how!" Granddad Teh-shun snorted.

The two of them fell silent, puffed at their pipes and pondered.

There is an old saying that "the new-born calf fears not the tiger." While the grown-ups reluctantly swallowed their anger, Rock showed he wasn't the least bit afraid of Chen Chan-ao. Day after day he stood outside Chen's house, fishing spear in hand, waiting for the despot to appear. Rock would not leave till Aunt Liu or someone else came to make him go home.

"Don't you know what's good for you? Can an egg crush a rock?" they would say.

Rock's reply would be: "I'm going to shove this spear through Chen. You just wait and see!"

As his mother could do nothing with him, she hid his spear.

But spear or no spear, Rock was set on settling scores with Chen Chan-ao or dying in the attempt. One day he tore out of his mother's grasp and ran to Chen's house where he hammered with his small fists on the iron-clad door, shouting, "Chen Chan-ao, you murderer! I'll get even with you; just wait!"

One night I tossed and turned in my sleep, dreaming that the Chens were having one of their lavish feasts. Then I saw Uncle Liu and father standing before me, dripping with blood. Rock and I were fishing out at sea when a mountain-high wave swept Rock into the water. It was pitch dark and I was frightened. In the grip of the nightmare I shouted wildly; Rock rose out of the waves and told me to keep my head and grab hold of a rope. I reached the shore and saw people running about in great alarm. Then I heard them shouting, "Black Wind and his pirates are coming!"

I woke with a start to hear hoarse voices shouting, "Fire! Fire!"

I saw the window lit up. Mother woke too, but she did not move for she was very weak. I jumped out of bed and ran, not bothering to find my shoes.

It was Aunt Liu's house that was burning. I pushed my way through the crowd of people fighting the fire to reach the door, which was already aflame. It was locked! I was shoved aside. Others battered down the door with a stout beam. The roof had caved in. There was no water near the house, which stood on a hillside. Someone carried water up from the bay. When it arrived, the house was already an inferno. . . . Only its blackened walls remained, standing ominously against a black sky.

"Aunty! Rock!" I screamed again and again as I fought my way through the crowd to the charred, smoking heap. I felt the clutch of a strong pair of hands. I saw and heard nothing more, only felt a great clawing at my breast.

Everyone knew that it was Chen Chan-ao who had locked the door and set the house on fire. This was a sample of the way he "liquidated" anyone who dared oppose him, as he had openly declared. Some people cursed him; a few blamed Rock for shouting revenge at Chen's gate. Many wept hot tears of sympathy for our two families.

People sighed, "How tragic! Two happy families broken up, decimated. Now there's only a widow and a girl left of the two families!"

It was mid-day, but mother still lay in bed moaning softly. I sat beside her weaving a net, working without pause save to stretch my fingers when they became numb and cramped.

"Take a rest, Hai-hsia," mother urged in a weak voice.

"I'm not tired, mother," I replied, but of course I was. I could not stop, for everything we ate and used depended on this little shuttle. Through the fine mesh I had visions of more medicine for mother, and dried sweet potato chips for us both. No! I mustn't stop weaving.

Presently mother groaned loudly. I said, "As soon as I've finished this net, mother, I'll get a doctor to look at you."

The frail door of brushwood suddenly opened and Chen Chan-ao's steward edged his way in. He sniggered and hemmed, "Um . . . so you'll call a doctor, eh? Um . . . now, that means you're pretty well off."

Mother turned on her side and, half reclining, said, "Mr. Yu, what brings you here? Get a chair for Mr. Yu, Hai-hsia!"

I went on with my work as if I had not heard. His bald, shiny pate and weasel eyes set me quivering with revulsion. And his "ums" froze me with loathing.

"So Li Eighty-Four has passed away, eh? Um . . . so let's forget about his debts to Mr. Chen. You know, Mr. Chen feels sorry about it, but . . . um . . . you'll have to move out of this house. . . ."

"Why must we move?" I demanded.

"Why? Um . . . now, you see, this house belongs to Mr. Chen. That's why! Um . . . Mr. Chen wants to pull it down to make room for a new pigsty."

Mother tried to placate him. "She's just an ignorant girl. Don't pay any attention to her, Mr. Yu," she said.

I had never heard that the house belonged to anyone but us.

"Wait till my mother is better. We'll move then!" I flung at him.

The steward suddenly flashed a cruel grin and said, "Um . . . where will you move to? Um . . . um. . . . Winter's coming. You want to kill your mother off with cold? Eh?"

"Go and feed your merciful heart to the dogs! Who wants your pity! You know we have nowhere to go and yet you're forcing us to move out! Do your worst! We can only die!"

The steward was not put off and continued, "Um . . . um. . . . What's the use of your tough talk? Now, let's put it this way. How about a job for you as a maidservant in the Chen household? Then . . . um . . . um . . . I could put in a word to Mr. Chen for you about your house."

So that was what was behind this sudden visit! They wanted to force me into servitude in their house by threatening to evict us. What wishful thinking! I shouted at him, "I'd sooner be a servant to a cur than to the Chens!"

"Mr. Chen is doing you a favour. Um . . . now, you're just a slip of a girl and don't know what's good for you. Now, you just come along with me!"

I was already simmering with rage and when he tried to take hold of me I turned on him and drove my sharp-pointed bamboo shuttle into his dirty paw.

No. 2 Dog left cursing with a bloodied hand, and mother shaking with fear.

"Now you've done it, Hai-hsia!"

"What's there to be afraid of, mother. I'm not afraid of death itself!" I said heatedly.

"It looks as if the Chens won't leave us alone until they've driven our two families into our graves," said mother resignedly, and began to cough loudly. "We might as well move now." She dragged herself up and wearily began to gather together our few possessions, afraid I might get into more trouble.

Where were we to go? Mother herself did not know.

As I began to take down my half-finished net I realized that we would soon be without a roof over our heads. This dark, low, cramped, little room suddenly became very dear to me. It leaked like a sieve and kept the winter wind out no better, but still this was our home. Without it, we were homeless. Where would we find another home? And mother was so very ill. I could no longer hold back my tears.

"Don't cry, daughter. It's our fate. We were born unlucky."

"I'm fourteen, mother, and I know we're poor. But I never knew even this poor flimsy reed house belonged to someone else!"

"We've been poor like this for more years than I care to remember," said mother bitterly. "I was seventeen when I married your father, and I had only a blue cotton blouse covered with patches. Other girls, no matter how poor, at least had a print blouse when they left their mothers. I remember saying to your granny, 'I won't marry unless I have a bright new blouse!' Granny was hurt and said sadly, 'You're grown up and should know better! Where am I to get you a new blouse, you silly girl! We have hardly enough to keep ourselves alive!'

"I was married in someone else's worn tunic. My mirror, no larger than the palm of my hand, and wooden comb with many teeth missing were both borrowed! At your father's house I found a coverlet for the bed, old and patched but still a coverlet. It disappeared on the third day. I thought your father had taken it out to give it an airing, and I looked outside. But it was not there. Could some thief have stolen it? I ran to tell your father. He gave a bitter chuckle and said that it, too, had been borrowed and he had just returned it. He came home, took a woven grass mat down from the rafters and handed it to me, saying, 'Here, use this. It's just as warm.'

"Later I found that even the chipped blue-rimmed bowl I ate from had been borrowed. I knew I was marrying into a poor family but never imagined it was so poor that even the rice bowl I used belonged to someone else. I burst into tears at the thought. Your father said with a straight face, 'Hey, what are you bawling for? When better days come round I'll buy you two big patterned bowls — one for each hand!'

I forgot my tears. 'Then how will I use my chopsticks?' I answered, consoled."

We had still to face the problem of where to live after leaving our house. Granddad Teh-shun wanted us to move in and live with him in his thatched hut, but mother wouldn't hear of it. It would have been too much of a burden on the kind old man, who had seen enough troubles already. So we lived in Dragon King's Temple, perched on the slope a little over a *li** west of the hamlet. The wind blew in through the broken-down doors and windows, sending sand and dried grass swirling in spirals about the big bare hall. It was cold and draughty, but luckily the weather began to grow warmer. So despite our thin, threadbare clothing we managed to survive.

Outside, the azaleas had turned the hill-slope opposite into a riot of flaming red. Ah, you blossoms so fresh and gay, why are you so insensible to the misery among men?

Every day mother and I went begging. My stomach cried out for food but I never mentioned hunger. I was weary to the

---

* One *li* = 1/2 kilometre or 1/3 mile.

bone, but never complained, just gritted my teeth. Mother knew how I suffered, and I knew how she suffered, too, for she was hungrier and more exhausted than I was.

Things were worse at night. Hunger and cold kept sleep away, and I could dimly see the hideous idols with their fearsome popping eyes glowering in anger and their white fangs, bared in spite, as if they were determined to drive mother and me out.

One day as we stumbled homeward, tired and famished, we ran into Chen Chan-ao. Tailing after him was his steward, that No. 2 Dog.

Chen Chan-ao had grown fatter than ever, his jowls, like lard, hanging heavier and three thick rolls of fat bunched above his shoulders. His eyes gleamed with malice.

"Why, if this isn't Li Eighty-Four's family!" he jeered. "What a terrible, terrible shame! How did you get yourselves into this condition? A pity, what a pity. You could be walking along fortune's wide road but you would choose the risky plank of insecurity! You're asking for trouble. You've only yourselves to blame. This really is a case of 'the carpenter in a cangue, self-made to fit himself'!" And he roared with laughter.

Mother, shaking with silent rage, spat blood as I helped her back to the temple. Her health took a turn for the worse.

Once, a kind old woman gave me a hot sweet potato larger than my fist. She said, "Begging alone and so young, too. Here, eat this while it's still hot." I was overjoyed.

Oh, how badly I wanted to eat it all up! Or even just take a tiny bite of it, but I stopped myself. Mother was sick and had not eaten for days. I hurried home to the temple with the hot potato.

A thick black cloud rolled over above the sea and pressed low over Tide-Watcher's Point, darkening the whole sky. A sudden cold wind almost keeled me over, and then drops of rain as big as copper coins splattered down, striking and numbing my face. I clutched the potato, not daring to put it in the tattered basket for fear of losing it as I ran.

39

The squall lashed down from the leaden sky, blotting out the hamlet. Tide-Watcher's Point was hidden in the clouds. Sea gulls, dogs and cats fled for shelter. Only I was out running madly about in the storm. How much farther to the temple? Mother must be frantic with worry!

I must press on, come hell or high water.

The storm seemed to have sought me out to vent its fury. It sent wind to pummel me, rain to pelt me, branches to claw at me, stones to trip me, and how it shrieked and howled to frighten me. I murmured to myself, don't worry, mother. Don't upset yourself. Your daughter is coming. She can see the walls of the temple. She will be with you in just a little while. Oh, mother!

I staggered through the door, the potato now a muddy messy mass like myself, for I had stumbled and fallen many times. I groped my way through the pitch darkness of the temple to mother's side.

Mother's life seemed at low ebb. Between heavy gasps, struggling for breath, she spoke. "Mother's sufferings . . . end . . . soon . . . now . . . but yours . . . yours. . . . Only you left. Only you . . . so young . . . two families . . . only you left. . . . Hai-hsia . . . if only . . . you were a boy. . . . Mother is very sorry . . . leaving you. . . ."

"Mother! Mother!" I clasped her chilled body to mine, shaking her gently while the wind and rain outside howled and hammered.

A hand pulled at me. My mind cleared. I found Granddad Teh-shun beside me, saying quietly, "Come, child, let's go."

Wives and children toss and whimper in their sleep,
When angry waves rise high and steep.

Granddad Teh-shun's lot in life was a hard one, too. He once lived with his only son, Ah-tsai, who was married and had a two-year-old child. One day, when the menfolk were fishing far out at sea, an unusually violent storm arose. Women and children huddled on the jetty searching the foaming sea with straining eyes as one by one the boats fought their way home, all except Granddad Teh-shun's. Just as everyone was about to give up hope of ever seeing those on board again, Granddad Teh-shun's boat came ploughing through the boiling sea. There were loud cheers and sighs of relief. As the men stepped ashore they were seized and hugged by their families. No one noticed anything wrong aboard the smack. The last man to leave was Granddad Teh-shun. He staggered like a drunken man, reeling and lurching. His daughter-in-law ran to him demanding, "Father! Where is Ah-tsai?"

He did not answer but hurried away, his hoary head bent.

"Father! Father! Where is Ah-tsai?" she cried after him. Still he did not answer, just stumbled doggedly forward.

"Don't ask him, now," some of the crew implored her. Then they broke the news to her, told her what had happened. . . .

When the storm broke, Granddad Teh-shun had ordered his son to furl the fore-sail, but a mighty wave drove the boat aslant and Ah-tsai lost his hold of the rope and a huge curling roller breaking across the deck had dragged him into the sea. They saw Ah-tsai surface once and heard him shout: "Father! Help!" Then he was sucked under again.

That cry shattered the old father's heart. His face turned deathly pale.

Anyone who has been to sea knows that a tiny vessel is just like a leaf in a storm. The waves lift it high on their crests and then drop it suddenly into a deep valley in the water. The boat must run before the storm. It cannot stop. If someone tries to turn it, the next oncoming mountain of water will crash down and splinter it. The eyes of all the crew watched Granddad Teh-shun, waiting for him to make the decision: risk the lives of everyone on board and save his son, or sacrifice his only son for the safety of the crew? They saw the old man's grip tighten on the tiller and heard him shout: "Forward!"

Men sobbed as they clung to the boat's mast and boom. Granddad Teh-shun turned sternly on them, "Stop that blubbering! You've got work to do!"

Granddad Teh-shun staggered home, picked up a jar of wine and gulped the fiery liquid down. Then he slumped over the table and cried as if his heart would break. The daughter-in-law remarried shortly after and left, taking her son with her.

Granddad Teh-shun lost all interest in life. He grew weaker daily and his hair swiftly turned white.

Granddad Teh-shun's house had two rooms, an inner and an outer. His son and daughter-in-law had lived in the inner room, and he the other. In the yard was a thatched shed where the stove had been, and the hay and firewood. After the daughter-in-law left, he put the stove into the outer room and moved into the inner. The first thing he did when he led me home with him was to smash the old wine jar. "I won't touch another drop of that stuff as long as I live," he vowed.

We set up a new home and lived, with Granddad Teh-shun as one prop and I the other. The fate that befell our families was not a rare one. It just shows how bitter and hard were the lives of those who lived by fishing in the old society.

I wondered, will life always be so harsh and bitter for us who fish? Is there no one to save us, someone who is not deaf to fishermen's pleadings?

CHAPTER 6

A TUB OF RICE, A BUCKET OF WATER

THE Kuomintang Coast Guards on the island milled about like a swarm of ants on a hot griddle. They dug trenches, put up fortifications and built strongholds on Tide-Watcher's Point. Chen Chan-ao did not know what to do. Rumour had it that the Liberation Army was about to capture the island. He was racked by gnawing fear and uncertainty.

People asked each other in whispers what the Liberation Army was like. It became a habit to get together in a group, spontaneously, at the settlement's edge and peer over at the mainland. Was the coming of the Liberation Army expected with joy or apprehension? I did not quite know.

Granddad Teh-shun had heard people say years ago that the Liberation Army was a good army. But that was only hearsay. Fisherfolk are realistic, down-to-earth people, who don't venture an opinion until they have seen for themselves.

After crumbling before the Liberation Army, the Kuomintang bandits fled to our island, sullen and savage, with bloodshot eyes and loud curses. They looted as they went, commandeered ships and men and created chaos on our Concord Island.

One day a gale arose, bringing with it such intense cold that granddad and I stayed indoors. Suddenly half a dozen Kuomintang bandits burst in and, kicking granddad aside, demanded grain. They threatened us with their guns, but granddad did not cower. "We have no grain!" he said.

"What do you mean you have no grain? What do you eat, you old liar! Hand it over, quick, or I'll run you through with my bayonet!"

"We eat this," said granddad, taking a basket of wild greens from behind the door.

"That's what you feed to your pigs. Do you think we believe that?" asked one of the bandits sneeringly. "I'll put a bullet in you when I find your store of grain, but first you're going to dig some trenches." Two other bandits seized granddad and dragged him off. He turned as if to speak to me but they hustled him away before he could utter a word.

Granddad was now an old man and a sick one too, yet they ruthlessly dragged him away to dig trenches. I wanted to explain things to them, but what would be the use? They were dogs, mangy curs. There was no reasoning with them. I wasn't going to go down on my knees and implore them to be merciful. No, never! I did not cry nor did I feel grieved. I was filled with an intense hatred fuelled by a burning anger. I stared at the knife by the stove, swearing to myself that if they tried to touch me I'd fight to the end.

The rest of the bandits tore the house apart, searching and prying, vainly looking for anything worth robbing. They found nothing. "Miserable beggars!" they cursed. "They haven't a damn thing worth taking!"

Just then another band of Kuomintang looters stormed into the house, carrying hens, ducks, chunks of meat, eggs and rice. They intended to cook them there and then. They found the water-tub empty and one of them yelled, "Go and fetch some water, girl!"

"It's too much for me," I said defiantly.

"You'll do as I say, or I'll beat you to a pulp with this," he threatened, throwing a carrying pole at me.

I suddenly realized that granddad had left without his padded jacket, and thought I must take it to him, otherwise his illness might get worse. "All right," I said, snatching up the tattered jacket the bandits had flung on the ground. Picking up the pails, I hurriedly left the house. When I reached the well I let the buckets sink, knowing that I could find them when I needed them again, and hurried off to look for granddad.

Early one winter morning in 1950, when the wind howled across the island, the night-long sounds of fighting, exploding shells and the crackle of gunfire slackened, but from Tide-Watcher's Point came loud noises indicating that the enemy was still resisting.

When the Kuomintang soldiers retreated up the slopes of the Point shortly after the fighting broke out, the inhabitants fled to the hills on the south, leaving the settlement almost deserted. Granddad and I stayed behind, for his heart was very bad after several days of digging trenches for the bandits. He was much weaker than before and lay in bed groaning softly, sick, angry, worn out and famished.

Kind-hearted Sister Ah-hung came and urged us to take refuge outside the village. Granddad said he was too sick to move, but he joined her in urging me to go to a safer place. Of course I refused. Despite their pleading, I refused to leave without granddad.

Both halves of the settlement were suddenly filled with Liberation Army men. A squad came along to live in our house.

"Countrymen, we're sorry to trouble you like this," one of the Liberation soldiers said smiling. They peered into the inner room and then, without another word, began to sweep and tidy the place. Some of them began cleaning their weapons. Their clothes were covered with mud. Everything about them indicated that they had fought all through the night and more than likely they had not eaten yet.

One of the Liberation Army men, thin and short, looked no more than sixteen. He wore a uniform several sizes too big for him and had a wide leather belt drawn tightly round his waist so that he looked for all the world like a human gourd. You could see immediately that he was as sharp as a pin.

45

"Why haven't you gone over to the southern part?" he asked granddad as he cleaned his rifle. "It's safer over that way. The Kuomintang are shelling this side of the island."

"I'm too old to move. Besides, I'm not well," replied granddad with a sigh.

The young boy-soldier looked up solicitously and said, obviously trying to comfort us, "There is some danger, but it won't be long now before we clear them out. We'll take that height in another two or three hours."

After the house and their guns were cleaned, the boy-soldier asked a tall thickset soldier, "Squad Leader, shall we use the owner's pot to cook our food?"

"Is it being used?"

The boy lifted the lid and saw the wild greens cooking in the pot. He turned to granddad and asked, "What's this you're cooking, grandpa? Is this all you've got to eat?"

"What else can poor people like us eat? Even that will soon be all gone," granddad replied wearily.

"There are only the two of you, why cook so much of it?" he asked, looking at us with sympathetic eyes.

"It takes a lot of fuel to cook wild stuff. Cooking enough for several days at one go saves fuel."

"That's true," one of the soldiers said.

"That's the way we do it at home too," another added.

Another Liberation Army soldier came in. He was about forty, of medium height, his face dark with bristles. In his hand was a pipe. As soon as he stepped inside, the boy-soldier said to him as if to an elder brother, "Platoon Leader Fang, how're we going to cook? Our host's pot has greens boiling in it!"

"Take the rice over to Squad Two, Li Tieh-chun! They've got a big pot and I'm sure they'll help," said the man addressed as Platoon Leader Fang.

So the young soldier's name was Li Tieh-chun. With a brisk "yes" he flew out with the sack of rice.

The platoon leader removed the lid from the pot and, looking thoughtfully at its contents, said to the men, "Are you comrades hungry? Here, help yourselves. A bowl each to begin with!"

"Right you are! We'll do that immediately!" The soldiers leapt to their feet and began fishing out the enamel mugs from their shoulder bags with a red star sewn on them.

"Hey, save some for me," cried the boy-soldier as he stepped through the door. He pushed his way forward and helped himself to a heaping mugful. I thought to myself as I glared angrily at him, you're a little fellow but you're the greediest of them all.

"Don't look so angry, lass," their platoon leader said to me, his eyes twinkling with amusement. "You won't have to eat this sort of stuff much longer. This is bitter, and tough too. You call them wild vegetables? Why, they're nowhere near as good as the greens from our Pingyang County!"

"Then why are you bolting them down, if they're so terrible?"

"Hang on there. We're going to give you our food in return."

"I won't touch it! I've had my fill watching you eat ours!"

The soldiers burst into laughter. Oh, how they laughed! I didn't see anything funny but I'm sure I looked very ferocious and angry.

They seemed to be laughing on purpose to make me angrier. They helped themselves to more and soon emptied the pot. Suddenly there was the shrill blast of a whistle outside.

"Mess time!" they announced. Several of them hurried out and soon returned with a tub of steaming white rice. The platoon leader filled a bowl and handed it to granddad, then Li Tieh-chun passed a bowlful to me.

Anger made me turn my head away.

"A hungry little girl filled up to bursting point with indignation," the platoon leader said with a smile. "Come and eat it while it's hot. We've already had ours."

When I realized what they were doing I was struck dumb. I did not say anything or do anything. I couldn't understand why these Liberation Army soldiers behaved in this way. As I held that bowl of rice in my hands a wave of warmth and fragrance flooded over me, healing the wounds and soothing away the hurts that had been heaped on me over the years.

47

Here before me were my own people, my liberators. My anger melted into hot tears which fell into the rice bowl I held.

While granddad and I ate our rice, the platoon leader pulled up a bamboo chair, sat before us, asked me my name and began telling us about revolution and class struggle, about the Communist Party and socialism. I didn't understand all he was saying, but I do remember him stressing that the Chinese People's Liberation Army was an army led by the Communist Party and Chairman Mao, that this army was the working people's own army and that it fought to win the world for the poor people.

This was all very new to me and I felt I was grasping a treasure more precious than anything I had ever had before. Granddad was getting on for seventy and this, too, was the first time he had heard about such things. If father, mother and Rock could only have been here to hear this!

The platoon leader's full name was Fang Shih-hsiung. His smiling, twinkling eyes, so kind and compassionate, made me feel he was closer to me than either my father or my mother. His squarish face dark with bristles had a martial look inspiring both affection and respect. By the time we had eaten our meal I had lost all fear and doubts, and just as I was about to ask him if we weren't going to arrest Chen Chan-ao, someone called from outside, "Platoon One, get ready for battle!"

The soldiers leapt up, grabbed their weapons and prepared to move off. Platoon Leader Fang slipped a bulging bag of parched grain from his shoulder and handed it to granddad. "Take this and get well soon." Then he turned to the soldiers drawn up in rank and shouted, "Let's go!"

Guns in hand and backs bent, they clambered up the slope behind the house. I ran out and watched them. I asked myself, "What kind of men are these? Why are they so good? What can I do for them?"

"Boil some water. They'll be thirsty when they get back," said granddad as if he had read my thoughts.

Granddad and I rinsed the pot clean, fetched water and chopped wood. I worked at the bellows with a will and soon the pot was singing and the water boiling. I filled a bucket. The rattle and crackle of gunfire outside became intense.

"I'm going to take them some water," I said.

"You can't do that. Listen to the guns."

"I'm not scared."

I took the bucket of water and headed up the road without waiting to hear granddad's reply. The wind was strong and cold as I doggedly made my way up the hill.

Bullets whistled overhead and shells fell on the hill-top immediately opposite with a loud crash, sending up showers of dirt. I climbed steadily, never thinking for a moment that bullets could kill and maim but occupied with the sole thought that I must get the bucket of water to the Liberation Army soldiers.

I heard a "bong!" and felt a burning sensation on my leg. A bullet had pierced the bucket and hot water was spouting over me. I felt like bursting into tears but I plucked a thick twist of grass, plugged up the hole in the bucket and continued to climb. Just as I neared the crest, Platoon Leader Fang saw me and sprang out of a trench. "What are you doing here? Get back down at once!" he ordered.

"I . . . I'm bringing you water," I stammered, not understanding his anger and ignoring him as I continued to climb upwards.

There was a high-pitched screeching. Platoon Leader Fang hurled himself on me, pinning me to the ground.

The shell exploded near us. The bucket was lying on its side empty. There was a buzzing in my ears. Platoon Leader Fang pulled me to my feet and brushed the dirt from my clothes.

"The water is all spilled," I gasped, looking at the bucket on its side some distance away.

"I forbid you to come up!" Platoon Leader Fang's voice was stern. The look on his face reminded me of the time father scolded me for a wrongdoing. He shouted into the trench, "Take her back down, Li Tieh-chun!"

I felt like a chastened child who did not know what she had done wrong. I gaped at Platoon Leader Fang. When he turned back into the trench I saw that his right upper arm was

49

bleeding. Blood stained the yellow earth in the trench. What had happened?

Li Tieh-chun grabbed my arm and started to drag me down from the crest. He was muttering, "You ninny, you! Look what you've done!"

When the hill-top was taken they carried Platoon Leader Fang down to a waiting stretcher. His right arm was badly injured.

I stood beside him as he lay on the stretcher. I felt wretched. With an effort he turned to face me and flashed me a faint smile. His face was like wax and his eyes seemed withdrawn into their sockets. His whiskers appeared to have grown much longer, making him look years older. I was miserable and disgusted with myself. Then I knew why Li Tieh-chun had muttered angrily at me and, as I looked at the platoon leader's pallid face, I felt a stabbing pang in my heart.

When they picked up the stretcher to carry him off, he said to me with a smile, "See you again, Hai-hsia! I'll be back to tell you more of those revolutionary stories you said you liked so much."

I moved my lips but no words came. My eyes were swimming with tears and I saw everything through a blur as I watched them carry him down the slope.

At that time I did not know about such things as class love and class feeling. I did not know why he was so dear to me. We had known each other for less than half a day and yet I felt drawn to him, related in some way. A tub of steaming rice, a bag of parched grain — these were things one could buy if one had the money, but where could one find a heart like that of the platoon leader? The water I had boiled but which not one of the soldiers had tasted was something more than a bucket of water. It was something right from the hearts of us poor and wretched fisherfolk.

More Liberation Army men charged up Tide-Watcher's Point. The sound of gunfire merged into one continuous thundering

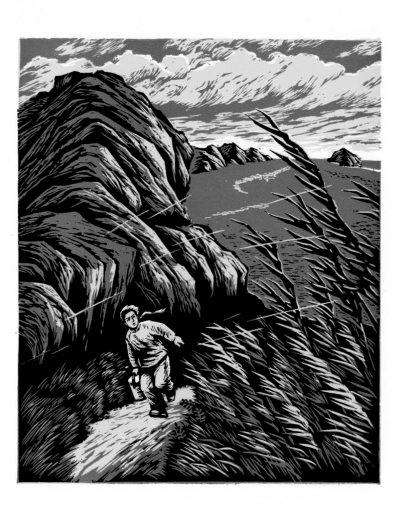

roar. I saw a red flag streaming out at the top and jumped for joy.

"Where's your grandfather?" Granddad Wang-fa asked sharply. He had appeared out of nowhere. In his hand was a fishing spear.

"He's home."

"Teh-shun! Come out, quickly! Get your boat and come along. We're going to catch some bandits!" he called out long before he reached the house.

"Where?" granddad asked, coming out to meet him although bent with pain.

"Ha! The Liberation soldiers have taken the Point and you're still home in bed! I saw some of the bandits take to the sea. I bet they're holing up on Tiger-Head! Let's go and get them!"

"Shall we get some of the Liberation soldiers to come with us?"

"Oh, come on! There's no time to waste. This spear of mine will do. Hurry! Get that boat of yours!" Old Granddad Wang-fa was bursting to go. He held on to Granddad Teh-shun as they hurried for the beach.

"I'm coming, too!" I yelled, racing after them.

"You can't. You stay and look after the house."

But I took no notice of granddad and followed them. They weren't going to get rid of me.

When our sampan neared Tiger-Head, Granddad Wang-fa said to me, "What's that floating over there, Hai-hsia?"

I looked carefully where he was pointing and then shouted, "It's a man! clinging to a log!"

"You've got a sharp pair of eyes. I'll bet you anything you like that it's one of those rats who jumped off the Point."

Granddad sculled the sampan towards the man.

"Ahoy! Help!" the man shouted in a voice tinged with hysteria. He probably thought we had been out fishing.

Granddad Wang-fa cupped his hands to his mouth and shouted back, "A — hoy! Coming!" We drew up to the man.

He was obviously at the end of his strength and thought we had come to his rescue.

The two old men exchanged knowing looks and granddad told me to take the sculls for a minute.

The bandit, looking like a half-drowned dog, clung to the side of our sampan. The two men seized an arm each, hauled him on board and quickly twisted his arms behind his back.

"What're you doing?" the bandit gasped.

"I have a score to settle with you," said Granddad Wang-fa. "You're the one that took a stab at my ribs with a bayonet!"

They tied him up securely.

"Elder uncle, you've made a mistake. I've never done such a thing in my life! Have mercy! I have a hundred pieces of silver in my belt. They're all yours. . . ."

"Who wants your dirty money! Where's your gun?"

"I threw it into the sea!"

"Where?"

"I rolled down off the Point and threw it away."

Granddad took over the sculls and said, "Let's take him along to find his gun."

A cold wind was blowing. Granddad's white whiskers were damp with sweat. I sculled as hard as I could in unison with granddad and could feel the sweat sticking my clothes to my body. Our sampan sped swiftly through the water and we soon arrived below the Point. The drenched bandit pointed out the spot where he had thrown his gun.

Granddad Wang-fa handed me his spear and dived overboard.

I took a firm grip of the spear and kept my eyes on the bandit. The spear was pointed at his chest as if I expected him to suddenly sprout wings and take off.

Next moment Granddad Wang-fa surfaced and glared fiercely at the bandit. "I can't find it here. If you're trying any tricks then it'll go badly with you. But if you're telling the truth then that gun will keep your head on your shoulders!"

"I swear it's the truth. If I'm lying then strike me. . . ."

Granddad Wang-fa disappeared beneath the water again without waiting for the bandit to finish. Suddenly a gun appeared, followed by the old man. His face was beaming as he climbed into the sampan. He fondled the gun as if it was the most precious thing on earth. "Well, here's the knife we said we would seize! Look at it!" He sounded very pleased.

CHAPTER 7

PLATOON LEADER FANG'S STORY

THE year my father and Uncle Liu were murdered by the Black Wind gang Uncle Shuang-ho fled to the mainland where he took part in revolutionary work. As soon as Concord Island was liberated and political power set up in the settlement he was appointed head of the township.

Very soon, with the help of a work team from the People's Liberation Army, Uncle Shuang-ho was leading the island people in a drive to clean up and struggle against the bandits and tyrants on the island. Chen Chan-ao was quickly rounded up.

The day Chen Chan-ao was to be struggled against at a big meeting I went along taking with me granddad's fishing spear. The meeting lasted two whole days.

People who had been wronged stood up and demanded that their wrongs be redressed and those who had been made to suffer cruelly spoke out against those responsible for their suffering. We fisherfolk were happy and elated, and we walked with our heads held high. Had it not been for the work team's intercession, Chen Chan-ao would have been torn to pieces by the angry people.

No. 2 Dog was made to stand beside his patron up on the platform and admit his crimes before the people. He enumerated several major crimes by Chen Chan-ao, such as how Chen had instigated and collaborated with the Black Wind gang to murder my father and Uncle Liu, how they had burnt the house over the heads of Aunt Liu and Rock to wipe out the whole family, and how they had forced us to move out of our house in order to make me a maidservant of the Chens.

Although his confession concerned things that everyone already knew, he spoke with "indignation and wrath" as if he was the injured party and not the other way round. When he came to the bad things he himself had done, he put all the blame on Chen Chan-ao, saying that he had been forced by Chen to do them, that he was just a dog in Chen's house that had to tear at a man when sicked on him, and so on.

He gave Chen Chan-ao several resounding boxes on the ear, exclaiming in a loud voice, "Um . . . isn't that so? Uh?"

"Yes! Yes! Yes!" Chen assented readily.

No. 2 Dog's barking grew more energetic. He foamed at the mouth and yelped, "Ah, fellow villagers! I was the Chens' steward but I was always at one with the rest of you. Um . . . ah . . . I want to accuse Chen Chan-ao! I want to expose him! Under that rockery at the back of Chen's house is a secret cavern. There's gold and silver hidden there, rice and white flour. . . ." Then he raised his voice higher. "I ask the government to call a big accusation meeting to try Chen Chan-ao! Shoot the heinous criminal and despot Chen Chan-ao! Um . . . um . . . fellow villagers, I regret what I did in the past and um . . . um. . . . I beg you to forgive me. I beg you all to let me make a fresh start! I shall turn over a new leaf!" Then he swaggered off the platform holding high a clenched fist, as if he were a great hero.

His words moved some people to pity but they left me cold. Every time I heard him "um" and "uh," it made my flesh creep.

While Dog was barking on the platform, people could be heard whispering their comments. Some doubted whether Dog really meant to turn over a new leaf and others said that he was more slippery than any eel.

Granddad and Wang-fa were muttering. Granddad was saying that No. 2 Dog had revealed nothing new. "I wouldn't put it past him to try some more tricks. His sort never throw away their butcher knives and become buddhas," said granddad with conviction.

"We'll see," added Wang-fa. "If that cur tries anything, we'll be ready for him with a big stick!"

I said to myself, "Even if a dog learns to speak, it's still a dog."

At the end of the meeting Uncle Shuang-ho declared that all of Chen Chan-ao's property was to be seized and the movables distributed to the fishermen. Chen was to be placed under arrest and sent to the district government the next day for prosecution.

I ran up to Uncle Shuang-ho and said, "Uncle, Dog should be arrested and sent with Chen to stand trial too."

"Dog has behaved himself quite well and wants to turn over a new leaf so we must give him a chance," Uncle Shuang-ho replied.

"He's a scoundrel!" I cried.

He tweaked my plaits, saying, "This is grown-ups' business. You run along and leave it to us."

I was furious and pushed away his hand, indignantly protesting, "You must be democratic. I'm a person every bit as much as a grown-up is!"

"You won't become a full-fledged citizen for another couple of years, so run along and play!" he teased.

I thrust my spear into the ground and glared at him. He was so exasperating!

That was another tempestuous night, that first night of the meeting to struggle against Chen Chan-ao. But, unlike the time when Uncle Liu led us to struggle against him, the island was now the people's. Power was now in our hands. People this time had no hindsight qualms and fears. It was just as Granddad Wang-fa said, "We hold the knife now!"

Granddad was no longer so much troubled by a pain in the chest, thanks largely to the rice that Platoon Leader Fang brought him and his happier state of mind. He smiled easily and more often these days and looked years younger.

One rainy night when granddad still sat by the lamp weaving fish-baskets and I was already in bed, he suddenly said to me, "Liberation has come, Hai-hsia. Chen Chan-ao has been knocked down and we've stood up. Better days are at hand."

"Isn't it wonderful!" I replied. "I'm going to make good nets and plenty of them, and I'm going to visit Platoon Leader Fang at the hospital too and tell the Liberation Army soldiers to go out and catch Black Wind and shoot him along with Chen Chan-ao!"

"You are right," said granddad quietly. "Life has been bitter all along for us fishermen, but from now on that'll be something entirely of the past. For this we have to thank the Communist Party and Chairman Mao."

Granddad's words let loose a flood of sad memories in me. Visions of those now dead, who had been near and dear to me, paraded past me deep into the night.

Bursts of gunfire could occasionally be heard above the noise of the wind and rain. What was happening outside? I felt uneasy and slept fitfully.

Early the next morning news of the night's happening spread through the island. Some pirates had landed under cover of the storm, overcome the two fishermen guarding Chen Chan-ao and taken him and his whole family away. The island had only just been liberated and no people's militia had yet been organized. The company of People's Liberation Army men stationed up at Tide-Watcher's Point heard the rumpus and rushed down to the beach just in time to see the pirates making off in their ship. They fired several volleys after them but as the bandits were already some distance from the shore and the night was dark no one could be sure if any of the bandits had been hit. Concord Island's biggest and most malevolent evil-doer had escaped across the sea.

The following day reactionary slogans appeared in Yungchiao. They read: "Chen Chan-ao will be back; the Communists will soon leave," "The Americans have reached the Yalu River and a third world war will soon break out" and "The Kuomintang will soon be back on the mainland."

The two islands opposite ours were still in enemy hands and, as our Concord Island had only just been liberated, the night attack and the reactionary slogans caused quite a great alarm. I could not read but I heard others read them to the groups of people standing around. I was fuming. Why don't we rip them down? I thought, and went up and tore them off without batting an eyelid.

A couple of timid souls edged away when they saw me do it. I overheard one of them say, "That Hai-hsia must have eaten tiger's liver for breakfast!"

"It runs in the family," the other answered. "Those Lis and Lius are always getting themselves into trouble!"

But there were others who supported me. Sister Ah-hung came up to me and said, "That's it, Hai-hsia! You're a true fisherman's girl!"

Before I could answer, someone slapped me on the back. It was Hai-hua. She said to me quietly, "A Secretary Fang wants to see you."

What's this about a secretary? And what did he want of me? At first I was inclined to disbelieve her but when I saw how earnest she was, I thought otherwise and felt apprehensive. What had I done? Was it because I had torn down those slogans?

"I'm not going," I said to Hai-hua. "Anyway, what does he want me for?"

"He's waiting for you at your house," she went on.

I ran home with a pounding heart and saw immediately that it was Platoon Leader Fang. "Ah, it's you, Platoon Leader Fang!" I exclaimed with delight. "That little devil Hai-hua told me that it was some Secretary Fang!"

"She wasn't wrong, Hai-hsia," he said standing up and shaking my hand. "I'm now Party branch secretary of Concord Island."

I then noticed that he was still in uniform but without a badge on his cap nor tabs on his tunic. I realized what had happened and took hold of his limp right arm. "It was because of me that you. . . ." The rest of my words were drowned in tears.

"Ah, you silly girl. What a thing to say!" he replied, patting my heaving shoulder. "The Liberation Army isn't fighting up and down the country for this or that person. It's for the revolution, for the liberation of all the oppressed and exploited. Who were you carrying that bucket of water to? Why? But we won't go into that here. When there's time, I'll tell you some more stories about the revolution."

"Tell me one now."

"Now, hold on a bit. I've got some matters to attend to. When I've time, I'll tell you a story. Meanwhile, I want you to take me to your township head."

Secretary Fang came again after the evening meal. Granddad and I plaited fish-baskets under the lamp as he told us a story about the revolution. And this is what he told us:

"One spring day in 1949 on the eve of our Liberation Army's crossing of the Yangtze River, our South Chekiang Guerrilla Column received orders to intensify our attacks on the enemy. The plan was to disrupt the enemy's rear and destroy his political power while the main body of our troops forced the river. The enemy, wanting to consolidate his rear, also stepped up his actions against us. There was plenty of fierce fighting as you can imagine. Sometimes we fought two engagements a day, and even three at times. One day I went with Platoon Leader Li Jung-sheng to a meeting to get our battle orders at Kuatsang where one of our detachments was located. On the way back we ran into a company of soldiers belonging to the puppet Fourth Chekiang Peace Preservation Regiment. They sighted us and we both started moving up the side of the hill for the crest. The enemy came at us from three directions and we fired as we retreated, hoping to slide down the other side with the help of the tangled vines. Just as we got to the ridge there was a burst of gunfire and the platoon leader had his legs shot from under him. I quickly hoisted him on my back, carried him behind a boulder, and then took up a position commanding the path the enemy had to use as they emerged from the brush. One man there could hold back the enemy, for the path was narrow and steep. After I had picked off seven or eight of the enemy they took cover and didn't dare make a move to come nearer. They fired at us from behind their shelter and I fired back. This went on for about half an hour before I ran out of bullets. I hurried back to my wounded companion and told him that I was out of ammunition. I suggested that we start moving down the back of the slope. He had lost a lot of blood and was lying there limp. In a weak voice he said, 'You get out of here as fast as you can. I can't make it. Leave a hand-grenade with me and I'll cover you.'

" 'I'm going to carry you,' I said.

" 'You want to see the two of us crash down this cliff?'

"Pulling the last of our grenades from my belt, I replied, 'Then we'll make a stand here together.'

" 'There's no need for that. Our troops crossing the river have got to be met. Remember? I order you to leave, now!'

"I was so upset and worried that I didn't really take in anything he said. 'I'm going to stay here with you!' I repeated stubbornly.

" 'Take 'em alive,' the enemy soldiers yelled as they got nearer.

" 'You mustn't stay,' the platoon leader said, looking steadily at me. 'I'm too weak and dizzy. I want you to deliver these papers to Shu-chin. They're very important.' He tremblingly took a small book from out of his blood-soaked pocket and handed it to me. 'It's imperative that this reaches her,' he said curtly. 'This is an order!'

" 'Important . . . imperative. . . .' Shu-chin was his wife and our underground liaison agent. I handed him my grenade and put the notebook securely away.

" 'Take this empty gun with you too. We're not going to leave any revolutionary weapons for the enemy.' I took his gun and slipped down the cliff.

"There was concentrated firing followed by the explosion of a grenade. I looked back, saw a cloud of smoke and knew that the platoon leader had pulled the pin as the enemy closed in on him.

"I handed the little notebook to Chu Shu-chin through a blur of tears.

" 'This is not a document, Comrade Fang! This is his diary!' she exclaimed.

" 'Oh, how could I be so stupid! And I left him alone!' I thumped my own thick skull. I could restrain myself no longer and I wept, clutching the bed.

" 'Bear up, Comrade Fang,' Chu Shu-chin said from the other room. 'A revolutionary sheds his blood but never tears.'

"I checked myself with an effort. Soon Chu Shu-chin's only son, Tieh-tan, came indoors from chopping firewood.

" 'Do you have a message for me to deliver? Give it to me,' he said to his mother as soon as he stepped inside. He did not know what had happened. He was only fifteen but had already proved himself to be a brave and resourceful messenger. He passed on letters, newspapers and documents and it was he who came and went silently and secretly, meeting or seeing off underground comrades on missions.

" 'Why, you've been crying, Uncle Fang!' he exclaimed after he had put down his basket of firewood and noticed my red and swollen eyes.

"I said, 'What rot! When have you ever seen me cry?'

" 'Comrade Fang, there's a slip of paper inside the book, a letter perhaps,' Shu-chin suddenly said. 'Read it for me, please.'

"I unfolded the sheet of paper and saw that it was a letter, written by the platoon leader to his wife. At that time I knew more characters than Shu-chin so I read it to her, stumbling now and again.

"I have a copy of that letter and I would like to read it to you, Hai-hsia. It was written by my platoon leader just before he heroically met his death. It is full of revolutionary spirit and the fire and ardour of battle. It moved me very much, and that's why I keep a copy of it."

61

Platoon Leader, no, Party Secretary, Fang took out a little red cloth-covered book and, opening it, began to read. I listened very carefully.

Party Secretary Fang read:

Comrade Shu-chin,

In the fighting today both my legs were injured and it seems I won't be able to get back. If that is so then I shall shed my last drop of blood for the people and take my last breath fighting for the revolution.

Chairman Mao has taught us: **Wherever there is struggle there is sacrifice, and death is a common occurrence. But we have the interests of the people and the sufferings of the great majority at heart, and when we die for the people it is a worthy death.**

Victory in revolution does not fall out of the sky; it must be fought for with blood, sweat and sacrifice and by overcoming countless difficulties.

The enemy soldiers are closing in, emboldened by their numbers. They're starting another all-out attack. Comrade Fang Shih-hsiung is putting up a plucky fight but he hasn't many bullets left and the position as I am writing is critical. I shall not be able to say much more. To die for the revolution is a most glorious thing. I shall die proudly, with a smile on my lips knowing that I give my life for the revolution. Don't be sad; turn grief into strength and fight with renewed vigour and bravery for tomorrow's victory.

A dozen will take the place of one fallen. Thousands will step forward and take up the fight. Tieh-tan is no longer a boy and you must not try to keep him to yourself. He was born for the revolution and should fight for the revolution. Please give him my gun. . . .

"That was as far as he got because the enemy rushed at us. He never finished his letter," said Secretary Fang. He put the diary away and for a long moment was lost in thought, then went on:

"I told Shu-chin that Platoon Leader Li had sacrificed himself for me, but Shu-chin wouldn't hear of it. She said, 'That's not true. He didn't die for any one person but for the revolution. In battle, comrades support and help each other, and to save another comrade's life with one's own life is a matter of course. There is nothing more precious nor loftier than the love between class brothers, between revolutionary comrades. . . .' "

I listened, drinking in the words.

Secretary Fang continued:

"That night I had been instructed to take part in another engagement and Comrade Shu-chin said to me, 'Take Tieh-tan with you, Comrade Fang.' I stared at her. 'He's too young. Let him stay with you,' I objected. She had just lost her husband, how could I take her son away?

" 'Age doesn't matter. Everyone can serve the people. His father wanted to take the lad with him to gain experience with the guerrillas but I'd stopped him. It wasn't right of me. What Li said in his letter is correct. Successors must be trained for the revolution. That's a revolutionary's responsibility. We can't refuse Li's last wish. A revolutionary's children should be dedicated to the revolution. Tieh-tan must take his father's gun and his father's place. . . .'

"What else could I do? I took Tieh-tan with me. When our army crossed the Yangtze we were enrolled into the regular army. I was made a platoon leader and Tieh-tan became a member of my platoon. . . ."

"Where's Tieh-tan now?" I demanded.

"Why, you've met him!" replied Secretary Fang. "He's Li Tieh-chun, the one who took you down that hill."

CHAPTER 8

STORM IN A RICE BOWL

SOON after Secretary Fang's arrival democratic reforms got under way. Guided by him the poor fishermen and poor peasants elected their representatives and a new political power was established in the settlement. The puppet heads were all tossed aside and the poor and oppressed people, now masters of the land, stood up with heads high.

Secretary Fang went to West Yungchiao to chair a meeting there, leaving Uncle Shuang-ho to preside over the elections in East Yungchiao.

At first people did not talk much when we were divided up into smaller groups. We did not quite know what was expected of us. Then suddenly someone said, "We poor folks can't write nor can we use the abacus and make speeches. What do we know about running things?" This was followed by another who said, "If we poor folks don't work, we don't eat. We haven't any time to spare."

No. 2 Dog's wife, commonly called "Smelly," took up the refrain: "You've put it right. An old saying has it that without book learning you're not cultured and therefore cannot reason things out. And being unable to reason things out, how can you conduct state affairs? Although we don't set much store by such talk nowadays, how can you run public affairs without knowing how to read and write?"

Dog's wife was a shameless hussy, and her reputation was a by-word. When she was still a girl she was nicknamed "The Little Salamander." After she married this name was replaced by her present one, "Smelly." Her mother lived over at the town of North Hollow on East Beach Island and had earned herself a name of ill-fame when she too was a girl. By the time she was in her thirties she was notorious for always prinking and painting herself and being deeply involved in necromancy, fortune-telling and such trash. Wherever there were death and disease, she was sure to be there, "sending the departed's spirit off" and "searching for the lost soul." In summer she would deck herself out in white silk, heavily powdered and rouged, arching and twisting like a reptile, and openly solicit. She early earned herself the nickname "The White Salamander."

With such a mother, the girl was soon dubbed "The Little White Salamander," though she never quite mastered the art and craft of her mother's trade and did not compete with her in this field. She struck out along a new path, concentrating her attention and affections on Kuomintang officers, and was the cause of numerous scandals. One led to open fighting among her rival suitors. Later she married a puppet village head on Half Screen Island. After being widowed she married No. 2 Dog and came to live on our Concord Island. Her liaison with Chen Chan-ao was rewarded by her husband being made Chen's steward.

And because she polluted the air wherever she went, East Beach Island, Half Screen Island and Concord Island, a more fitting name was soon given her, "The Notorious Smell," shortened to "Smelly."

She was such a vile, deceitful woman that it would be strange for anyone to take any notice of what she said. Yet stranger still, some people actually listened to her.

Right after Dog's wife had raised the question of book-learning, someone said, "I think Mr. Yu can do it. He can speechify and click those beads of the abacus real quick. He's the sort that'll be able to conduct public affairs."

And so Dog was nominated. His nomination was followed by that of a former puppet soldier.

"But can these men represent the poor?" I askcd myself. Suddenly Sister Ah-hung leapt to her feet, exclaiming hotly, "I'm not afraid of hurting anyone's feelings, and I say Dog won't do!" Her face had flushed the colour of a ripe persimmon.

"I agree! I agree!" I shouted.

"I am all for Mr. Yu," another former puppet soldier cried, scowling at Sister Ah-hung. "He did his bit during the struggle against Chen Chan-ao, and Shuang-ho the township head praised him for it. Can't a man change?"

For a few moments there was a dead silence.

Suddenly Dog leapt to his feet and cried, "I propose Hai-hsia! Her family is one of the poorest and was made to suffer bitterly by the despots!"

I was astounded! Why is he nominating me? Is he really a changed man? I am only sixteen and cannot write nor do sums and cannot even make myself understood. How can I be a representative? I was seized with apprehension.

I looked imploringly at Uncle Shuang-ho, and he didn't disappoint me. It was getting towards the end of the meeting when he said, "I think Hai-hsia is too young. We should propose someone else instead."

I sighed with relief. But just then Secretary Fang returned from West Yungchiao and joined us.

"I think Hai-hsia will do fine," he said decidedly. "She can learn as she goes along. She's young and we must take pains to bring up our successors to the revolution."

"That's it. That's settled. Hai-hsia is young but she's got a good head on her shoulders," agreed the others at the meeting, and so the matter was decided.

I glared reproachfully at Secretary Fang. This was going to be beyond me. Secretary Fang was addressing the meeting again but I did not take in a word he said. I felt as if a huge boulder was crushing me down. When the meeting ended, Secretary Fang went out of his way to have a dig at me, calling me "junior representative," which did not put me in better humour.

I went home very ill at ease to wait for granddad to return from the "little harvest"* so that I could talk things over with him.

Stroking his beard and chuckling to himself, he advised me, "Since Secretary Fang says you can, then take it up. But, mind you do a good job of it. Don't let us poor fisherfolk down." Very good, but how was I to go about it? Even granddad was not very clear about that.

Granddad asked who else had been elected, and when I told him what had happened he shook his head and asked slowly, "Dog and Chen San? How can they act for poor folk like us? How on earth did they get elected?"

"All the others didn't want to, so those two got elected."

"I suppose changes can be made after elections, can't they?" granddad asked.

I said I didn't know. Granddad urged me, "Now that you're a representative, you must be more careful. And you had better speak to Secretary Fang about it. It'll be wise to change the other two."

I put down my bowl and went off quickly to look for Secretary Fang as I thought this was important. I did not find him. He was out.

The next day we were given forms to fill in and then asked to decide on a leader to head this group.

As soon as Dog saw me he sidled up and said, "Um . . . now, Hai-hsia. What are you making such a face for? Um . . . I'm progressive and um. . . . I want to turn over a new leaf. We're all members of one big family now. Um." His face wrinkled up as he gave out a low hollow laugh. I thought I could see foul tricks and cunning schemes hidden in every fold of his skinny wrinkled face.

"Oh, stop that umming," I told him sharply. "You're oil and I'm water. We just don't mix, see!"

---

* "Little harvest" refers to the harvest of shrimps and small fish from the near shore after the shoals have passed.

"Um. You're only a kid but you've learned to harbour grudges." He shook his head and looked hurt.

"Let's fill those forms in," Chen San said impatiently.

Dog began to fill in my form for me, writing down my name, age and occupation. But what my occupation was I didn't know.

"Um . . . well, now, we'll say, 'Unemployed,' " said Dog, wagging his head. "Um, we'll leave it blank."

I could not read or write and for this reason I was very much on my guard. I heard Chen San whine, "What are our occupations, Mr. Yu?"

"Write down 'fishermen-peasants' " was Dog's terse reply.

I was astounded and, in a burst of fury, demanded, "Secretary Fang told us to fill in truthfully, didn't he? How can you say he's a fisherman-peasant when he's a puppet soldier!"

"Now, you're a little girl, and don't know what's what," he lectured me as he would a child. "I've filled in your form, so go out and play!"

So that was it! They took me for an ignorant little girl whom they could fool.

That evening I went in a huff to talk to Secretary Fang in the township administration office. I found him scrutinizing the forms we had filled in under the light of a lamp. I blurted out what had happened.

"You've given us a lot of help, Hai-hsia," Secretary Fang said. He placed a chair for me to sit in. "Now, come and tell me about each of those representatives. Who is this Yu Erh? Isn't he the steward of Chen Chan-ao?"

"That's right," I said. "He's Chen Chan-ao's steward and a real bad egg. People all call him Yu the No. 2 Dog behind his back."

"And who is this Chen San?"

"Chen San was a puppet soldier. He's always drinking and gambling and goes round bullying people. He's a brute!"

Secretary Fang turned over another form, then asked, "Who is Chen Ta-cheng?"

"He's Yu-hsiu's father. He used to be very poor and is very simple and honest. When they told him he had been elected, he was so upset and worried that he couldn't eat his meal that night."

"Why were these people elected?" he asked me as if to another adult.

"I don't know," I answered. "Poor people are afraid of taking posts and things like that, because they think they can't run public affairs."

Uncle Shuang-ho came in just then and Secretary Fang turning to him, said, "Have a look at these, Shuang-ho. I think we've got to have a re-election in East Yungchiao."

"Why?"

"Why? People like Yu Erh, or No. 2 Dog as the people call him, and Chen San have been elected. Can they act on behalf of the poor people? You belong to this place so you should know what sort of people they are. . . ."

"They're not despots or capitalists," broke in Shuang-ho, as if he saw nothing wrong with them.. "They were just earning their living. They were just doing what they were told to, weren't they? If we're going to set up an administration to run things we've got to have people who can write and speak. They'll do whatever we tell them to do. After all, won't they be working under us?"

Secretary Fang and Uncle Shuang-ho fell into a long discussion. I did not understand what they were talking about, but caught snatches like, "holding on to political power," "a question of class line," and "mass viewpoint" and so on. I gradually came to understand what they were talking about — who were to hold the reins, who were to rule.

"Comrade Shuang-ho, political power is the fundamental question in a revolution. . . . This election has taught us a big lesson!" Secretary Fang was saying.

In the end Uncle Shuang-ho admitted that he was at fault. "I thought only of getting some people to look after the administrative side of things, getting things going. I never thought I'd made a political error," he said.

69

Then Granddads Wang-fa and Teh-shun came in. They weren't satisfied with the election, they said. The election had not been sufficiently prepared, the masses did not fully know what it was all about and many of them had doubts and fears. As it was only said that one member of a household should attend, some families had sent a child along, the one who ought to have gone staying at home. How could a successful meeting be held like that? they argued.

"We'll have a re-election tomorrow," Uncle Shuang-ho announced.

"No, not tomorrow," Secretary Fang broke in. "We mustn't be in too much of a hurry. It can wait another few days. We've first to raise the political consciousness of the masses. An election held before the masses fully understand the issues won't bring good results. Our job now is to go and speak individually to the activists among the masses. We can't let class enemies hold power!"

A few days later there was another mass meeting chaired this time by Secretary Fang. A new election was held and Dog and Chen San were replaced by Granddads Teh-shun and Wang-fa. I was indescribably happy. After the meeting the representatives met to elect a chairman. Secretary Fang's proposal that I should be elected chairman was unanimously passed with loud applause.

I protested a great deal, but Secretary Fang told me in a stern voice, "This is revolutionary work and not only must you accept, you must also make a good job of it!"

During the early spring when the island was threatened with a famine, the enemy was very active out at sea. U.S. imperialist warships moved arrogantly through our waters and sometimes Kuomintang gunboats came close in and shelled our island. Things were getting tougher for our fisherfolk because they were unable to put out to sea.

Eventually, Uncle Ta-cheng insisted on putting out. The colder water near the land was barren of fish so he went further out to the deeper water, where the fish were feeding. That was the end of him! All that ever came back were a few splinters of wood from his boat, washed ashore by the incoming waves. People said he had been killed at sea by the Kuomintang reactionaries. He left Aunt Ta-cheng and their fifteen-year-old daughter Yu-hsiu.

Aunt Ta-cheng was born of the poorest of poor parents. They had come from Fukien to fish, ran into a thunderstorm and had their boat smashed up. They sold their six-year-old daughter to someone on the island for a small sum of money, sufficient to pay for their return home along with their seven-year-old son. That happened thirty and more years before and never a word had been heard from them since. Now, Aunt Ta-cheng's daughter Yu-hsiu was sick in bed and there wasn't a grain of rice in the house. They were in terrible straits.

Then the People's Government relief grain arrived, 30,000 *jin* of it! I was told by Secretary Fang to count and study those families in East Yungchiao who were in dire need and then decide on how to share out the grain. Before he left, he instructed me, "Don't just listen to what a person says, ask his neighbours too. Don't forget to discuss it with the people when you are not sure of something. . . ."

That was typical of Secretary Fang, careful and considerate, pointing out every step of the way to me in my work.

Which family needed help most? The first family that came to my mind was that of Aunt Ta-cheng. But before I called on them I made inquiries among their neighbours. When I walked into Aunt Ta-cheng's house I saw Yu-hsiu eating from half a bowl of rice.

Aunt Ta-cheng put her work aside and hurriedly found a seat for me. I told her what I had come for and she hastened to explain that she had just that moment borrowed half a bowl of rice for her daughter as she was having hunger pains.

Aunt Ta-cheng was so afraid that I would not believe her that she showed me the empty grain bin. Actually, I hadn't taken much notice of what Yu-hsiu was eating.

At the group meeting everyone had agreed when I proposed putting Aunt Ta-cheng's name on the most needy list. But as

I was on my way to take the report to the township administration I was accosted by Smelly, who demanded, "Why have you been spreading rumours at the poor fishermen's association about Yu-hsiu having good rice to eat?"

"Who's been spreading rumours?" I retorted in a burst of fury. "I saw her with my own eyes! Anyway, what does it matter?"

"People who have good rice in the house aren't allowed a share of the relief!" Chen San broke in. "Look at us, we haven't even dry chips to eat!"

Just as I was about to answer him, Dog joined in. "Um. . . . Why are you trying to make it hard for Hai-hsia!" he demanded noisily, addressing himself to his wife. "And . . . um . . . the matter can be cleared up just by asking Ta-cheng's wife."

"That's right," I said, seizing on this unexpected remark from Dog. "If you don't believe it, we can ask Aunt Ta-cheng."

In the twinkling of an eye Chen San had Aunt Ta-cheng before us. "You mustn't say things like that, Hai-hsia. It's not true. We've no rice to eat." As she said this she was looking at the ground, her eyes avoiding mine.

"But I saw the rice with my own eyes!" I exclaimed.

She stuck to her assertion that Yu-hsiu hadn't eaten any rice. I stared at her, feeling a dull anger rising in me. She was an honest woman and the lie she was telling made her wriggle uncomfortably, her face flushed red and her eyes lowered. She dared not look at me. Then she turned and with head lowered hurried away.

By this time quite a crowd had gathered in the street.

"Um . . . now, one says she ate rice and the other says she did not," Dog declared.

"One of them is lying, and that's a fact. Arguing like this won't show up the liar. Get the bowl and we'll see." Smelly darted away and quickly returned with the bowl Yu-hsiu had been using. She showed it to the spectators. It was all done as quickly as a conjuror's trick. The rice had been eaten so what use was it showing an empty bowl?

But people loudly backed up Aunt Ta-cheng. Some said that I was being unfair, and I had only just been made group chairman too. I heard someone call me "a young liar."

What a mess I was in! As sure as day is day it was she who was telling a falsehood and yet I was being called a liar! Above the loud accusations Smelly was heard shrieking, "She should be kicked out of office!"

If I had shouted my protests to high heaven no one would have believed me then. I fought back my tears and thought, you don't have to kick me out, I'm not going to be chairman a minute longer even if you go down on your knees and beg me!

"Why did Hai-hsia say such a thing?" someone demanded. "She isn't that sort of person."

"Look at the stuck-up little hussy! That little baggage!" reviled Smelly. "You want to know why she's lying? She wants to grab another share of the relief grain for herself, that's why!"

I winced as if she had struck me with a whip. If ever a foul-mouthed serpent crawled on this earth it was she, that viper!

As soon as I reached home I flung myself on my bed and bawled. Granddad was stunned and frightened. "Whatever's the matter? What happened?" he asked frantically.

"I want you to speak . . . speak to Secretary Fang, grand-dad," I sobbed. "Tell him I don't want to be chairman of that group. I'm not up to the job!"

"Who's been bullying you?" he asked anxiously.

"They're all bullying me! I just don't want to be chairman!"

"Hey, you mustn't throw childish tantrums like that!"

"I won't and that's that!" I replied, crying louder than ever.

After a while I heard Secretary Fang come in and felt him patting me on the shoulder. He sounded cheerful and gay.

"Little Hai-hsia, Hai-hsia. You cry too easily. Remember what Chu Shu-chin said? 'A revolutionary sheds his blood but never tears.'"

"Then what sort of revolutionary am I!" I turned and flung at him.

His reply was a loud chuckle.

"Go on and laugh! But I'm not going to be chairman!"

"Then who do you want for chairman?"

"Anyone but me!" I flared back.

"Then we'll get No. 2 Dog to take on your job." I left off crying. "Him? Never!"

"Think it over, Hai-hsia. If you resign, who will be pleased? Dog and his like will gloat. You loudly declare that poor people must rule but the moment you are asked to help rule, you back down."

"The injustice of it! I can't stand any more of it. The poor have stood up and are not trodden down any more. Doesn't it mean that they are ruling the country? Besides, Uncle Shuang-ho said I was too young to vote!" I remembered I wasn't pleased to hear that at the time but I now used it as an excuse.

"You mustn't back down like this. You've just reached the front line and you want to retreat. Now, tell me exactly what happened."

I briefly described what had taken place, and Secretary Fang asked, "Can't you see that someone is deliberately making trouble for you? Someone hates you. Remember that it was you who exposed them fraudulently filling in those forms."

He went on to point out that I had gone about it in a wrong way and that I shouldn't have confronted Aunt Ta-cheng the way I did.

"But why did she tell such a lie?" I argued.

"Can't you see that if she had admitted it, she might not have got any relief grain?"

"Who said she wouldn't? Why, I had already put her name on the list of the most needy!"

"How was Aunt Ta-cheng to know that? Someone frightened her by telling her she wouldn't get relief grain if she admitted having some rice, so naturally she wasn't going to admit it."

I hadn't realized that it was so complicated but Secretary Fang made everything clear to me.

"You mean I've fallen into a trap laid by the enemy? What shall I do?"

"If you want to see a thing clearly you must not only use your eyes but must use this too," he said, pointing to my head. "Use it!"

Three days later relief grain was distributed and I took a 50-*jin* sack of rice to Aunt Ta-cheng. When I walked in I found her, back towards me, cleaning some wild tubers she had gathered. They were the knotty and spindly kind, very bitter to the taste.

"Here's your share of the relief grain, aunty," I said, putting down the sack.

She twirled round and, shaking the water from her hands, rose to her feet. She gazed unbelievingly at the sack and could only say, "Is this . . . is this. . . ?"

"Relief grain is being given out to three categories of people, according to need. Fifty *jin* for those in the first category, the most needy; thirty *jin* for those in the second and twenty *jin* for those in the third. You're getting fifty *jin*, aunty. Will you check and weigh it?" I said as I wiped the sweat from my face with the back of my hand.

"Aiyah!" she stammered, her lips trembling. "Why should I weigh it? The very idea of it! Sit down! Sit down! You must be exhausted." She hurriedly found me a seat.

"I can't stay, aunty. Will you get me something to tip this in. I've got to use this sack again."

As she went about finding containers for the grain, I went over to ask Yu-hsiu how she was.

"You are so good, sister," she cried, throwing her arms about me. "Mother was foolish. . . ." Then she burst into tears and I cried too.

As I was leaving with the empty sack, Aunt Ta-cheng suddenly took my arm and said apologetically, "I'm sorry, child. I meant you no harm. I was afraid I'd get no grain and then we'd starve."

"Let's forget that," I said, for her pained expression had blotted out all my sense of injury. "I'm so glad you're not angry with me any more."

CHAPTER 9

A CLEAR HEAD FOR SEEING CLEARLY

IN the spring of 1951 the U.S. bandits in their war against Korea were worsted in one battle after another. Finding things getting worse and worse they ordered their Chiang Kai-shek running-dogs to step up harassment along the coast to co-ordinate their war efforts in Korea. We on our island had two tasks to carry out in order to frustrate their schemes — fight the enemy on the one hand, and construct and produce on the other. Class education on the island was carried out at the same time as we campaigned to suppress the counter-revolu-tionaries, carried out land reform, organized the fishermen into mutual-aid teams, built up the people's militia and held mass meetings to condemn the crimes of the U.S. imperialists and the Chiang Kai-shek gang. Secretary Fang, acting as our great leader Chairman Mao instructed, called on the fishermen to take up arms to defend the island and safeguard production and construction.

Secretary Fang declared: "We poor people won the right to live our own way of life by the use of the gun, and we must rely on the gun to defend what we have won. Chairman Mao has said, **Without armed struggle neither the proletariat, nor the people, nor the Communist Party would have any standing at all in China and it would be impossible for the revolution to triumph.** We must remember and grasp the great truth that

Political power grows out of the barrel of a gun and here, I would like to commend Granddad Wang-fa. His life has been a hard one and he has an undying hatred for the class enemy, and for the old society. He has a most profound love for the new society. Some people say that our Granddad Wang-fa is a crusty old fellow and cannot express himself. But listen to what he says: 'The gun is the poor man's guarantee, it is his very life!' He has put it well! There is profound truth in his words. Young people should learn from him and join the people's militia."

Hardly had Secretary Fang said this when Ah-hung jumped to his feet demanding to join the people's militia. Sister Ah-hung and I applauded at once and I saw dour old Granddad Wang-fa smiling as he clutched his beloved rifle. This was the first time I had ever seen him smile so heartily, and what a wonderful, bright smile it was!

Granddad Wang-fa was in his seventies when our island was liberated and he captured his gun, the gun he was now holding. He loved it passionately, and spent days with the Liberation Army soldiers learning to strip, clean and use it. No one could get him to part with it, not even Uncle Shuang-ho.

"I'm not going to give the gun to anyone, whatever you say," he affirmed stubbornly, his face set hard. "I may be old but I can use this gun to defend our land. I can still stand sentinel despite my years." Then abruptly turning to Uncle Shuang-ho, he said, "You wouldn't let me guard Chen Chan-ao that night because you thought I was too old, didn't you? If I'd been there that night, he wouldn't have got away. He'd have been a dead Chen Chan-ao!"

When this was reported to the comrades at district administration, they readily gave him permission to keep his rifle and also commended him. This incident helped enormously to get the drive going to build up the people's militia.

The meeting lasted until midnight but when I finally got into bed, I could not sleep. I lay there tossing and turning, my thoughts chasing each other like a shuttle weaving a net. I heard a cock crow before I fell asleep and even then my sleep was troubled. I saw Chen Chan-ao and his bandits standing before me, their guns pointed at my chest. They gave vent to an ugly laugh and stretched out their filthy claws as if to tear me to shreds. "Granddad! Help!" I cried soundlessly.

In my dream I suddenly heard someone say, "Here's a gun for you!" It was Secretary Fang. "But I don't know how to use it," I protested. "You do know," he replied. I took the gun and pulled the trigger. There was a terrific "bang" and all the bad eggs vanished.

I woke to find sunlight streaming through the window onto my face. I still felt as if I was holding a gun in my hand. I looked and found myself clutching the whisk I used to sweep the bed.

Chairman Mao has called on us to join the people's militia and I will join, I mused, and when I am a militia woman I shall have my gun.

After breakfast I went over to talk to Sister Ah-hung about it. She asked doubtfully, "But will they accept women?"

"I remember Secretary Fang telling me once about women taking part in the revolutionary struggle and that some of them became outstanding heroines in battle," I reassured her. "If they can become soldiers, real soldiers, what's to stop us from becoming militia women? After all, we're not asking to join the regular army!"

Sister Ah-hung was even more eager than I was to become a militia woman. She put her baby safely on the bed and, taking me by the arm, hurriedly escorted me to the township administration office.

The administration office was formerly Chen Chan-ao's front court. Behind its iron doors was a huge, wistaria-covered partition-wall in the centre of which had been painted the character *fu* (fortune), larger than a fish-basket. There was a rockery in the yard and many exotic flowering shrubs.

When Sister Ah-hung and I walked into the yard we found Uncle Shuang-ho and some fishermen arguing. "All right, all right," he said, "I'll fix it for you tomorrow. All this arguing is going to drive me mad." He finally got rid of them, looked up, saw us and asked impatiently, "What are you two doing here?"

"We want to join the militia!" Sister Ah-hung answered briskly.

"Oh, no!" he groaned. "Why must you come now, of all times!" He quickly vanished.

"Let's go and find Secretary Fang," I said to Sister Ah-hung. Secretary Fang was busy writing in the eastern room.

Sister Ah-hung strode inside as if entering her own house and said in a loud voice, "I'm thirsty! Let me have a drink of water, will you?" Without waiting for a reply she helped herself to water from the jug on the table. Secretary Fang raised his head and watched her with a quizzical gleam in his eyes. Then he asked with a chuckle, "Is there anything I can do for you?"

"Why weren't we women consulted about the setting up of the people's militia?" I asked bluntly. "Don't you want us?"

"We thought we'd wait a bit. The island has just been liberated and a lot of feudal ideas have to be abolished before we can do that. The masses' political consciousness has to be raised first."

"What! You're afraid of difficulties and you call yourself a Party secretary?" Sister Ah-hung said scathingly. She had a quick tongue and never bothered to hide what she thought.

"I'm not afraid of difficulties. I was afraid of making things difficult for you women," he said with a smile. "What is your name?"

"My maiden name was Chao Erh-man but I left it behind when I left my family to get married. Now I'm called Ah-hung's wife."

"Who have you got in your family?"

"My parents-in-law died some time ago. There are three children. Ah-sha is seven, Little Two is four and Little Three is one. Then there is the children's father, Ah-hung."

"Have you talked it over with the children's father?"

"What's there to talk about? Can't I decide for myself?"

79

"Ah, but are you aware that the militia has to stand sentinel and do guard duty? You must discuss this first with your husband, for you have three children, and I'm sure with all the housework you will have plenty to do."

She replied truculently, "You're a very biased Party secretary. Hai-hsia was just telling me about women who became heroines. If other women can, why can't we join too?"

I nudged her. What I had told her and what she was now demanding were two totally different things.

Confused by her forthrightness, Secretary Fang stammered, "Er . . . er." Then he realized what it was all about and burst into laughter, but Sister Ah-hung looked a little resentful.

Why was Secretary Fang pouring cold water on our request? Was he trying us out? Did he doubt our sincerity?

"We fisherfolk have a saying that 'the ship's strength lies in its sails and a person's in his heart.' We can do anything if we have the will for it," I told him with conviction.

"Quite right, too," said Secretary Fang, nodding approval. "I'll ask the district Party committee about it. You go home and talk it over with your families, then come and see me again tomorrow afternoon. I'll let you know then. You women prop up the other half of the sky!"

"What's there to ask?" Sister Ah-hung demanded. "You say 'all right' and that'll settle it, won't it?"

He laughed as he said, "I can't do that. I can't decide on my own, I must consult the district Party committee about it."

As soon as we got out into the street, Sister Ah-hung said in a loud voice, "Bah! That man there is not at all like a military man. Shilly-shallying about like an old woman!"

"Shush! He'll hear you."

"So what? I want him to. What's there to be afraid of? He's not going to eat us up like a tiger, is he?"

I discussed it with granddad at home and he was all for it. "If Secretary Fang says it's all right, then join by all means," he encouraged me. "In the old days there were plenty of women warriors and generals, too."

"But how can you talk about today and yesterday in the same breath?" I asked him.

"And why not?" he countered. "You have to have plenty of pluck to be a militia member, don't you? Besides, why could those Kuomintang scoundrels, pirates and Chen Chan-ao do as they liked with us in those days? Because they had guns and we didn't! Why have they run away now? Because we have our Liberation Army! If we have guns too then they'd better not try coming here again. Your Granddad Wang-fa has a good head on his shoulders, he has. Keeping that gun he got out of the sea was a clever thing and he's been commended for it by the district."

"I'll have a gun too when I join the people's militia!"

The next day I went to call on Sister Ah-hung to ask if she had talked the matter over with her husband. But before I could open my mouth she flung the broom aside and said fiercely, "I've mucked it up!"

"What do you mean?"

"Ah-hung says that the militia has nothing to do with women. Women should stay at home, see to the cooking and washing and look after the children."

"And what did you say?"

"I told him housework was a private matter while militia affairs were a public concern. Then I asked him which came first. I also told him that militia work wouldn't interfere with housework!"

"Then what did he say?"

"He glowered at me, probably would've tried to beat me like men beat their wives in the days before liberation. He said, 'How many pairs of hands have you got?' I answered, 'Why can't you help with the housework?' That really made him lose his cool! He banged on the table and kicked over a stool. 'A man do housework! Never heard of such a thing!' Then he stormed out of the house and stamped his way aboard ship."

"What's to be done? I think I'll have to go on my own to see Secretary Fang."

"No, you won't! Do you think I'm going to let a man have the last word? Why didn't he ask me before he joined the militia? I clapped when he did it and now when I want to join he kicks. I don't care what he thinks, I'm coming along with you. And if you tell the secretary about this I'll wring your young neck!"

Secretary Fang didn't return until the third day. That evening we went early to his office. When he saw us he called, "Everything settled?"

"Of course, otherwise why are we here!"

"That's splendid!" he said jovially. "We need enthusiasts like you. The island has just been liberated and there's much to be done."

"Then we're accepted?"

"That's right. And a lot of others too. District has told us to organize a platoon of women militia. We've got to make a good job of it as the other villages are going to follow our example."

"Then give us our guns!" I demanded impatiently.

"They haven't arrived yet," he apologized with a smile.

Dismayed, I asked, "You expect us to fight with bare hands?"

Sister Ah-hung slapped her knees and stood up saying, "I'm leaving. Got to feed the baby. Everything, the whole works, has changed since liberation but nothing has changed for us women!" She flounced out of the room.

When I caught up with her she was still muttering and griping. "What sort of militia are we without guns! He's not much better than Ah-hung. Looks down on us women!"

"But that's not true," I protested. "He has a very high opinion of women. Didn't he say the other day that women hold up half the sky?"

"And that's true. But why doesn't he give us guns?"

"Probably there aren't any left. But we'll get guns later!"

"Then can you tell me why the men have been given guns? And when it comes to us women, he has no guns to give? Doesn't it mean that he belittles women?" she demanded fiercely.

I had no answer to that. Time was getting on and night was falling. I knew that she had to go home and cook the evening meal for the family so I said nothing more. I went back to talk to Secretary Fang.

"Probably she and her husband don't see eye to eye about this," Secretary Fang said affably.

"How do you know?"

"I could see this might happen. You girls will find it tough. There'll be plenty of difficulties in setting up your women's platoon and plenty of difficulties afterwards. And we mustn't forget that the enemy will try to sabotage too."

"They won't get very far!" I assured him.

"Don't be careless. Once you become careless the enemy will put you into an awkward position. By the way, have you got to the bottom of that matter about half a bowl of good rice?"

"It's all over. Ta-cheng's wife and I are friends again, so that's the end of that."

"You think so? My, my, Hai-hsia, you have very big eyes and can look piercingly at a person, but for all that you don't see the heart of a problem, the essence of it."

"What do you mean?"

"There's class struggle involved in that business of half a bowl of rice."

I was mystified. How could there be class struggle in half a bowl of rice? From Secretary Fang's stern face I could see that the matter was serious and tried to figure out what he meant.

"Chairman Mao teaches us, **Who are our enemies? Who are our friends? This is a question of the first importance for the revolution.** If you can't distinguish enemies from friends, Hai-hsia, what use is a gun to you? Who are you going to shoot? Would you consider people like Dog friends?"

"Most certainly not! He's a bad egg, an enemy, and will never be at one with us!" I declared passionately. "Anyway, he wouldn't dare try anything funny when the gun's in our hands!"

"That's where you're wrong. His like will never be reconciled to their defeat. Every minute, every second they are up to some mischief. You haven't noticed it, that's all. That matter about half a bowl of rice was his doing. He was behind it."

"Oh? So they were at the back of it?" I was surprised and a little shocked. Of course I shouldn't have been, for Secretary Fang had said the same things to me just before the relief grain was shared out, only I hadn't really understood then.

"That's right. And let me ask you another question. Who did they borrow that rice from?"

"From Smelly."

"Have you ever known her give food to anyone even when poor people were on the verge of death from starvation? Why did she do that — when the People's Government is distributing relief grain? Do you think she has changed, or was she up to her old tricks again? And who was it that urged Aunt Ta-cheng to come out and deny it?"

"Smelly!"

"And who accused you of spreading rumours? And demanded your dismissal?"

"Smelly!"

Things were becoming clear to me under the stream of prodding questions. As an old saying has it, "No waves without wind" and this adverse current was surely whipped up by class enemies. But I still could not get right to the bottom of it. Why did they do it?

"Don't just have Smelly in view. Remember those hiding behind her, those who prompted and directed her, people like Dog and Chen San."

"So, it was them, those heartless scoundrels! They are vile!" I cried out in a fury and, as if waking from a dream, at last saw it. "I'll find them and confront them with this!"

"All this is only deduction. You must investigate and clear up the mystery."

"How am I to go about it?" I asked in dismay.

He looked at me and then patiently explained, "Investigation means getting to know a thing clearly. It's something you must learn to do in revolutionary work. If you don't understand a thing clearly then you can do nothing correctly or well." Then he went on to tell me how to go about it. "You're good friends with Yu-hsiu, aren't you? You could talk to her first and then have a talk with her mother if you think what she has told you requires that, or else you could ask her to speak to her mother. You've got to use your brains if you want to have a clear picture of a thing."

I am by nature impetuous and cannot eat or sleep well if I leave something undone. That very day, acting according to what Secretary Fang had told me, I learned the whole story. It was like this:

The trouble-makers were Dog and Chen San. When the government relief grain arrived they pretended that they pitied Aunt Ta-cheng and offered to lend rice to her because her daughter was sick. When she said she had no rice to repay them with, Smelly said, "It doesn't matter. We've all been liberated and the poor and the rich are now members of one family."

The half bowl of rice was handed to the sick girl only after I had arrived and was making inquiries among the neighbours, which was why I saw Yu-hsiu eating it. After I left, Smelly went and asked Aunt Ta-cheng whether I had seen Yu-hsiu eating the rice. She told her that I had. Then Smelly exclaimed, "That's the end of any relief grain for you! You won't be getting any of it."

"Oh, what shall I do? What shall I do?" wailed Aunt Ta-cheng.

"There's only one way, and that's to deny it, deny that you ever had any rice," advised Smelly.

"But that's a downright lie!" protested Aunt Ta-cheng.

"You're a fool not to see what's more important to you. Can't you see that if you don't you won't get any relief grain?"

"But Hai-hsia saw it."

"What can she do if you deny it? There's no one except you and me who know about it."

And so Aunt Ta-cheng did as Smelly said.

In an excited voice I told Secretary Fang all that I had learned and, when I had finished, he said, "Let this be a lesson to you in class struggle. In the future you'll have to pass plenty of such tests. It's good training."

"This has taught me a big lesson, but there's still something I'm not clear about. And that is, how did you see it right from the start merely from what I had told you?"

He laughed at my bewilderment. "Oh, that is what is called 'being armed ideologically.' Experience is useful, but first of all you must have class struggle in mind. That is the important thing. If you bear class struggle in mind then you can see things clearly. You must keep a clear cool head, otherwise you'll get duped and fall into a trap."

I looked at him in awe and admiration and said, "I'm just an ignorant girl. But now that you have pointed it out to me, I can see it very clearly. You must give me more pointers, otherwise I'll come a cropper with every step I make. I promise you I'll do exactly as you say."

"I'm much older than you and have a bit more experience and I have had the benefit of being taught and trained by the Party and Chairman Mao a little more than you have. I can and should help you, but every one of us must make revolution as Chairman Mao instructs and go forward along the road he points out."

"Chairman Mao is in Peking, thousands of *li* away from our little island, how can we be instructed?" I asked in a puzzled voice.

With a smile he pulled out a drawer and took from it several books of varying sizes. "Chairman Mao's instructions are written down in these. They're all in here. On the question of class struggle, this is what Chairman Mao says." Secretary Fang picked up a book and, turning some pages, he came to a

part underlined in red and read: **"After the enemies with guns have been wiped out, there will still be enemies without guns; they are bound to struggle desperately against us, and we must never regard these enemies lightly."** Then taking up another book he read a passage similarly underlined. **"Make trouble, fail, make trouble again, fail again . . . till their doom; that is the logic of the imperialists and all reactionaries the world over in dealing with the people's cause. . . ."** He explained the content to me and then asked if I had understood.

"I think I understand now that you have explained it," I nodded. I really did feel that I was seeing things clearer, not just observing them but really understanding. I saw that Dog, Chen San, Smelly and those like them were enemies without guns. "Did Chairman Mao say that?" I asked.

"Yes."

I looked at the books on the table and asked, "What has Chairman Mao to say about our people's militia?"

Secretary Fang quickly found the passage and read it to me: **"What is a true bastion of iron? It is the masses, the millions upon millions of people who genuinely and sincerely support the revolution. That is the real iron bastion. . . ."** Again he explained what he had just read.

"Why, these books are a treasure!" I spluttered.

"That's right. If you study these books well, you won't go astray and will be able to see everything clearly and correctly. It will give you greater foresight and widen your horizon so that no matter what difficulties you meet you will be able to overcome them."

"How wonderful it would be if I could read these books!" I sighed, adding, "but I'm letter-blind. I can't read."

"You can always learn. We'll be organizing literacy classes soon and getting people to attend night school."

"When?"

"Let us wait till winter when there is less work."

"I can't wait till then. Write them down for me and teach me to read them right away," I begged him.

It was dark now and Secretary Fang lit his little oil lamp, appearing quite pleased at my impatience. "Very well, I'll be your first teacher and we will have our first lesson today. But it's already dark and no matter how impatient you are you must have your evening meal. How about coming back after that?"

I reluctantly assented.

I bolted down my meal and then hurried back. He was still having his meal so I plied him with questions.

"How did you learn to read and write, Secretary Fang? How long have you been studying? And where?"

"I studied at the guerrilla university," he said with a smile.

"Where is this university?"

"In the forests, caves, huts and thatched houses. In fact everywhere."

"Ha! You're pulling my leg. What sort of university do you call that?"

"You mustn't underestimate this guerrilla university of ours. It has turned out a lot of revolutionaries and revolutionary intellectuals."

His meal finished, we began our first lesson. I repeated after him word by word: "After . . . the enemies . . . with . . . guns . . . have . . . been . . . wiped . . . out. . . ."

It grew late. The moon peeped in through the window as if asking what detained us to such a late hour. When I could read the words, Secretary Fang got up and hurried off to a meeting in another village. I sat there by the lamp reading the words aloud over and over again but no sooner had I read them than I forgot them, and was unable to recognize them again. So this is what studying was like — hard work!

I was so engrossed that I didn't hear granddad enter. "It's very late, Hai-hsia. Time you came home," he said.

"You go on home, granddad. I'll be home when I can read this passage."

He looked pleased to find me learning to read, and picked up a book. He caressed the smooth pages with his hard calloused hands. "Hai-hsia, you're lucky. We fisherfolk never so much as knew the feel of a book in a dozen generations." His voice was charged with emotion. After a pause he again urged me to go home. "If you can't learn it tonight, there's still tomorrow. Learning to read and write is not one day's work. Come, let's go home."

There was reproach in my voice as I said, "You go, grandpa. Can't you see I'm busy?"

Granddad, who knew my perverse temper, admitted defeat and, taking off his jacket, gently draped it over my shoulders. He then set off for home.

The lamp dimmed. I refilled it with oil and went back to study. The tung trees outside the window swished and swayed as if in time with my reciting: "After . . . the enemies with . . . guns. . . ." Night passed and the first light of another day suffused the window when at last I mastered the passage.

I was overcome with joy and made a bee-line for Sister Ah-hung's house. I pounded at the gate.

I heard her hurrying to open it and then saw her dishevelled hair and her hastily thrown-on clothes. "Where's the fire?" she demanded. "Ah, you giddy-headed girl!"

"I have armed myself!" I exclaimed.

"We've been given guns? Where are they?" I saw her eyes light up at the mention of guns.

"Here!" I pointed to my head. "I'm learning to read."

CHAPTER 10

THE WRITTEN MESSAGE

THE women's militia platoon was organized and all the girls whom I had grown up with were in it, Yun-hsiang, Hai-hua, Tsai-chu and ever so many others. Yu-hsiu was only fifteen so she couldn't join until another year, poor girl!

We were all daughters of poor fisherfolk but our natures were as different as our looks. Hai-hua was a roly-poly girl and short, which made her look even dumpier and sturdier. She was a simple downright girl, impulsive and eager, and said whatever came into her head, heedless of the result. She was rough and ready and somewhat careless.

Yun-hsiang was almost all that Hai-hua was not. She was tall and slender, had an oval-shaped face and was by nature careful, patient, considerate and more given to listening than to speaking. When she did speak she chose her words like a marksman taking aim.

I liked both of them, one for her reserve and the other for her bluntness, but of the two I preferred Yun-hsiang. She had many fine qualities, among them her quiet reserve. She had been well known ever since she was a small girl for her fine singing but hadn't let that turn her head. She was an affectionate, warm-hearted girl who felt deeply, but one had to know her well to know this, for she did not readily show it. She was only a fortnight older than I.

As for Tsai-chu, she was unlike either of them. She was spoilt and finicky. If her whims were flouted she would fly into tearful tantrums.

I was elected platoon leader at the meeting which set up the women's militia platoon, and Secretary Fang, as if going out of his way to see that I had my hands full, nominated me a member of the public security committee. He told me, "A committee member must keep an eye on the whole of the island, so don't devote all your time just to your own village."

"I am not fit to be a committee member," I protested. "I don't even know how to look after myself!"

"You'll have to learn as you go along, like I had to. This is the first time here that poor people are sitting in the saddle, so everything has to be learned from scratch. I wasn't born a Party secretary!"

"All right, I'll give it a try," I answered, still unconvinced.

He turned, gave me a stern look, then said, "It's not a matter of giving it a try! You've got to take it on and make a good job of it."

As we weren't given guns there was no rifle drill and we spent the days guarding the roads to and from the settlement with fishing spears, keeping an eye on people's comings and goings. It was not at all fun. Our only other activity was attending meetings to encourage production and the like. Then after the wheat had been harvested and the sweet potatoes had been planted there was a break in field work and we began attending literacy classes in a temple.

I studied hard but made little apparent progress. The only thing which kept me plugging away at it was a desire to be able to read and understand the books that Chairman Mao had written.

We found a teacher for our women's class in Chen Hsiao-yuan, a clerk in the township administration office. When the class was told who their teacher was to be, the girls got very excited. Chen was a junior middle school graduate. He liked to show off his little learning and prided himself on being the island's scholar. And he had a way of nodding and rolling his head about priggishly whenever he spoke. Not many of our militia girls took kindly to him.

"Why him of all people!" cried Hai-hua. "He's like green grapes — smooth outside and sour inside."

"That fellow's like a crab pedlar in summer, hawking wares which contain very little meat!" Sister Ah-hung added.

"Keep your voice down or someone may hear you," Yun-hsiang entreated Hai-hua. "Someone not outside either."

It suddenly dawned on me that Yun-hsiang was referring to Tsai-chu, Chen Hsiao-yuan's fiancee. A glance at her flushed face told me she had heard.

But Hai-hua was not to be headed off. She darted a look at Tsai-chu and, raising her voice higher, cried, "My, my! Protecting family secrets already!"

A stool went crashing over and Tsai-chu flew out of the room. Hai-hua let out a roar of laughter and shouted, "The Beauty and the Scholar! What a perfect match! Ha, ha, ha!"

"What are you up to, Hai-hua, trampling down the vine to pluck the melon!" I said sharply. "Watch that tongue of yours. Driving away students before the teacher has even arrived!"

She realized I was angry and hastened to say, "I can't keep that tongue of mine in order. Before I know it I've gone and said it, and I regret it afterwards. I feel like biting off my tongue!" And she poked it out saucily.

That made everyone burst out laughing, but I was getting hopping mad.

I ran after Tsai-chu, who was crying as she walked away. I said, "Come, Tsai-chu, let's go back to our lesson. It's only a joke. Don't take it to heart. Besides, he has his faults. We'll help him correct them later, all right?"

"As long as he's the teacher there, you won't see me ever coming to class!" she solemnly declared and stalked off.

The first lesson was a noisy one. No wonder some people say that "three women together are like a gaggle of geese." There is some truth in that. Our classroom sounded like a food market. and no one made any effort to keep still either.

As soon as the teacher wrote "Lesson One" on the blackboard, Hai-hua got up and proposed, "We're militia women so I move that we learn to sing a song!"

"That's it! Hurrah! Teach us a song!" the girls cried in chorus.

"Very well. We will begin with a song," he pompously said, putting his textbook on the table.

"Here it comes," someone whispered.

Chen Hsiao-yuan did not hear this remark and went on in an affected voice, "We must have silence. Will everyone please keep quiet? I shall now teach you all to sing *Militia Drill*. As this song which I am about to teach you is for male voices, that is, for militia men, you women will have to sing loudly, and with a swing, to give it a martial air. It must be rendered with feeling, deep feeling. . . ." What a wind-bag, I thought. Then he went on, "Now will you all please repeat after me?" He raised his arms high and began, "With bright rifles and bayonets gleaming, the spirited militia men are training. . . . One . . . two . . . three. Sing!"

Not a voice joined his. We were all too self-conscious. It was terrible. A moment before we had all been jabbering like mad and now that we were supposed to sing, suddenly everyone lost her voice!

Chen Hsiao-yuan began again and once more he was singing a solo. I saw those "eager students of singing" grinning from ear to ear, hardly able to stop themselves from breaking into loud laughter at the sight of Chen Hsiao-yuan's wide-open mouth and joggling shoulders.

"Sing!" cried the teacher.

"Sing!" shouted several of the girls, imitating him.

"Now, after me!"

"Now, after me!" echoed the girls.

Getting to my feet, I said, "Let's have some discipline. What sort of a militia unit are we?"

Some giggled, others whispered quite loudly and suddenly the whole class burst into uproarious laughter. I joined in, unable to check myself. We laughed until tears came to our eyes, until our sides ached, yet no one really knew what we were laughing about.

Someone hummed, "With bright rifles and bayonets gleaming, the spirited militia men are training. . . . How does it go from there?" Only then did we discover that the teacher had disappeared. The girls were indignant and said contemptuously, "What sort of teacher is he, running off like that!"

Then someone started off another peal of laughter and it was on that note the first lesson ended.

The following day it fell on me to call and apologize to Chen Hsiao-yuan and promise him it would not happen again. He came the next day, but Tsai-chu did not. She kept her word and never put in an appearance when he was there.

Chen Hsiao-yuan brought his primers to the class, the books he had used when he started school before liberation. The first lesson began with Going to School and the second was Posture, then it went to Dog, Cat, Ball, Tree, Horse and so on and so forth. At first I tolerated this but as the classes went on I could stand it no longer and said to him, "Teach us about something else, Hsiao-yuan. We're militia women and all this stuff about ball, tree, cat and dog doesn't interest us."

"You're learning to read and write so what does it matter what it's about?" he argued.

"You're wrong there. We want to learn something about politics, not learning words merely for the sake of learning them," I retorted.

"And what do you know about politics? What is politics anyway?" he demanded challengingly.

"I can't tell you what politics is, but I do know that we're learning to read and write so that everyone can understand the revolutionary truth, so that we can read Chairman Mao's books!" I flashed out.

"Very well, if you give me those books I'll use them, but I haven't got them," he said sulkily, backing down.

That night I went to get some teaching material from Secretary Fang. He approved of my demands, saying, "Learning to read and write should be linked with politics. Studying is not merely for the sake of being able to read and write, it's to enable us to study Marxism-Leninism-Mao Tsetung Thought, so that we can serve the people better and do our revolutionary work better." Before I left he gave me three books by Chairman Mao. They were *Serve the People, In Memory of Norman Bethune* and *The Foolish Old Man Who Removed the Mountains*. The militia women found these books were exactly what they wanted.

On the fifth evening it began to rain and, as we waited for our teacher, all of us militia girls sat there chatting about this and that.

"I don't think our Mr. Big Airs is going to come," said Sister Ah-hung.

Even patient Yun-hsiang showed some impatience. "If he isn't going to come, he should at least have let us know and not keep so many of us waiting."

It rained harder and harder as we waited. I said, "I'll go and get him. Don't go home until I come back. Start reviewing yesterday's lesson."

When I stepped out into the night I couldn't see a thing and bumped my head against a wall. The wind was blowing fiercely. My reed rain-cloak hindered my movement so I bundled it up and carried it in the crook of my arm as I made my way through the wet darkness for East Yungchiao. I was soaked through by the time I reached the township administration office and pounded on the door.

"Come in," said Chen Hsiao-yuan curtly.

I pushed open the door and found him half reclining on his bed with a book in his hand.

"You've made yourself pretty comfortable!" I exclaimed hotly, grabbing the book and throwing it on the floor. "Do you know we've been waiting there for you!"

"Can't you see how hard it's raining?" he said.

I stood there shivering, my clothes clinging to me and two pools of water forming round my feet. I was furious. "Are you coming or not?" I demanded. "They're all waiting for you!"

"What is there to get so heated over? Go back and tell them to go home. And while you're at it, tell them there'll be no lessons when it's blowing or raining."

"And would you like us to send a sedan-chair to pick you up too?" I asked bitingly.

The sarcasm was lost on him. He didn't bat an eyelid. "There is no need to send a sedan-chair," he said condescendingly, "but I do need a flashlight."

What an intolerable person!

I turned and ran out of the room. I was so angry that I plumb forgot how I got back to the classroom through the storm.

"Is he coming?" the girls asked.

"He's not coming tonight, nor any other night from now on," I answered.

"That suits me just fine. I'm getting sick of these lessons," one of them said.

"We've stood up since liberation and husbands don't dare beat wives any more. What do we want all this studying for?" another asked.

I lashed out, venting my anger on the whole lot of the militia women. "What a lot of spineless creatures you are! To be looked down upon is nothing so terrible, but it *is* terrible if we don't have any self-respect."

"We've no teacher, so what can we do?"

"Find another one, can't we?"

It was easier said than done. For all our efforts we couldn't find one suitable. Were we going to let our night class fold up just like that? "No!" I declared determinedly. "Not even if I have to do the teaching myself!"

I had said this in anger but the girls took me at my word and greeted my outburst with a round of loud applause. What could I do? Without a teacher the class was sure to collapse. Like it or not I had to take the job, studying and teaching at the same time. Just as Secretary Fang had said, "Necessity compelled it."

96

One evening it was raining cats and dogs and the wind reached tempest proportions as I hurried to class. I had not properly prepared for the lesson and as I made my way over the bridge thinking about it I slipped and fell off. I got thoroughly soaked and hurt my leg. I got up and staggered painfully for the temple and would have collapsed on the floor if I had not clutched hold of the door.

"Aiyah!" cried Sister Ah-hung running up. "What has happened to you?"

"Never mind that. Let's get on with the lesson," I said and went up to the blackboard. There were only twenty-five characters in this new lesson and I copied them on the board: **Comrade Chang Szu-teh died for the people, and his death is indeed weightier than Mount Tai.**

I knew without anyone having to tell me that I was a pretty poor teacher. Those words on the blackboard weren't written; they were drawn, and some of the characters obviously lacked a stroke or had one too many.

One day I asked Secretary Fang, "Isn't there a quicker way to learn?"

"You don't bolt down a meal at one gulp. And when you're walking you take one step after another," he answered.

"Step by step, one following another. At that rate my hair will be grey long before I can study Chairman Mao's works," I protested. "I'm an impulsive and impatient person and I like to hop and skip along."

"If you hop and skip you'll also be liable to trip, won't you?" he asked with a smile that told me that he was pleased.

"If I trip, I can always get up again, can't I?"

"That's the spirit. That's the sort of spirit to have in making revolution," he said approvingly. "That dogged, plucky, persistent spirit."

I plugged away at my studies but it didn't seem to be getting me anywhere. It took me nearly four days just to learn to recognize those twenty-five characters, let alone to write them. When would I be able to study Chairman Mao's works? At the mere thought I felt a wave of despair sweep over me.

97

I got impatient with the "pupils" too, lost my temper all too frequently and blamed them for being slack and inattentive. Trying to force them to be more attentive and diligent, I made those who did not know their lessons stay behind until they did. The result was that the "pupils" began to lose heart. Sister Ah-hung said to me one day, "It's no use getting impatient, Hai-hsia. Despite all your efforts I can't grasp it. I'm not made for studying. I'm a blockhead, so let me out of it. I'll just listen." So, I thought, even Sister Ah-hung is losing confidence! What am I to do?

For days on end the wind whipped the sea, churning its sparkling blue into a muddy yellow. One day as granddad sat by the door mending his broken oar with wire and I was at his side tackling my lesson, he said to me, "You're thinner, Hai-hsia. Can you really learn to read without going to a proper school? It's not all that easy, you know."

That added fresh fuel to my growing frustration. There was so much to learn; I wondered if I would ever be able to read. Secretary Fang had said that three thousand or so characters would be enough to read newspapers, but learning that number seemed to take ages.

"Comrade Platoon Leader!" I looked up. It was Ah-sha imitating a military salute and saying, "I've got a note for you."

"What did you say, you little scamp?" No one had ever sent me a note before. I thought he was teasing me until I noticed a piece of paper in his hand. I reached out for it and unfolded it. It *was* a note!

I read: "Comrade Hai-hsia, there is to be a meeting this afternoon in the township administration office to discuss the work of the militia. It will start right after lunch. Come on time." It was signed "Fang Shih-hsiung."

I was able to make out every one of the characters without a mistake. I don't know how a blind person feels when he suddenly finds his sight restored, but it must be very much like I felt at that moment. How wonderful it was to be able to know, through a note, without anyone having to tell me in spoken words, when and where a meeting was to be held and what the meeting was to be about! And the name of the sender, too! I flung myself at granddad and hugged him. Unfortunately, in my excitement I sent poor granddad staggering. When he had managed to steady himself, he protested, "Have you gone mad?"

"Oh, granddad, dear granddad, I can read! I've just read the note!"

"Really?" he asked.

"Really and truly."

"Read it aloud to me," he said, laying the oar aside and waiting attentively. I read it to him slowly, word by word.

"You've read every word correctly?" he inquired a little dubiously.

"Every word correct," I answered confidently.

"All that lamp-oil wasn't wasted after all," he chuckled. "Now we have a scholar in Hai-hsia."

"And I'm going to be a big military officer, too," I added, teasing him.

Granddad made no comment but stroked his beard and chortled happily.

"I'll soon be able to read Chairman Mao's works to you, granddad, and then you'll know all that Chairman Mao has said."

"Will you really, Hai-hsia?" he asked, looking very pleased.

I lived quite close to the administration office and there was no need to send me a written message, but the way it spurred me on in my study showed that Secretary Fang had done so purposely so as to give me confidence and encouragement.

What enthusiasm, patience and consideration Secretary Fang displayed in training people! He taught me about Mao Tsetung Thought, used revolutionary stories to enlighten me and a variety of ways to lead me forward. He criticized my faults unsparingly and gave unstinted encouragement to me to press ahead.

99

He was continually making higher demands on me and constantly increasing my responsibilities. I knew he was doing it on behalf of the Party. His considerate help and teaching were spurring me on to forge ahead.

That evening when I told the militia members in our class about the note and the way Secretary Fang went about guiding, encouraging and leading us, the enthusiasm of the girls for study soared and their confidence hardened. And through that I came to see the importance of ideological work.

When class broke up Yun-hsiang sought me out. She seemed unusually excited. "You used to be just full of push and energy, but now you've learned to do ideological work as well. The way you told us how Secretary Fang sent the note to you was simply wonderful. It encouraged us no end. That was skilfully and cleverly done. You have made progress, Hai-hsia." It made me feel good to hear how glad my comrades-in-arms were. They were sincerely happy about my progress and saw it as progress made by all of us. Which it was.

"Every forward step that we make is inseparable from Chairman Mao's instructions. We have all made some progress but we're still a long, long way from what the Party expects of us."

Yun-hsiang's words, "have learned to do ideological work," echoed in my mind and made me uneasy. I didn't know the first thing about it in fact. Look at the way I had handled the problem with Chen Hsiao-yuan. I was too curt and brash, my emotions had got the better of reason and made me completely disregard the consequences. What did I know about doing ideological work! I hadn't told Secretary Fang how I behaved towards our teacher and I expected a good ticking off when he got to know.

As luck would have it, that incident came up the very next day. I had just finished speaking to Secretary Fang about my application to join the Party and had reached the door when he called me back. "I want another word with you, Hai-hsia," he called.

"What about?"

"I hear you've driven the teacher away. Is that true?"

"We didn't drive him away," I answered, rankled by the thought of it. "We begged and implored him to come, but he didn't seem at all keen. What else could we do?"

"And so you took up the job in his place?"

I walked up to him at the desk and said, "I was forced to!"

"I like your spirit of daring to do and I've told you that before. We need that spirit in the revolution, but at the same time you mustn't forget to mobilize the masses. One person's strength is small however strong he is. We should rely on the masses, believe in them and fully mobilize them. Nothing can be accomplished without the people. You must learn how to do work among the masses if you want to be a revolutionary. Chen Hsiao-yuan has his faults, plenty of them, but who hasn't his faults and shortcomings? You càn't expect anyone not to have faults. No one is perfect. And precisely because we all have our faults we must study, really study, Marxism-Leninism-Mao Tsetung Thought. We must stress the fact that political-ideological work must be done well, ideological struggles energetically pursued and criticism and self-criticism carried out."

He was right. Where now was the "have learned to do ideological work" that Yun-hsiang had praised me for only the other night?

CHAPTER 11

THE RIBBON OF ROAD
ROUND THE ISLAND

T HE relationship between Ah-hung and his wife became
so strained at one stage that they were like flint and steel
— sparks flew whenever they met. On top of that, old women
who knew no better because they were steeped in feudal thinking constantly fed fresh fuel to the flames by mocking Ah-hung
with, "Call yourself a man? Why can't you even keep your
own wife in her place!"

Others remarked, "Our Ah-hung is too complaisant and
easy-going. Soon he'll be doing all the cooking as well as washing the baby's diapers for his wife!"

"Probably washes his wife's feet for her too," barked Smelly,
outdoing everyone else. "He's worn two holes in the floor by
the side of the bed kneeling to her." Baring her large yellow
teeth, Smelly almost choked herself with her own spittle.

Ah-hung had a fiery temper and the chipping and sniping
drove him mad. He had opposed Sister Ah-hung's joining the
militia right from the start and now he was dead set against it.

One day he came home from sea to find no one there. No
hot meal was awaiting him and even the stove was stone-cold.
Ah-hung locked the door and stormed off to have his supper

at the village restaurant. When Sister Ah-hung returned from a meeting, she had to prise open a window to get in.

When they finally met he complained, "I'm more of a bachelor than a married man. I'm much happier at sea than ashore."

"You've said it! With you out of the way I feel exactly like a prisoner freed from jail," she responded.

There was an armistice only when Ah-hung left for his fishing. Don't think it was just an ordinary squabble between a man and wife. It was a fight to the finish between two determined powers! It makes one laugh to think of it now, but in those days it was no joke.

Ah-hung came home one day carrying a big basket of fish. "Where's your mother?" he gaily asked his son.

"She's weaving nets under the banyan tree," Ah-sha answered. "Didn't you see her?"

We had seen Ah-hung striding home happily with the fish and told Sister Ah-hung to hurry home and cook. She left and upon entering the yard heard her husband saying to their son, "Your mother is too busy to bother with us, son. But never mind, we'll show her we can get along quite well without her."

"I'll run and call her," Ah-sha volunteered.

"Don't bother. We'll cook for ourselves. You give me a hand with the fire. Put a bowl of rice in the pot and a couple of bowls of water and we'll have enough for the two of us. Let your mother look after herself."

After hearing this father-to-son conversation, Sister Ah-hung ran back to us, hardly able to stifle her laughter.

"Ah-hung is doing the cooking!" she laughed.

"Good!" I said, feeling very glad. "It shows he's making progress. I heard that aboard ship he refuses to even so much as touch a pot. Just takes on the rough work and leaves cooking and washing-up to the others."

Sister Ah-hung picked up her shuttle and resumed her weaving. Suddenly she leapt to her feet. "Oh, I must be going back!" she cried, dropping her work and running off. We heard her shout something about, "They'll be making pop-rice. Just you see!" What did she mean?

Ah-hung started to clean his catch after telling his son to put the rice on the stove. Every now and again he would urge Ah-sha, "Stoke up the fire, son."

"Will we get our rice cooked, dad?" asked Ah-sha. "It's always mum who does it."

"Our rice will be better than any rice your mother ever cooked. Keep that fire high and hot," he said as he went on cleaning the fish.

"Dad, I can hear popping sounds inside the pot!" Ah-sha said.

"That's the rice getting cooked, silly. Stop making such a fuss and keep that fire hot and high like I told you!" He continued cleaning his catch, blissfully unaware that Ah-sha had forgotten to put water in with the rice.

"I smell something burning, dad!"

Ah-hung got up and, lifting the pot lid, saw popping grains of rice, black, brown and white.

"I suppose I've arrived just in time to try your pop-rice?" Sister Ah-hung giggled as she stepped in.

Ah-hung tossed the fish aside, picked up his bed-roll and went to live on the boat.

Sister Ah-hung laughed as she watched him go. When his receding back vanished from sight she began to cry.

Secretary Fang criticized faults in my work at the meeting of the militia. I readily admitted them, saying, "We have many faults, for instance, we have not been conscientious enough about attending class, and some comrades have been a bit slack about sentinel duty and. . . ."

"Not those faults! I'm not referring to those," Secretary Fang broke in. "I'm referring to that matter about ideological work I spoke to you about earlier. You must pay attention to what the masses have to say. For instance, why doesn't Hsiang-lien call her mother-in-law 'mother'?"

Can that be counted as a fault in our militia work? I stared at him, then asked resentfully, "Hsiang-lien's mother-in-law was her aunty before she married, so Hsiang-lien simply found it awkward to address her either as 'mother' or as 'aunty.' Anyway, what has that got to do with our militia work?"

"A lot. People are saying that she's become too proud since she joined the militia and doesn't even address her mother-in-law as 'mother.' And by the way, why doesn't Tsai-chu turn up to work?"

"But what has that got to do with me?" I argued. "Even before there was a militia she always stayed at home and did embroidery. She's never worked in the fields."

"People will say that you militia women don't like manual labour. Don't you see?"

"Fancy blaming us for that!" I couldn't help complaining. Before we had our militia no one said a thing when women did not go to the fields, or when a man and wife had a quarrel or when mothers-in-law and daughters-in-law fell out. Now everything was blamed on the militia.

"No one is being unjustly blamed," said Secretary Fang. "Tsai-chu wasn't a member of the militia before, but she is one now, and she should be taught to work like a member of the militia. That's a job the militia should carry out!"

A couple of years ago he would have tweaked by plaits and said, "Ah, Hai-hsia, little Hai-hsia!" and I would feel as safe and snug as if in my mother's arms. But today it was "Comrade Hai-hsia!" Now I was given all the hard jobs and got all the blame too! "You're pushing me!" I muttered.

"Of course I am," Secretary Fang said sharply. "Can gulls soar if they don't try their wings? How can they learn to fly if they don't leave their nests?"

"Oh, very well then, we'll do all that and more."

"And how are Ah-hung and his wife getting along?" Another hard question!

"Getting along as well as oil and water. They're even talking about getting a divorce."

"The rich and the poor are like oil and water. I say they're like fish and water. You should help them patch it up."

Good grief! What a job and so much else to be done. I couldn't sleep that night. Granddad heard me tossing about and asked, "Had a hard day of it, Hai-hsia?"

"Hard day!" I exclaimed, suddenly remembering how I had begged granddad to ask Secretary Fang to let me off my job as group chairman.

"You can't dodge a wave at sea. You must take it squarely, head-on! You must seek help from Chairman Mao's works, Hai-hsia," granddad advised.

He had a point there. I got up, lit the lamp and, taking up Chairman Mao's works, turned to "On the Chungking Negotiations," in which is said: **What is work? Work is struggle. There are difficulties and problems in those places for us to overcome and solve. We go there to work and struggle to overcome these difficulties. A good comrade is one who is more eager to go where the difficulties are greater. . . .** This was a passage that Secretary Fang had told me to underline in red pencil. At that time it hadn't made much impression on me. Now, on reading it over again it made me feel that Chairman Mao had written it especially for me and I felt a surge of new strength. Sleep being out of the question, I dressed and went to find Sister Ah-hung.

As I stumbled along the ribbon of a road rounding the island mountain, I thought, work is like this path, full of ups and downs and twists and turns that must be traversed carefully step by step.

Sister Ah-hung was still up. Her eyes were red and swollen.

"Been crying again?" I asked.

"I work myself to the bone and yet he doesn't appreciate it. He even refuses to let me wash his clothes!" she grieved.

What a woman! Says she is overworked and in the same breath complains that her husband is not giving her his dirty clothes to wash! Indignation made me forget what I had come for. "Then let him do his own washing!" I cried passionately. "We can't let men bully us women!"

"But you don't understand. I want to do his washing," she sobbed. "And only the other day he tossed back at me the new pair of shoes I had taken specially to the boat for him."

"Well, then let him wear out his feet!" I said angrily.

"But you don't understand at all, Hai-hsia! You're too young."

Don't understand? Me? I thought. What a funny character she is, how unlike the Sister Ah-hung that I knew, who was harder than granite. The Sister Ah-hung before me now is softer than dough.

"I'll find him tomorrow and drag him back!" I said.

Dawn was breaking when I reached the boats. I found Granddad Wang-fa chiding Ah-hung.

"That wasn't right, Ah-hung. She came all the way here to wash your clothes and she brought you a pair of new shoes too. Yet you treated her like that! She was putting down a gangway for you to reach her. Why do you want to go on making her and yourself unhappy?"

"I'm not going to be walked over by any female!" protested Ah-hung, his cheeks flushed with anger.

All my good intentions vanished when I heard him disparaging women like this. I forgot I had come to persuade him to go home. "What's all this about females, eh? Why do you look down on women?" I rounded on him.

"Ho, our comrade lady soldier is here!" he said, only then realizing that I was standing near. "Women have been liberated and have risen in the world, eh? Your feelings are not to be hurt but at least you can let us keep out of your way, can't you?"

"Will you be reasonable or not?"

"Who's not being reasonable? As the saying goes, 'If justice is on your side you can travel anywhere in the world; if justice is not on your side you'll find it hard to move even an inch.'"

"All right. How much land have you reclaimed? And how many loads of manure have you carried to the fields?"

"I've been fishing."

"And how did you look after your three children?"

"I've been fishing."

"Who chopped the firewood? Cooked? Fed the pigs? The poultry? Who did all that work?"

"I have been fishing."

"Fishing! That's all you can say. And you call yourself a man? Your wife has been busy standing guard, studying and doing all the work about the house. Did you lend a hand? No! And yet you try to hold her back. Who's bullying who? Answer me that!"

"Who's holding who back? I've moved out, haven't I?" he argued.

"You're the bully, and yet your wife is still making excuses for you! Washing your clothes and bringing you new shoes. You're more bigoted than any old woman! Yet you call yourself a man! What kind of a militia man are you! If I were Sister Ah-hung I'd soon move you out — with a fishing spear!"

"That's just it. We have men for the militia and yet she just goes off without so much as a 'by your leave' and joins the women's militia! Why did she have to do that?"

So that was what was behind it all. He had been holding this against Sister Ah-hung all this time.

"Let me ask you something. Why have we organized a militia? How much do you understand of Chairman Mao's thinking that everyone should be a soldier? How much do you understand about Chairman Mao's thinking on people's war?"

"Enough, enough of that!" he shouted, waving his hands at me. "My tongue can't get the better of you, but men have their reasons, every bit as much as women have theirs. I know all about her kindness. Stood there laughing at me when I came back from a hard day's fishing and didn't even cook a meal for me. I'm not going to stand that."

"What a fool you are! She had been weaving nets and went home to cook for you as soon as she saw you, but you would insist on cooking the meal yourself!"

When I thought of that incident I began to laugh. "Don't try and put us off with 'been fishing.' You reckon we women can't go fishing too? One fine day Sister Ah-hung and I will swop places with you. You stay home and look after the children and do the cooking and washing and we'll go out to sea and fish!"

"You think I can't do it?"

"Sure you can. You can make pop-rice!"

He lowered his head and gave a surly grin, admitting defeat. My ire melted away. I tugged at his sleeve and said, "Come and make it up with Sister Ah-hung. Come on!"

Granddad Wang-fa had Ah-hung's bed-roll already packed. He pushed it towards him and Ah-hung and I left the boat. We made our way back across the beach, he in front and I behind, feeling very much like someone escorting a prisoner of war.

CHAPTER 12

AFTER THE GUNS WERE DISTRIBUTED

TIME passed swiftly and it was soon the spring of 1952. Rain had washed the wheat on the slopes a clean young green, and near and far the hills were a blaze of red azaleas. The very air tasted cleaner and smelled more fragrant. It made one feel refreshed and cheerful.

Today was going to be a big day for the women's militia platoon. We were to be given our rifles.

It was two months since East Beach Island had been liberated and granddad was once again plying his ferry-boat back and forth.

Secretary Fang and granddad had gone to that island to bring back rifles for us. That was why we were all waiting with straining eyes on the quay.

When the boat docked, there were loud cheers and shouts of greeting. "Here are the rifles!" "We've got rifles too!" "Hey, there's even a machine-gun!" "Wait till the militia men find this out!"

Every one of us seized a rifle and began a minute inspection, fiddling with this and that and patting them lovingly.

"Now take those guns to my office. We're going to have a handing-over ceremony," Secretary Fang said with a smile as he got off the boat. "Don't get too excited now. If you don't pass the test I'm going to give you, there'll be no rifles for any of you."

"Oh, don't wait until then. Give us the test now, or I won't be able to sleep tonight," pleaded Hai-hua.

"All right. What is the basic task of the people's militia?"

"That's easy," said Hai-hua. "Fight the enemy and catch enemy agents!"

"You've failed on the first question! One down."

Hai-hua poked out her tongue in dismay and hid behind me. Secretary Fang gave me a long look and said, "Hai-hsia, you're the platoon leader, can you answer that question?"

"Try me," I answered.

"Let's hear it."

"Actively participate in socialist construction, take the lead in productive labour and work with the People's Liberation Army to consolidate coastal defence, air defence and fight against enemy agents. Maintain social order and be prepared at all times to join the army and fight to defend the motherland."

The militia women appeared to be highly satisfied with my answer and looked with expectant eyes to Secretary Fang for approval. Their looks seemed to say, "Well, you didn't catch us out with that one."

"Hai-hsia's answer was not complete. Especially the last part," he said. "It should be pointed out that our people's militia should be ready at all times to counter imperialist aggression and give the aggressors a resolute rebuff." Then he continued, "Which of you can tell me what the character of our people's militia is?"

"Let me try," said Yun-hsiang. "Our people's militia is a body of armed people which is led by the Party and not divorced from production. The people's militia is an important instrument of the Chinese people for defence externally against imperialist aggression and internally to carry out the people's democratic dictatorship. It is a good assistant of the People's Liberation Army and is its powerful reserve."

Well spoken. I wanted to give her a clap.

"And it is the basis from which the army draws its recruits. It is a military organization, an educational organization and a physical culture organization," added Secretary Fang.

"Good heavens! I haven't been questioned yet and I'm already in a cold sweat," Sister Ah-hung exclaimed.

The sky had cleared but underfoot it was still wet and slippery and we had to tread carefully lest we slipped and damaged our precious rifles. We tried to look serious and business-like because a lot of girls and women were gathered outside the village to welcome us.

"They look like a militia platoon," someone exclaimed.

"And they've got brand-new rifles, too," shouted another.

A swarm of happy children trooped at our heels and there was a festive atmosphere about the place.

I heard Aunt Ta-cheng say, "Women soldiers. Can't bear the sight of them, rolling and crawling all over the ground. If there are women who like that kind of thing, let them. But I'm not going to allow my Yu-hsiu join them rolling in the dirt."

We heard but it did not dampen our high spirits. We now had guns and every one of us was full of smiles and go. We didn't even know how to use them, yet Sister Ah-hung, Hai-hua and the others were already thinking about catching enemy agents and shooting up bandits.

"We've got to catch an enemy agent for the militia men to see, otherwise they'll go on making fun of us. When they see us with guns they'll say, 'What's the use of giving them guns, they don't know how to use them! In their hands the rifles are no better than pokers to stir the fire with!' "

Remarks like this were maddening, yet at the same time it was amusing to listen to them. Not many days before, when Hai-hua had been standing guard with her fishing spear at the entrance to the settlement, she saw the militia men returning with their rifles from the sea and asked Ah-hung to let her have a look at his rifle.

"Mind you don't hurt your eyes with looking!"

"My, how cocky you are! But wait till we get ours. Secretary Fang says we'll be getting them soon and they'll probably be much finer than yours!"

Ah-hung slapped his rifle and said proudly, "Our guns may not be good enough, but we captured them ourselves. If you've got it in you, go and fight some of those bandits out at sea. You're just all blah-blah!"

The militia men had their reasons for speaking in such proud tones. A month ago when mists still shrouded the sea, some fishermen had reported sighting a motorized junk off-shore from Tiger-Head Isle. It was a "sea rat," the militia men decided, one of those Kuomintang pirate ships which raided fishing vessels and merchant ships, sabotaging production. Under cover of the fog the militia men, commanded by Secretary Fang, went out in three rowboats to take the pirate ship by surprise. He instructed the militia men not to do anything rash and not to use their guns until they were absolutely certain, when he would give the order to fire. When they were within thirty metres of the ship the militia men found that it had dropped anchor, and the crew were drinking and feasting after dividing the spoils.

Secretary Fang ordered, "Open fire!" The enemy was thrown into a panic. Someone cut the anchor cable and others tried to start the motor. They trained their machine-gun on the militia. Several militia men slipped into the water, swam towards the ship, then silenced the enemy machine-gun with a few well-aimed hand-grenades. The first to board the pirate ship was Ah-hung. He picked up the axe used to cut the cable and waded into the pirates, hacking at them right and left. One of the Kuomintang officers was taking aim with his revolver when Ah-hung hurled himself at him. The momentum carried them both into the sea where Ah-hung made him drink his fill of sea-water before dragging him up a prisoner.

From that day the militia men seemed to walk a little jauntier whenever they met a militia woman.

I had just finished my breakfast when Yu-hsiu came sobbing to me.

"Now what's the matter? Why are you crying?"

"You mean you've forgotten? And you the platoon leader?" she wailed.

"Ah! I remember," I said with an embarrassed laugh. "You're sixteen! But what is there to cry about? All I have to do is put your name on the militia list."

"Will you really? Then you had better talk to my mother first, for she won't hear of it."

I was mystified. After that relief grain episode we had become good friends again, especially after we had a good chat. We were getting on better than before, though I did hear Aunt Ta-cheng say things against our setting up the women's militia platoon and I had criticized her for it at a meeting. She held that against me, I know, for later she ignored me when we chanced to cross each other's path. This had been going on for some time now.

It was part of my work, so I had to see her. I reached her home in the middle of the morning and found her still cooking breakfast. I greeted her, "You're late cooking this morning, aunty."

She quickly fetched a bamboo chair for me and returned my greetings warmly like a good hostess, for after all I was calling on her. "I've been cutting faggots up the hill and got back late. That daughter of mine gets more wilful each day. When she saw you getting rifles she was green with envy. Now she won't even cut faggots. She went out early and hasn't turned up yet, that good-for-nothing girl!"

"I want to ask you to do something, aunty."

"What is it? Tell me," she answered, adding warily, "I'll try and do what I can."

"Yu-hsiu is sixteen now. Don't you think she should join the militia?"

Aunt Ta-cheng's face fell as soon as she heard me mention her daughter and the militia. "We're too backward for the militia. And besides, isn't it voluntary?"

"Yu-hsiu wants to join," I told her.

"Why, my Yu-hsiu is even afraid of a mouse! Someone has put that idea into her head. She couldn't have got it herself." She continued to feed the fire to avoid my eyes.

"Her wanting to join the militia is right."

"I don't care if it is right or if it is not right but my Yu-hsiu isn't going to join any militia."

"Think it over, aunty, before you decide." I saw there was no further purpose in staying any longer and arguing with her so I made for the door. As I went out I heard her say, "What a way to behave! She should be married instead of traipsing round all day cutting a dash! Humph!"

I was very hurt. I have come to her with the best of intentions, without a bit of ill-will, I thought, and she treats me like this, hurling abuse at me. So that's what the old saying that "cold meals are not hard to swallow, but cold words wound the heart" means. I had a good cry when I reached home. I could carry two pails of manure when others carried one; I could do two turns of guard duty when others did one, and although I ached all over I was happy at heart. But I could not stand the way Aunt Ta-cheng treated me.

In my mind's eye I suddenly saw Secretary Fang's face and seemed to hear him say, "Little Hai-hsia! Tears come too quickly with you. Have you forgotten the story I told you about a revolutionary shedding his blood but not tears?" I took out the application I was making to join the Party and read it again — "Fight to the end for the cause of communism, fearing neither hardship nor sacrifice." I felt a flood of shame and admitted to myself that I was afraid of difficulties.

I recalled the time Secretary Fang criticized me for the way I had shoved Chen Hsiao-yuan aside. I thought I had understood what he meant. That was a mistake. But now I knew. My clash with Aunt Ta-cheng today had taught me a lesson. I had to do more patient, painstaking work. I must be bold, brave and resolute and also broad-minded.

I made up my mind to take the bull by the horns.

"I'm here again, aunty!" I said and found a seat for myself.

"It's no use your trying to persuade me. I won't be persuaded."

"Then I won't be persuaded to leave until I have persuaded you," I replied, trying to sound jovial.

"You can talk and argue as much as you like, but I owe you nothing," she said frostily.

Her words chilled me from head to foot and sparked the memory of those grim days not so long past. I found myself talking earnestly, pleadingly. "That's very true. You owe me nothing and I have not come to collect any debts. But do you remember when Chen Chan-ao came to collect debts? Remember how your husband was beaten and you went down on your knees crying and begging them to have mercy? Do you want those days to return? Your husband's death has not been avenged yet! . . ."

"What are you saying!" she broke in. "Who wants those days to come back!" Her eyes reddened and I knew my thrust had hit home. "We didn't owe Chen Chan-ao anything. It was the other way about. He owed us our wages and when Yu-hsiu's father asked for them Chen Chan-ao said that we were telling lies. 'A rich fish merchant like me owes you money! Why, you impudent beggar, get out of my sight!' he shouted, and when Yu-hsiu's father protested Chen had him beaten until he was covered in blood."

"Chen Chan-ao is still alive and hoping to come back!"

"He wouldn't dare with so many Liberation Army soldiers here!" Suddenly she saw where I was leading her. With a low laugh she asked, "Why are you militia women always after Yu-hsiu to join? You can do without her, can't you?"

"If everyone thinks the way you do then there'll be no militia. Those Liberation Army soldiers have mothers and fathers too and yet they've come all this way to liberate our island and stay to defend it. Why? What do you think of people who refuse to defend their own island?"

After some deliberation she asked tentatively, "You mean that the militia does good for us poor people? Then why does

116

Dog's wife say that the militia is a waste of time and energy, that you militia women staying out every night will create terrible scandals?"

"What else did she say?" I asked quickly.

"She also told me that if fighting starts, the militia will be the ones to be put right in the front, and when the Kuomintang come they'll kill every member of the family which has someone in the militia."

"Why do you listen to her? No good ever comes out of her mouth. Remember how she made a fool of you over that half bowl of rice?"

And as the devil would have it, Smelly just then pushed her way into the house. She turned to escape as soon as she saw me, but I cried out, "Hey, there! Come in!"

She saw she wasn't going to get away and, baring her long yellow teeth, broke into a smile, saying, "Ah, the platoon leader is here. Had nothing to do so I just dropped in. I see you have some business. I'll leave you to it. I'm going now." she tried to leave but I said, "I was just going to look for you."

"Me? What for?"

"To ask you something. But come inside," I replied, trying to keep my voice even.

"Well, what is it you want to ask about?" She tried to look unruffled but dared not step into the house. She leaned against the door as if ready to run away any moment.

"What do you think of women joining the militia?"

"Fine! Wonderful! Excellent!" she replied.

"But isn't it a waste of time and energy? And if the Kuomintang return won't they kill every one of a family that has someone in the militia? What's so fine? What's so wonderful about that?" I pursued.

"Whoever says things like that are backward elements. Who said them?" Her expression changed, and turning to look fiercely at Aunt Ta-cheng she went on, "People who say such things should be taken before a struggle meeting! That's what I say!"

117

Aunt Ta-cheng's face contorted with rage. "It was you! You said all those things! You said them to me! You said you were giving me and my daughter good advice. You also said that Hai-hsia was slandering me behind my back, calling me a backward element and so on!"

Smelly lost control of herself and shouted, "You . . . you're mad! Be careful what you say!"

"You needn't shout and bluster," I rasped. "What's wrong with joining the militia? Come and tell that to the whole militia. Don't say things behind our backs. We'll call the entire militia out to hear you!"

She saw that she wasn't going to get away easily. She realized it was serious and began beating herself with her fist. Hitting herself across the mouth she cried, "That's for you, you bad tongue! You loose tongue!"

"Go on, strike that tongue of yours! Knock that mouth of yours out of shape and you'll still spread vile gossip and slanders!" cried Yu-hsiu who had returned home.

"A nice niece you are!" she shouted as she turned and fled.

"So that's what she is!" said Aunt Ta-cheng after Smelly had gone.

"You shouldn't let that sort come anywhere near you," I said.

"I'll never let her darken my door again, never!" Yu-hsiu's mother said.

"You'll let Yu-hsiu join the militia now, won't you?"

"Yes. Let her join. I think she'll be able to take it."

"You really mean what you say, mother?" Yu-hsiu flung her arms about her mother and clung to her.

"Ah, look how spoilt and childish you are. Don't blame me if you come to regret it!" Her tone contradicted her words.

"Yu-hsiu, you can consider yourself a lucky girl to be able to have a rifle the moment you join," I said to her as we went out. "We're going to start shooting practice tomorrow, and try to make a good job of it."

After I left Yu-hsiu, I kept thinking of Smelly. I had always known that she was a coquette and a bad woman who loved

to spread rumours and ferment trouble and mock at others'
woes. Now I saw she was also meddling in politics. What had
she to do with the militia? What was the militia to her? Why
did she spread lying rumours about the militia? Chairman Mao
teaches us that we should see things in terms of class struggle
and we must on no account underestimate rumours. As the
old saying goes, "Puppets dance at the end of a string." Behind
the scenes someone was manipulating the string. I was sure it
was Dog. A fox may pose as a man but it cannot hide its tail.

Chapter 13

SELF-CRITICISM

POLITICAL studies and military training were started by the militia of both sexes with the help of army units stationed on our island. Every Monday, Wednesday, Friday and Sunday the army and militia held joint exercises. We studied and trained with the Liberation Army soldiers, and worked together with them in the fields. The Liberation Army men taught us a great deal. They told us what they gained from studying Chairman Mao's works and spoke to us about domestic and international affairs. They explained to us the performance of various weapons, and how to strip, clean and re-assemble them. Also how to hit the target. From them we learned to carry out training with a thorough hatred for the enemy.

As the men were frequently away fishing, our women's militia had more opportunities than they for study and training. And as we were eager and keen, we frequently carried out exercises on our own. One day I assembled the women for sighting and aiming practice. We stuck targets on the slope of the hill and lying prone on the beach we aimed at them. The scorching sun beat down mercilessly and the sweat ran down our faces. Our clothes stuck to us and we were soon covered in sand and mud. This was the first time I had led our platoon on an exercise without the help of the Liberation Army men and I realized how important it was that I should make a good job of it. I found it quite a job!

Tsai-chu suggested that we pick a shady spot but I quickly turned that down. I told her, "We militia must be like the Liberation Army men. We mustn't be afraid of hardships, but must go out of our way to meet them so as to be able to adapt ourselves to the needs of actual fighting."

Tsai-chu said nothing. She applied herself to aiming and re-aiming her rifle at the target. After a while she spoke again. "What's the use of just pointing our guns," she complained. "When will we do some live shooting?"

"What's the hurry?" I asked. "We can't even line up our target, foresight and rearsight properly yet and our hands shake. You can't grasp the key points of shooting overnight, can you?"

"I don't see much sense in this," she said and got up. She took out her towel and began fanning herself.

"Practice makes perfect. You've got to practise and practise, otherwise how can you shoot properly?" I admonished her.

"That's what you say. If I can't hit the target I'm sure there's something wrong with the gun. Anyway, it's too hot. I'm going to take a rest from all this aiming and aiming." And Tsai-chu walked off to the shade under the banyan tree.

Sister Ah-hung gave her a look and said, "Why don't you tell your Chen Hsiao-yuan to stick a sunshade over you as well? That'll protect your delicate complexion from the sun!"

"My, aren't you dainty!" Hai-hua added, and made Tsai-chu still angrier. "Why did you join the militia in the first place?"

"You think a lot of yourself, don't you?" Tsai-chu flung back. "I'm leaving. I didn't join the militia to get insulted." She picked up her rifle and strode away.

This sort of thing did not happen just once. If you merely made a mild remark, more likely than not she'd just laugh it off. If you were a bit stern, there'd be tears and she'd be running home.

"What sort of militia women are they!" I asked the next time I saw Secretary Fang. "They've no sense of discipline at all. Why, they're just a pack of civilians!"

He broke into loud laughter. It was infuriating. I was all worked up and he merely laughed.

"Keep your shirt on. They *are* civilians and what's more they're housewives too," he said when he got over his laughing fit.

"But they're militia members," I protested. "I don't know what to do with them — they're really impossible!"

"You think putting their names on the roll makes them all regular militia members? As easy as that? Don't kid yourself. See that peak up there? If you want to get to the top you've got to climb it step by step. Iron comes out of a fiery furnace."

"I know all that, but it's easier said than done."

"I don't think you know at all," he said with a laugh. "If you really understood you wouldn't be talking like that. Ignorance is no excuse. You've got to learn. Why are you always blaming them for being backward and slow? Why don't you shoulder some of the responsibility yourself? What would you say if you saw a peasant cussing his crops for coming along so slow when other farmers' were doing well?"

"He'd do better to ask himself what he hasn't done. . . ."

"That's just it," Secretary Fang broke in. "He should blame himself for being a bad farmer. But, you know, there are people who think that all they have to do is put the seed in and expect a harvest the very next day. . . ."

"You're meaning me. . . ." I interrupted him, smiling in spite of myself.

"Meaning your impatience and your overlooking your responsibility. Any good farmer knows that to get a good crop he must water it, keep down the pests, weed and manure and so on. He's got to work for it. When he sees his crop languishing he first asks himself a lot of questions — has he given it enough water, manure, or has he been slow with the hoe? The earth will look after you if you look after it. You're the platoon leader so ask yourself if you have done all you could. Blaming the militia members is letting yourself free from your own responsibility, isn't it?" Then he abruptly asked me another

question. "How many years has this island been liberated?"

"You know as well as I do. Close on two years."

"And how long were the women of China oppressed and exploited in the feudal society? How many years have they been influenced by old habits and customs, burdened with conventional ethics and trammelled by superstitions?"

I did not know what to say, for I did not know what he was driving at.

"Two thousand years, comrade! Two thousand and more years!" He stopped, lit a cigarette to let his words sink home and let me compare two years with two thousand. Then he continued, "Unlike you, I don't think your militia women are backward at all. I think they've made tremendous progress. Let's take just one aspect. They've thrown off feudalism, superstition, conventional ethics, antiquated customs and habits. They've taken up rifles to defend the island. That is something tremendous, a gigantic stride forward. That one stride of theirs covers centuries. A cataclysm has taken place in their thinking and way of living. Comrade Hai-hsia, if you would teach others, you must first learn, teach yourself to look at a problem in an all-round way. See both the achievements and the failures, the positive as well as the negative. When you look at a thing, observe, see the main stream, the essence of the thing. Don't be subjective and one-sided about it. Do you follow me? You're a cadre now and you must always bear this in mind."

"I admit I've been one-sided, but don't you see that I want them to be real, regular militia members as quickly as possible? That's why I'm impatient."

"Your impatience has its roots in one-sidedness. And there's also the question of the mass viewpoint. Impatience doesn't turn iron into steel. A lot of hard work goes into making steel from iron." Hammering home the point about our militia work, he went on, "If it is like you think it is, and women become ideologically awakened, their fighting quality enhanced and they become a disciplined body merely by joining the militia, then why were you made a platoon leader? Does all that take place of itself and things just happen? If that were so, then revolution would be a pretty cushy job with everything all cut out for you. But let me tell you now, comrade, the revolutionary road is full of trials, setbacks, hazards and tribulations, and there's plenty of hard work to be done. Aren't you studying Chairman Mao's "The Foolish Old Man Who Removed the Mountains"? Then remember these words: **Be resolute, fear no sacrifice and surmount every difficulty to win victory.** That's the spirit one must have if one is going to make revolution. Difficulties must be surmounted if victory is to be won. . . ."

Secretary Fang drove his points home to me and made me see things in a new light. His criticisms were well-aimed, I thought, I should really be armed mentally.

"I came to make complaints to you, little suspecting that you would give me a good talking-to!" I laughed and ran off.

At last the longed-for day arrived. We were to have a live target practice. Then, all the women warriors balked the issue. One was afraid the magazine would blow up in her face. Another was afraid the bullets would come out from the butt end! Still another was afraid the sound would split her eardrums. If you asked one girl to shoot she would push another girl forward. No one was willing. At last Yun-hsiang hit on the idea of letting me fire first. "Once you set the ball rolling, the rest will follow," she pointed out.

To be frank I was a bit afraid myself. But as there was no way out of it I steadied myself and tried to look as calm and capable as possible. I fired off three shots and all three bullets hit the target.

"Why, it's all quite simple," one of them said with relief. The others agreed.

Then the practice got under way.

When she saw the red flag waving denoting a hit, Hai-hua dropped her rifle without even bothering to eject the cartridge-case, and flung her arms around my neck exclaiming in high glee, "I hit it! I've hit the target!" She pulled me down on the ground in her joyful elation.

Tsai-chu burst into tears when she saw the marker flag "no hits."

"What's the use of crying? You've refused to practise all along," Hai-hua pointed out to her acidly.

Yu-hsiu's turn came. As soon as she had joined our ranks she had pestered me to let her handle the machine-gun. When asked why she wanted that job she replied, "It'll be so much fun! I like its rat-tat-tatting sound and the way it spits out the bullets in succession."

"So you're thinking about having fun, eh?"

She pestered the life out of me and would not take no for an answer. When I finally agreed to give her the machine-gun she made a deep bow, picked up the machine-gun and ran off as if afraid I might change my mind.

She was conscientious in her practice and studied diligently, but now she was saying she was scared! "I even jump if a firecracker goes off," she pleaded.

I tried to bolster up her courage. "You'll do fine. You've always practised hard. What's there to be afraid of? You've seen how the others have done it."

"Yes, but they were using rifles. This is a machine-gun!" She looked at me piteously. I was furious but I saw that wouldn't help. Was she turning out exactly as her mother had predicted she would?

A sudden idea flashed into my mind. I slipped a bullet into the chamber when no one was watching and then said to her, "All right. If you're really scared then just go through the motions as you would on a dummy practice."

"Pow!" She leapt up and covered her ears. Then she exclaimed, "Who fired that shot? Who was it?"

"You did," the others laughingly echoed.

"Me? I don't believe it! I wouldn't have dared. . . ."

Then the marker was heard shouting, "Eight points!"

Yu-hsiu was astounded at what she had done. But I was in hot water.

When Secretary Fang heard what I had done he sent for me immediately. His face like thunder, he asked, "Do you realize what you have done? You've violated regulations! Don't you know you can't fool around in a live shoot?"

"Who was fooling around?" I protested weakly. "I had taken precautions and no harm's been done."

"But it could have been serious. Anyway that's not the point. This is a question of what attitude to take towards your work, towards discipline and regulations. You should be punished for this sort of mistake."

"All right, then. Punish me." But even as I said that I was silently defending myself. "What else could I do? She was scared stiff!"

Secretary Fang saw the unrepentant look on my face and glared at me. "It's easy enough to mete out punishment. Getting you to understand your error will not be so easy. Go and think it over and then write a self-criticism."

Oh heavens! I never bargained for this when I took up learning to read and write!

Writing that self-criticism weighed heavily on me. I took it very seriously; a self-criticism was for something which was very wrong. After I had thought the matter over and written the self-criticism down, I took it to Secretary Fang.

"Are we asking too much of you, Hai-hsia?" he asked.

"Yes," I admitted frankly. "I try to do my best but I get myself into trouble all the time and get criticized and reprimanded. I'm hanged if I know why. Sometimes I'm clear and other times I get muddle-headed and confused. I've just corrected myself for this fault and then another one crops up. When will I stop making mistakes?"

"It's hard not to make mistakes on the job you're doing. You're very young and haven't much experience in leading a militia platoon," he said patiently. "No one is born knowing everything and able to do everything. Take fishing, why does an old fisherman catch more fish than a newcomer? He's got experience! When the newcomer learns and acquires experience he'll catch plenty of fish too. It's the same in your work of leading the militia platoon. This self-examination you've been asked to do is intended to help you find out why and where you went wrong. Having done that you learn the lesson and know better next time. This process is unavoidable if you want to make progress."

"The way you put it, self-examinations aren't a bad thing then?"

"That's right," he grinned. "Self-examinations are inevitable in turning a bad thing into a good thing. You know the saying: 'Failure is the mother of success.' If an experiment succeeds at the hundredth time it is because ninety-nine failures preceded it. If every experiment were successful then there would be no experiments. Without experiments there can be no achievements."

"I've learned something through doing this self-examination," I told him. "When I don't make high demands on myself I feel it's very unfair. I feel grieved. I feel I have been trying very hard and yet I get blamed and criticized. But when I make high demands on myself I feel that I haven't done my very best and could do much better. . . ."

"That's a very fine conclusion," he said, nodding approval. "You must ask more of yourself and if anything doesn't turn out as it should you must look for the cause in yourself. That way, you'll make quicker progress. And another thing, enthusiasm and good intentions in work are not enough. You must know how to go about it." He passed me a book. "Study this. Chairman Mao wrote it. It's called 'Some Questions Concerning Methods of Leadership.'"

"I will do whatever Chairman Mao instructs," I promised, accepting it with gratitude and great respect.

CHAPTER 14

MOTHERLAND AND MOTHER

THE meeting that evening went on until nine, but the moon still did not show its face. Generally, after a meeting Yu-hsiu and I went home together as she was afraid of the dark. But tonight I said to her, "You go on home, Yu-hsiu. I've got to check the sentries."

"I don't believe it. You're kidding."

"But I can't always escort you home. You're a member of the militia now."

"You think I'm scared to go by myself?"

She went off in a huff and had only taken a few steps when she turned and said in a wheedling tone, "Hai-hsia, just this time. Once more. It's so dark outside."

"All right. Just this one time and no more."

I went with her and as we walked I said, "What is a good militia member? What must she do?"

"Be politically highly conscious, have a good ideology, be a good sentinel and able to fight well."

"And not afraid of difficulties," I added.

"Yes. Not afraid of difficulties," she repeated wistfully. "But I'm so timid. I daren't even go outdoors at night."

"What are you so scared of?"

"Ghosts and spooky things like fox fairies and hanged men and things like what Smelly tells us about. She says she's seen them with her own eyes."

"In future don't listen to her," I warned.

Yu-hsiu's mother was still up, waiting for her. She said to me, "What a fine militia woman Yu-hsiu makes. You have to see her home every time. Isn't she a burden?"

"She must learn to get over her fears."

"Can't you think of something to help her? Though, mind you, people do say that 'them that's born timid stay timid to the end of their days.' "

"I don't agree. People can learn to be fearless."

Yu-hsiu asked, "Why aren't you ever afraid, Hai-hsia? You're only a year older than I am."

"I wasn't always so brave. When I was little I also was afraid to go out of doors at night. Then Uncle Liu told me a story. He said that people scare themselves. He told me a ghost story. Want to hear it?"

"This is the story he told me years ago. It was said that a phantom haunted Dragon King Temple on North Slope. No one dared visit the temple after dark. One day Bold Wang and Stouthearted Chang went to sell their fish over at North Hollow. They did not get their business done until dark. Bold Wang set off for home a little earlier as Stouthearted Chang still had something left to do. It began to rain cats and dogs and Bold Wang decided to shelter at Dragon King Temple. He said, 'Others may be afraid but not me. I'm not called Bold Wang for nothing.' When he went into the temple, actually his heart was in his mouth. He could hardly breathe, his heart was hammering away so hard. He gripped his carrying-pole expecting a ghost to come for him any minute. The more he thought the more firmly he decided to leave at the first sign of lull in the storm. He took a peek outside and suddenly there was a tremendous flash of lightning. It lit up the whole sky and Bold Wang could see, clear as day, a monstrous object taller than a man wobbling and bobbing along the road towards the temple. Bold Wang's hair stood on end. The monster was barring the only route of escape. There was no way of avoiding it. He raised his pole and charged out in desperation, striking out blindly. His pole struck the black thing on its head with

129

a resounding crash. There was an unearthly shriek and the thing fell down. Bold Wang fled for dear life and did not once pause for breath until he reached home, where he immediately collapsed. He said he had seen a ghost and that he was not long for this world.

"A doctor was called in next day. After being told what had happened, he diagnosed 'severe shock.' Suddenly a messenger came hurrying in yelling for the doctor. Stouthearted Chang, too, was desperately sick. He, too, had met a ghost the previous night at Dragon King Temple. The doctor hurried to Chang and asked what had happened.

"Chang said, 'I sold my fish and bought myself a large pot. I carried the pot over my head as it was raining hard. When I reached Dragon King Temple there was a tremendous flash of lightning and a phantom rushed out of the temple and. . . .' 'And bashed you over the head with a pole,' the doctor finished for him. 'That's right. How did you know?' asked Stouthearted Chang. 'Luckily I was holding the pot high above my head, otherwise my head would have been smashed to pieces like my pot.' 'Listen to my prescription,' said the doctor. 'You go and call on Bold Wang. You'll cure him and he'll cure you.' "

Both mother and daughter broke into loud laughter. "Hee-hee," chuckled Aunt Ta-cheng. "They should have been called Fainthearted Chang and Jittery Wang. Why, they scared each other out of their wits. That's what they did."

"And from then on you were not afraid of the dark, is that right?" asked Yu-hsiu earnestly.

"No. Not at all. All my fears were driven away for me by life in the old society. Aunt Ta-cheng knows how Chen Chan-ao drove mother and me out and how we were forced to live in Dragon King Temple, which everyone said was haunted. We slept at the foot of the altar and every time I opened my eyes I would see Dragon King looking down fiercely and frighteningly at me. I would snuggle close to mother but never utter a sound. For if she knew how scared I was she would have moved out. And where would we find another shelter?

"Later, when mother got too ill to move about I went out alone to beg for food. I seldom got home until after dark. It was spooky walking back up the path to the temple, but I had to, for mother was lying sick and hungry, waiting for me. I just had to forget my fears and reach mother."

"Those were terrible days for you," Aunt Ta-cheng said quietly.

"They were indeed and that's why I'm not afraid of night duty and things like that today. I wasn't afraid in those days because I had my mother to think of. Now I have my motherland to think of and that's why I'm afraid of nothing, absolutely nothing, not even death itself!"

"You are politically highly conscious, Hai-hsia. I'll do sentry duty tonight," offered Yu-hsiu.

There was a resolute firmness in her voice and I believed she could do it, but I said, "What's the hurry? I've already put someone on. Let's wait till there's a night when there is a moon and I'll stand guard with you."

In the end Yu-hsiu did sentinel duty but I had to accompany her each time. Even so, it was a big step forward.

"I'm not afraid of anything when I'm with you," Yu-hsiu confided.

"What do you think about when you're on duty?"

"I often think about the time when I shall be able to stand guard by myself," she answered.

"Is that all you think about?"

"Well, I sometimes wonder what's the use of us standing guard day after day when the enemy's not even making an appearance. Isn't that a waste of time?"

"Not at all. You know the old saying about 'staying up all night to catch one thief.' For the security of the island and the motherland we should stand guard a hundred nights, even several thousand nights and still think it worthwhile. Look at it this way. Our island is at the entrance to the motherland. Guarding this doorway the way we do frees millions of our peo-

131

ple to build, work and sleep in security. So how can you say you see no use in our standing guard!"

The night sky was clouded over, threatening rain. We could sense it coming, and had only one reed rain-cape between us. We used it as a mat when we lay down to make observations.

"Yu-hsiu," I called softly, "will you be brave and stand guard while I go back and fetch another rain-cape?"

After a long pause she said, "All right."

I threw the cape over her and hurried away.

"Wait, Hai-hsia! The two of us can use this one cape. I'm . . . I'm . . . a little scared," she cried in a small voice.

There was no real need for me to fetch another cape but I wanted to use this occasion to test her. I had tried several times to get her to stand guard alone but without success. What was I to do? I couldn't go on nursing her. I knew what Secretary Fang would have done. He could be stern when it was necessary and he could be extremely gentle too, if the occasion warranted. Losing patience with her was no good, nor was mollycoddling. I decided to be firm.

"You're not a new militia member, Yu-hsiu. You know why we have to stand guard. This is an assignment I'm giving you! This is an order! The safety of this post rests in your hands tonight. I'm holding you responsible for the safety of the island! You've always said you would defend the island and the motherland, well, here's a chance for you to prove it in deeds!"

I knew she understood the import of my words and I could sense the mental struggle she must be having with herself.

"Very well!" she said, a catch in her voice.

I stamped away heavily to let her know that I meant to leave her on her own and then quietly slipped round to a close-by trench. She did not know that I never took my eyes off the approaches from the sea.

Then the storm broke. Lightning and thunder rent the sky and the sea threw itself madly across the shoals. The noise was frightening. The rain lashed down and the sea and air and land seemed to roar and writhe in unison.

"Hai-hsia!" I heard her cry above the noise of the storm.

I made no reply. But I could see her. She was scared obviously, for she gripped her rifle tightly and made a move as if leaving her post. Was she going to desert her duty? As I watched, my anger mounted.

But she steadied herself and stood there erect and straight, straighter than before as if some new force had found its way into her and filled her with courage.

I heard her slide a bullet into the breech of her rifle and repeat to herself in a desperate undertone, "I'm not afraid! I'm afraid of nothing!"

I felt a surge of warmth for her at this. "She's fought down her fear!" I said to myself triumphantly. "A militia woman has been born!" I was soaked with rain but did not feel cold. I looked at the wild tossing sea below and thought of that lone girl standing there erect, guarding the eastern coast of our motherland, defying the elements and victorious over her own fears.

Above the noise of the wind and rain I heard hurried measured footsteps approaching. It was Hai-hua coming to relieve us.

Yu-hsiu, too, heard the approaching steps and said, "You're back, Hai-hsia?"

Hai-hua reproved her in a quiet voice, "What's this about Hai-hsia? Why didn't you challenge me! What! You're alone?"

"Yes."

"Anything happened?"

"Nothing."

"All right, you can go."

"I can't. I've got to wait for Hai-hsia. She's gone back to fetch a cape. She told me to wait for her." Yu-hsiu added in an aggrieved tone, "She said she'd be back in a couple of minutes and she's still not here!"

I got up and walked out of the trench saying, "Don't wait. Let us go home."

133

Yu-hsiu turned and, seeing I was wet through, asked playfully, "Did you come out of the sea? Didn't you go home?"

"I was watching you all the time," I admitted. "You were brave, Yu-hsiu." If it had been anyone else I wouldn't have thought anything about it but with Yu-hsiu this was a great leap. She was fearless now, no longer the scared girl.

"Stop making fun of me," she said in a miserable tone. "I feel guilty."

"What's the matter?"

"Didn't you see? I was going to leave my post."

"But you didn't. You stayed at your post."

"Yes," she answered weakly, "but after you left I was so afraid. The hills and rocks all suddenly took on queer shapes and seemed to be crouching there ready to spring at me out of the night. I wanted to beat it but my legs refused. I thought I could see your eyes, and those of all the other militia members, reproaching me. It was terrible. If I leave I'll be a deserter, I thought to myself, and would deserve to be scorned. I decided that I just had to stay. Then I forgot all my fears. The rain, wind and thunder were nothing to be afraid of, but deserting was cowardice. . . ."

I was moved by Yu-hsiu's confession. "You did fine, Yu-hsiu. Some day when you become a platoon leader you must tell this story to the other militia girls."

The lightning and thunder and rain and wind continued unabated but we took not the slightest notice.

CHAPTER 15

SINGING ON THE SLOPE

EAST Beach and Half Screen alongside our island were liberated in turn. This brought more changes to Concord Island. The three islands were combined into a district to be known as the East Beach District. Secretary Fang left shortly afterwards to become district Party secretary. This took place shortly after the Spring Festival. After he moved over to East Beach, Uncle Shuang-ho took charge of Concord. But before that happened, granddad and I were admitted into the Chinese Communist Party. With the liberation of the other off-shore islands our fishing boats could go north in the spring to the Shengszu and Choushan Islands, and fish. The round trip took three months.

At that time only key off-shore islands were defended by regular troops. Company Six was transferred from Concord to the outer island of East Beach. The defence of Concord fell entirely on the shoulders of the militia, and specifically on the shoulders of the women militia, as most of the men were out on the fishing boats.

When they were ready to leave, Political Instructor Wang said to me, "Hai-hsia, you women have a heavy responsibility."

"Don't worry, we'll manage," I told him. I didn't say that to comfort myself. I knew our women militia could be depended upon, for we had made much progress.

At the end of spring and the beginning of summer the cuttle-fish season began. The beach was covered with cuttlefish drying in the sun. The oysters were also being harvested. Their shells piled mountain-high outside the village and the kilns were kept busy day and night. Uncle Shuang-ho was up to his neck in work directing production. There was so much to do but he did not neglect to invite half a dozen P.L.A. men over from East Beach to come and help us blast rock to build a dyke enclosing a part of the sea. We had to get this done before the typhoon season arrived.

One day Uncle Shuang-ho came up to me and asked, "There's a lot to do and we haven't enough manpower. How about organizing a shock force of your militia women and showing what you can do?"

The militia women were a shock force in production. The year before when there was a drought we had mobilized to get the planting of sweet potatoes done in time. Our women's platoon carried water up the slope day and night and got the potatoes planted in time.

We had also played a big role in the collection and delivery of manure. We did ten days' work in five and every time there was an urgent job that needed to be done Uncle Shuang-ho came and asked us. Again it was, "How about organizing a shock force and showing what you militia women can do?"

I accepted the task of building the dyke and immediately called a meeting of the militia to discuss it. The girls readily accepted the task and the battle was on right from the word "go." Our first job was to get the rock from the quarry down to the beach. We divided ourselves into three shock teams and the competition between us really got under way. We went at it with soaring spirits and even those who were not members of the militia were drawn in, including the aged and the children. Sister Ah-hung brought her family. Little Ah-sha was our messenger and water carrier. The site was a hive of activity.

By noon our shoulders were bruised and bloody, and our backs ached. Our legs were stiff and sore. After the noon break work began again but this time the tempo of work was slower and there was none of the morning's snap and verve.

"How about giving us a song, Yun-hsiang?" I called to our songstress. "Make up a ballad or work-song and liven things up."

"I'm all out of breath. How can I sing?" she replied wiping the sweat from her forehead.

"Stop carrying rock and start singing. Your job now is to sing and give people towels to wipe off their sweat. We'll work in time to your singing and we'll join in the ai-yo-hai chorus."

She thought for a minute and then raised her voice in song.

> *Tide-Watcher's Point is so steep,*

She sang a line and we followed up with the ai-yo-hai chorus, and so it went.

> *Blasting rock the whole day through,*
> *Ai yo hai!*
> *Carrying rocks in pairs and singly,*
> *Ai yo hai!*
> *We hurry along like sailing with the wind,*
> *Ai yo hai!*
> *Women's militia to the fore,*
> *Ai yo hai!*
> *Our shoulders are made of steel,*
> *Ai yo hai!*
> . . . .

Then Yun-hsiang said, "I've run out of ideas!"

"Start singing about good people and the good deeds you have seen," I told her. "Start with Sister Ah-hung."

"That's an idea. You give me the subject and I'll do the rest."

After a pause her voice was again heard.

> *Sister Ah-hung is strong and sturdy,*
> *Ai yo hai!*

Moves rock all day steadily,
Ai yo hai!
Works hard despite the sun,
Ai yo hai!
Works hard despite the aches,
Ai yo hai!

. . . .

"I'm not shirking because of aches and the sun," cried Hai-hua to me, making a face. "But I know someone who is. What about singing about those who are dragging their feet, too?"

I knew she was alluding to Tsai-chu.

Tsai-chu's family were classified as poor fishermen but there were plenty of able-bodied workers among them. There were the father and elder brother who went to sea to fish and brought home a tidy income. The mother was in good health and the sister-in-law was a hard worker, so even at home Tsai-chu did not have much to do. As the baby of the family, she was outrageously spoilt by her parents, and her brother and sister-in-law were very tolerant towards her. They indulged and thoroughly spoilt her. After she joined our militia organization she made some progress. She would carry water and manure and she took part in harvesting and planting and other activities readily enough but she seldom pulled her full weight. She was regarded only as a semi-able-bodied member. We had sharp-tongued Hai-hua with us, and one never knew when Hai-hua would goad her into a tantrum or into throwing down whatever she was doing to run off home.

That day we were carrying great rocks. It was heavy work. Tsai-chu came up to me at about mid-morning and asked to be let off duty. She said her shoulder was bruised and bleeding.

During the noon recess I called at her home.

"How's her shoulder?" I asked her mother, who opened the door.

"Aiyah! Her shoulder is bruised black and blue," she clucked. "She's not used to that sort of work. She should stick to militia work. There is no reason for her to do all that heavy work. Our family can do without her work-points. We've enough workers without her having to do that sort of job."

I said, "I admit I haven't taken good enough care of her, but she must take part in work. She's not just working for herself or her family. She's working to build socialism and everyone should do his or her bit. The militia is a work force and a fighting force, but mainly a work force. We're all of poor fisherman stock and if we don't work we'll forget our class origin."

Tsai-chu, who was lying in bed, heard every word we said. She got up and with tearful eyes asked, "Why am I not as good as the others? Why am I looked down on?"

"What are you saying? No one looks down on you."

"Then why is Hai-hua always calling me Miss Dainty?"

"She's only joking. You know what she's like. Says whatever enters her head. You mustn't take her seriously, you know."

"I try and work like the rest but I just can't do it. Look." She loosened her collar and exposed a purple, bruised shoulder.

"I'm to blame for that. I should have told you to wear a shoulder-pad. I forgot you weren't used to it like the rest of us. Our shoulders are hardened so we don't feel it so much. Work is tempering. The first two days are tiring but if you grit your teeth and stick at it things get better the third day. We're not working for ourselves or to win admiration and all that. Labour is one of the basic tasks of the militia and it's the glorious duty of the militia to build up the motherland. . . ."

"I'll be along this afternoon!" she said firmly.

"If you come, keep to filling the baskets. Don't carry rocks. One can only do what one is capable of doing. It's no good attempting what is beyond you."

I thought Tsai-chu deserved encouragement. After all she was willing to try and wanted to make progress, so when I went back to the site I sought out Hai-hua and cautioned her to hold her tongue and leave Tsai-chu alone.

"I'll give her a grand kowtow and apologize," she said, making a funny face.

When Tsai-chu arrived as promised, Yun-hsiang was singing a song about her pluck and her wanting to test and temper herself in labour despite her injured shoulder. Of course Tsai-chu was very happy and worked willingly and earnestly.

Hai-hua and I were putting down the empty baskets for Tsai-chu to fill when suddenly there were shouts and loud cries from higher up the slope. "Run! Get out of its way!"

I looked up. A boulder the size of a pillow was rolling down the slope, gathering speed as it approached us. Tsai-chu, who was bending to pick up rock to fill the baskets, was right in its path.

"Get out of the way, Tsai-chu!" I shouted.

Tsai-chu straightened up and stood there dazed. I picked up an empty basket and hurled it and myself before the oncoming rock. Luckily the wicker basket deflected the boulder, although it got smashed up in the process. I was thrown to the ground, luckily unhurt. People were stunned, fearing the worst, but as soon as they saw that I was uninjured they let out an audible sigh and came running to me.

Tsai-chu flung her arms about me, her cheeks wet with tears.

Uncle Shuang-ho ran up, his brow in a lather of sweat, and began to order precautionary measures to guard against possible future accidents. The whole site was soon bustling with activity again as we continued with our work.

Uncle Shuang-ho was very pleased with the way we militia women worked and, in between giving instructions and working, he found time to bring water for us to drink. He plunked down the pail, wiped the sweat from his brow and called, "Simply wonderful! Come and have a drink and rest. It's still quite early in the day and we've completed more than we had planned."

After that we worked harder than ever and pledged that we'd finish two days' work in one. And to the ringing swing of the work-song we threw ourselves into the job.

> *Make revolution through hard struggle,*
> *Taking on heaven and earth,*
> *The Foolish Old Man* of today*
> *Will fill in the sea to grow grain. . . .*

"Do you want to kill yourselves?" yelled granddad running up to me. He was angry. "Call it a day. Now I'm not going to let you all overwork yourselves."

---

* The Foolish Old Man is a legendary character embodying perseverance. It was said that in ancient times this old man lived in a house facing two big mountains which blocked the pathway to his door. He led his sons persistently to remove them. In 1945 Chairman Mao referred to this story in his article "The Foolish Old Man Who Removed the Mountains."

CHAPTER 16

A MAN AND WIFE

IN July 1952 several typhoons swept over our island, forcing the militia men to stay ashore. This provided an excellent opportunity to get in some target practice. Army Day (August 1) was approaching and a shooting match was proposed between the men and women to mark the occasion. Chen Hsiao-yuan came to us to present the challenge. "Do you respected women soldiers dare accept?" he asked, pompous as ever.

"Taken! Who's scared of you!" I replied curtly.

We couldn't very well refuse but I wasn't so sure we should accept either. After all we militia women had put in only one live practice at a hundred metres and all that had been demanded of us was that we hit the target. This time it was different. We were going to shoot for points.

"Aren't you big brave men ashamed of yourselves, challenging us who have had only one real practice when you've had at least three!" cried Yu-hsiu, stroking her cheek with a finger in mockery.

Secretary Fang saw that we weren't at all confident and came over to give us a pep talk. "I'm not sure they'll win, although they have had more practice in shooting," he said. "You girls have had more dummy practice than the men. You must have confidence in yourselves. That's a very important condition."

He's right, I thought. We have had more practice and we did practise very hard too, so we should have confidence in ourselves.

I remember one day in spring, when I was going home to cook the mid-day meal after attending a meeting, I saw a solitary target propped up on the slope. There was no one in sight. I had asked myself, "Who's forgotten to put her target away? Is that the way to look after militia property!" I was about to pull up the target when I heard Sister Ah-hung shout, "Leave it alone!" I turned and saw that she was doing aiming practice while attending to her cooking stove.

"That's a cute idea," I told her. "I thought someone had forgotten to take it in after practice."

"What's so cute about that?" she giggled. "I blundered into that idea, you know. I've got so much on my hands these days that I just can't find much time to practise, so in desperation I hit on this idea."

If this had happened some time earlier I'd not have thought of summing up this advanced idea, let alone popularizing it. I'd not have known what to do apart from thinking it was a smart idea. But now all was different, since studying Chairman Mao's article, "Some Questions Concerning Methods of Leadership" in which he says: **All correct leadership is necessarily "from the masses, to the masses."** Sister Ah-hung's resourcefulness and keenness gave birth to this excellent idea of combining work with military practice, I said to myself, it must be popularized within our women's platoon, and I told this to Secretary Fang. "That's an excellent idea. You must popularize it," he approved. By his look I could see that he wanted to say something more, a few words of praise, but he merely tightened his lips and said nothing. Anyway, that idea of Sister Ah-hung's sparked a drive to "be prepared against war during production and for remembering to practise with weapons while at work."

The coming match would be a real test of how well we had done our training.

In the end we decided among ourselves to enter five representatives. Long before the match began the competition site was thronged with spectators, most of them resigned to the idea that the men would beat the women.

The five militia men fired three shots each, completing their shoot in twenty minutes, and scoring an average of twenty-five points. It was good shooting and I was loud in my applause.

"Give us some tips, will you?" I asked the men. But all we got were hair-raising warnings.

"The kickback is terrific so look out for your arms!" Chen Hsiao-yuan cautioned. "It could dislocate your shoulder."

Sister Ah-hung clapped a heavy hand on his shoulder. "Oh, keep quiet! We didn't see your shoulder being dislocated!"

"But our shoulders are more solid than a woman's," he persisted, still trying to tear us apart.

Then it was our turn. From the looks of our team I could tell that they needed a pep talk badly.

"Sisters," I said in a loud voice, "today's match will prove our ability to shoot. We've learned to shoot because we want to defend our island, defend our motherland, and not because we want to win matches. We women suffered from the reactionaries in the old society, so shoot to kill! That target out there is the enemy!"

"Sister Ah-hung get ready to shoot!" I ordered. "And the rest be prepared!"

Sister Ah-hung took up her rifle, turned and looked at me. I saw that she was pretty tense. She was the first to shoot and how well or how badly she did would affect the others. I wanted to encourage her with a few words but realized that this wasn't the time. I put my confidence in her untiring efforts during practices.

"Show them what you can do, mum," Ah-sha advised his mother.

She rolled up her sleeves and took up her position. Her three shots followed quickly one after the other. I saw the dust spurt up behind the target and felt a wave of relief sweep over me. She had put her shots into the target but I did not hear the marker call the score. What was wrong? Didn't she hit the target after all?

A militia man commented, "Not at all bad. The bullets struck the earth!"

"With all the 'eggs' you women are going to take home you'll have enough to feed the whole family," another remarked bitingly.

The "eggs" he referred to were intended to represent noughts or zeroes.

I saw Chen Hsiao-yuan, the marker, poking about the ground like a hen. I was sure Sister Ah-hung had scored. I ran up and sure enough I found three holes clustered about the bull's-eye.

"What have you got for eyes? Can't you see! Look!" I shouted at him.

Chen Hsiao-yuan turned lobster red and stammered as if he had swallowed a fish bone, "I never thought to look there. I thought if any of the shots touched the edge of the target it'd be a wonder." Then a glimmer came into his eyes and he added, "Anyway, those holes could have been made by the men. I'd forgotten to paste them over."

The devil take him! I ignored him and shouted the score: "Three hits. Total twenty-nine points!"

"A dead rat falling into a blind cat's clutches —sheer luck!" I heard some of the men say.

But I also heard the applause from the crowd and I saw Secretary Fang clapping very hard in approval.

The result of the contest was an "Excellent" for both the militia men and women, the women leading by one point.

"These women soldiers aren't at all bad," said Chen Hsiao-yuan.

Secretary Fang said, "So don't slight our militia women. Everyone has his or her strong points and it's the same with the militia. Both the militia men and women should learn from each other."

When the prizes were being handed out I saw Chen Hsiao-yuan go through the motions of clapping but no sound came from him. He was a bad loser.

We tied our pennant high on a pole and Yu-hsiu ran up shouting, "Well? How do you feel now?"

Chen Hsiao-yuan answered back, "Stop crowing. I can see you have done pretty well in peacetime shooting but let's see what you do in a real shoot out!"

I searched high and low for Ah-hung to see his reaction but I did not find him. Nor did I find Ah-sha. I found Little Two who told me gurglingly that his father and brother had rushed homewards as soon as his mother had fired her round.

"What a difficult man! Ran away home just because his wife beat him at shooting!" I said to myself.

The militia men dispersed and we militia women marched up to headquarters to put the pennant away. We went with heads high and chests out. Arriving there we stopped for a while to talk about the match and by the time we had finished it was almost noon. When we broke up I fell into step with Sister Ah-hung, for I wanted to call at their home to find out how she and her husband were getting along. She had told me that Ah-hung had changed but I wanted to find out for myself.

Ah-hung had got hold of his son after he had heard me announce his wife's score and they had gone home.

Ah-sha protested, "I want to see the rest of the match. Why are we going home?"

"Your mother shot up an 'Excellent' today so let's go home and kill the speckled rooster to show her our appreciation," he whispered into his son's ear. "I'll cook dinner today. You give me a hand with the fire."

Ah-sha looked at his father dubiously and then said, "But not like the last time."

"That was rice, silly. This time we're going to stew a rooster!"

And so father and son went home.

When Sister Ah-hung arrived with me the rooster was simmering in the pot. Ah-hung looked at us sheepishly.

"I've killed the rooster in honour of the occasion," he said with a nervous laugh. "In honour of our militia women."

"How nice. Come on, Hai-hsia, let's try some of the chicken soup our fine militia man has prepared!" Sister Ah-hung walked over to the pot and lifted up the lid.

"Ah-hung! Why is the soup so green?" she exclaimed.

"Probably put in a little too much ginger," he said as he laid out the bowls.

"Ginger wouldn't turn it so green!"

"Probably a little over-cooked," suggested Ah-hung casually.

Sister Ah-hung took a spoonful and quickly spat it out. "Aiyah! You've left the gall bladder in!"

"What! Can't be. Let me try it." He took a spoonful and closed his eyes in anguish. "You're right. It is bitter. What'll we do now?"

"Toss the soup out and eat the meat."

"And I did mean well!" wailed Ah-hung.

I was laughing fit to die.

"We really appreciate your good intentions," said Sister Ah-hung, laughing, "but from now on will you please leave these things to me or else ask for instructions first?" Then turning to me she asked, "Would you like to try some of it? It's real bitter!"

"Of course I'll have some of it."

"I killed the rooster in honour of the occasion but what I really had in mind was to get her in a good temper so she'd pass on some pointers in shooting to me."

"Ah, bribery, is that it?" demanded Sister Ah-hung.

Listen to them singing to each other's tune! Well, I'll have my own dig at them.

"When did you get rid of all that male chauvinism, Ah-hung?" I asked sweetly.

Ah-hung knew he couldn't better anyone in a word combat although he could trounce anyone in a fight. He adopted a defensive position. "This isn't the time for jokes. I really admire you militia women."

"Just listen to him, sister. He says he admires us, but let's hear him make a self-examination. Remember how he used to look down on us militia women?"

"You mustn't be too hard on him. He's admitted his mistake. Didn't you tell us that a fault is nothing? What is serious is not to correct faults." This was quite unexpected. She was actually defending him!

"I see you two have set up a united front! But he must make a serious self-examination, otherwise he'll repeat his error. Faults must be as ruthlessly handled as an enemy. I see you're soft inside despite your hard shell, sister. Next time he starts to bully you, don't you come running to me for help!"

"You are terrible, Hai-hsia. Shut up or else I'll get real angry!"

The soup was tipped out and we began to eat. The meat did taste a bit bitter but we ate it with relish, enjoying ourselves and having a good laugh over it.

Chapter 17

SPRING FESTIVAL

EVERY year from the twenty-third of the twelfth lunar month the fishermen stop going to sea and stay on the island to observe the Spring Festival (lunar New Year). In the old days this festival was marked by orgies of drinking, gambling and other unhealthy pastimes, and there were no few drunken brawls. In those days the fishermen led hard lives, their days were full of anxiety and suffering and no one knew what the morrow might bring them. On top of all this there were all sorts of superstitions and villains by the score enticing the fishermen to dissipate and go whoring. Bawdy opera troupes were brought along, singing lewd songs and spreading reactionary ideas. The fishermen's hard-earned money disappeared into the pockets of these scoundrels, and many a wife and child cried the whole night long. To many a family the festival was a time of tears and sorrow.

On the island in those days there were all kinds of sayings: "Money from catching fish isn't worth a damn." "A man will die and money will rot, so eat, drink and make merry and let tomorrow look after itself." Fishermen would climb ashore and go on a spending spree, eating and drinking away their hard-won cash.

This was the third Spring Festival since liberation and some of the old habits still survived. Secretary Fang called on everyone to give up gambling and steer clear of the bawdy opera troupes. The militia decided to organize a get-together to celebrate the Spring Festival freed from those bad old customs and habits. We women were given the task of writing and putting on a play.

On Lunar New Year's Day the People's Liberation Army units sent a film projection team along to show us films. Then on the day after we were to put on our own number, called "Sisters-in-law Stand Guard on the Coast Throughout a Rainy Night."

When the news got round that the militia women were going to put on an original play, people flocked to attend. At first a few had been reluctant to come but we called on them repeatedly until they did. They came all right, but many merely out of curiosity, promising themselves that they would have a look and if it was not to their taste they would leave.

We hung up a canvas sail under the big banyan tree for our curtain. It was a fine idea and worked well. For lighting we used a pressure lamp which hissed loudly, but it gave out a bright light.

Our play was based on a tiff which really had taken place between Hai-hua and her father. What did they fall out over? It was like this:

One windy night as the rain poured down, Hai-hua came home and, after a quick meal, went into the inner room and took out her rifle.

"What! Surely you're not going out on a night like this?" cried her father.

"Of course I am. You know very well that we've got to be extra careful in weather like this."

He glared at her and grumbled, "You've carried manure all day long, and you still want to run about the hills in this dirty weather! Do you want to break a leg or something? What's the use of standing guard on a night like this? I see no sense in it!"

She gave him a queer look and without another word vanished into the howling night. Then suddenly she peered in through the open door and said, "No one's broken a leg standing guard duty, dad, but I do know someone who had his leg broken by Chen the despot!"

That touched a sore spot with the old fisherman. He was the very man alluded to and that was why he still walked with a limp.

"Why do you bring that up?" he muttered. "The past is the past."

"Past, indeed! Why, only last year you were saying, 'Hai-hua, don't you ever forget how I got this game leg!' And now you're saying the past is the past. Don't forget that the dogs who broke your leg are still alive and want to come back into power! You've forgotten that we must be prepared against war. You've let peaceful days blunt your vigilance, dad." Then she vanished again, rifle in hand, into the rain.

"So it's come to this, eh? My own girl telling me what to do!" fumed the old fellow as he bit the stem of his pipe.

His wife, however, took the daughter's side saying, "But she's right, you know."

This was how the play came to be. At first we did not even change the names of the characters. Later on, when we staged the play, we used different names because we were afraid the dour old fellow might kick up a row if he heard his name being used. We made up the other acts.

Of course we had to include Yun-hsiang, because she was the best singer of fishermen's ballads. Ordinarily she was a quiet, timid, self-effacing girl, but when she sang she was a different person altogether. When asked to sing she never hesitated nor refused. This time we cast her as the elder sister-in-law and Hai-hua as the younger. They were natural actresses and played their parts well.

Seated beside Granddad Wang-fa I watched the play. When the father on the stage objected to his daughter going out, Granddad Wang-fa muttered angrily beneath his breath, "That old codger has forgotten the pain now that his wounds have healed! That girl has guts, she has."

Aunt Ta-cheng who was sitting beside us interposed, "Of course she is more progressive than her father. She's been educated in the militia women's platoon."

A woman with a baby sitting behind us said, "Will you please put that baby of yours down on the ground, granddad? It gets in our way, and we can't see what's happening on stage."

The woman was referring to the rifle Granddad Wang-fa was holding. He had carried that rifle since the day he captured it, when Concord Island was liberated. It never left his side if he could help it. If he appeared without it — which happened only once in a blue moon — people inevitably asked, "Hey, where's your other half, granddad?" When the woman behind asked him to put his "baby" down, he turned on her angrily, "This is a gun, woman, not a kitchen poker! Why don't you put your baby on the ground?"

"Oh, stop squabbling, you two. We want to hear the play, not listen to you!" someone said resentfully.

On stage the sisters-in-law were out on night patrol. It was a stormy night. Yun-hsiang sang:

> *The waves roar and the wind howls in the night,*
> *Out in the rain two girls are patrolling the coast,*
> *They crouch out of sight and gripping their guns they*
> *   watch,*
> *Watch the enemy walk into a waiting trap. . . .*

From the audience came the shouts, "Well done!" "Bravo!" when Yun-hsiang reached this part. She had altered the melody and we never expected that it would be so well received.

The sisters-in-law marched across and off the stage. Chen Hsiao-yuan and other militia men, made up as enemy agents, crawled furtively on stage. Chen Hsiao-yuan was the enemy leader. He wore a big false nose and his face was smeared white, giving the audience the impression of an American imperialist. Actually his role was that of a runaway despot commanding a gang of bandits and agents.

Chen Hsiao-yuan gave a good performance. I didn't think he had it in him. As he directed his gang he sang a queer tune:

> Hurry, hurry, but coolly,
> The night is dark and the wind is high
> And the rains do pour down so,
> The militia men
> Are all in bed sleeping soundly,
> The beaches and passes are left unguarded. . . .

Bandit A, his face a mass of black and white stripes, sang in a tremulous voice:

> How I shake and how I quake,
> Slithering about like a snake,
> After crawling my way up from the sea.
> One false move and that's the end of me.

The gang leader with a toss of his head urged his men on.

> Hurry, hurry, don't be chicken-hearted,
> Remember what the American advisors have taught us.
> "If you pull this through
> I'll give you a fat reward. . . ."

People in the audience started asking, "Aiyah! What are those sentries doing? Why don't they open fire?"

Granddad Wang-fa muttered, "What do you know about it! Let them get closer and then grab them alive!"

The younger sister suddenly challenged the intruders and fired. The enemy fled.

Granddad Wang-fa said with unhidden disgust, "Bah! Now you've spoilt everything. Should've waited until they came closer and then nabbed 'em!"

There was a blast from the conch trumpet and the militia hastened to assemble. The curtain dropped.

Someone in the audience remarked, "What, it's ended already? Why weren't the agents caught? That would be a better finish."

"Who said it's finished?" retorted someone who had been at our rehearsal. He explained to those around him what was to follow.

The play went on to show the villains scatter and lose their way. Their leader forced his way into the house of Yu-hua and at gun point tried to get her father to help him escape across the sea. The old fisherman recognized that the bandit chief was none other than the despot who had once broken his leg. He grabbed his fishing spear and lunged at the bandit chief. The gangster raised his pistol to shoot down the old man when Yu-hua returned and in the nick of time shot the invader dead.

Chen Hsiao-yuan muffed this bit by falling flat on his face before Yu-hua fired. Some of the audience were furious and demanded that this should be re-enacted.

But the curtain fell and the play was over.

Our little play was badly written and poorly acted but was received much better than we expected. There were calls, "More! More!" and repeated bursts of clapping.

We could comply with an encore for a song, but this was a play and even if the play was a hundred times better we couldn't put it on again the same evening. However, the crowd refused to leave. People pushed up to the stage and waited. We got Yun-hsiang to sing another song and finally managed to persuade the people that the show was over.

We could hear people talking animatedly about our play as they walked home.

Uncle Shuang-ho was also very pleased with the play. "Not bad at all," he said. "Do you think you girls could put one on about production? That'd help boost people's spirits in production, you know."

Production, that's all he ever thinks and talks about! "Of course we will," I told him. Then I added, "While we militia members will set the pace in production we can't devote our entire energy to it. We've got to think about class struggle and being prepared against war too!"

Chapter 18

CONFLICTING VIEWS

THE launch ploughed its way through the waves towards the sun rising out of the sea. Shimmering sunlight turned the sea into a vast sheet of gold. A myriad of sea birds wheeled in the vessel's wake.

Aboard were militia members returning home from the military sub-area spring shooting competition. Pinned on one side of the hold was the coveted pennant awarded this time to the East Beach militia company. The militia members were cleaning their guns, singing and making merry.

Someone shouted, and a loud burst of clapping backed up their request, "Give us a song, Concord!"

I noticed some of our girls hung their heads as if the applause was a shower of blows. I knew the reason, for we had lost our pennant.

When there was no response, the East Beach militia could be heard whispering, "Of course they feel bad about it. After all they've held it for two years running."

"Go on, what's there for you to grin about?" muttered Hai-hua darting a reproachful look at me. She blamed me for the loss of the pennant because I had refused to take part in the match.

We had lost to East Beach by four points. I had delegated a squad to take part in the match instead of picking the best shots to make up a team. So, of course, there were good shots and not-so-good shots in it, and on top of that Tsai-chu had scored only seventeen points with her three rounds. This lowered our average and put us out of the running for top honours. Hai-hua fumed and raged throughout the match and when we got back to our quarters, she tossed her rifle onto her bed and lammed into me. "We lost because of you, Hai-hsia!" she accused. "You're the platoon leader yet you don't care a fig for the honour of our platoon!"

I suggested, "Don't get excited. Let's talk it over calmly."

"What's there to talk about? It's clear as daylight. If you had taken part we'd have got at least twenty-seven points instead of that paltry seventeen by Tsai-chu. We'd have won by at least six points if not more!"

I patiently pointed out to her, "That's only your guess, and besides I'm not a member of any squad so how could I take part? You're right to blame me for losing but not for not taking part. The blame for losing that pennant lies on me because I didn't get all our members to become crack shots. You can't blame Tsai-chu. We're all to blame, particularly me, for not giving her enough help. We used to send our best sharpshooters along but that's not right. They're not representative of our whole platoon. They've had more practice and more training than most of the others.

"Furthermore, I don't think you should accuse me of not caring enough for the honour of our platoon. We have to be honest about it. Our standard was the best that we could achieve. The other team won because they were better. We should face this and learn from them and be glad to see that others have made such rapid progress. We used to think that the more pennants we collected the greater the honour to our platoon. This is looking at it too one-sidedly. That's being medal-crazy and contrary to Chairman Mao's line for army building. Had we persisted and collected plenty of awards then our mistake would have been even bigger. We should cultivate the style of tackling difficulties and leaving the glory and honour to others."

"Style, style, style. What's the good of style? You can't see it and you can't feel it and you've got nothing to show for it. How are we going to face the others when we get back home?" And big tears coursed down her cheeks.

Then Tsai-chu came running over as soon as Hai-hua left. She too was crying and blaming me. "I told you I was not good enough but you would insist on my entering the match, and now look what I've done! I've lost the pennant for all the others!" She sat down beside me sobbing bitterly.

The contest showed that there was a good deal wrong with our training. More important, it showed that we had neglected to do political-ideological work. I saw the seriousness of this situation. In the past we used to discuss a lot about shooting techniques and skills during our post-contest meetings, only lightly touching on the political and ideological aspects. I was firmly set against repeating this mistake. I was determined to make the summing-up meeting an occasion for taking a thwack at this craziness about medals, and thoroughly repudiating it. This was to be the first serious ideological struggle since setting up our militia women's platoon. I saw that the conflict was a struggle over principles, a struggle between two lines, and I hoped that through struggle our platoon would advance along the line laid down by Chairman Mao for building up the militia.

At the summing-up meeting Hai-hua turned all her artillery on me and fired away. She blamed me for not taking part and for putting Tsai-chu on the team. She said that she would rather die than acknowledge that the East Beach militia were the better marksmen, and so on. She had said all this to me before.

I told the meeting why I had decided to put Tsai-chu on, and then turning to Hai-hua I asked her, "What year was our platoon set up?"

"Spring of 1951."

"And when was the East Beach company set up?"

"Spring of 1952."

"Then that makes us the senior by one whole year, and yet they can shoot this well. Aren't they better than us? Tsai-chu is a veteran militia member and yet she made a poor showing. Doesn't that prove the standard in our platoon is not too high? And she's not the worst shot either. There are some worse than her in our platoon. Doesn't that reveal our weakness? And what is a contest for? It's to gauge the level of our fighting capability, not for the sake of letting a few sharp-shooters compete for pennants. . . ."

One of the girls remarked, "I couldn't agree more with you but that still doesn't make me any happier."

Soft-spoken, sagacious Yun-hsiang said, "I agree with Hai-hsia. Losing the pennant is a good thing as it enables us to see our weaknesses in training and in thinking. A very good thing indeed. Let us see what 'I couldn't agree more with you but that still doesn't make me any happier' means. Who has the pennant? None other than our own sisters-in-arms, our own comrades. But haven't we one common goal? A revolutionary goal? We should congratulate them and not feel depressed. Why should we feel depressed? If on the other hand we had won the pennant, how would we feel if they felt upset about it? What's the good of holding matches if it's just to enable one team to win and make the rest unhappy! That's not what a revolutionary contest is intended for. We shouldn't harbour bourgeois egoism, we should have proletarian feelings. . . ."

"Oh, I know now," Sister Ah-hung broke in. "If we had won, when we knew that most of us aren't as good as the opposite team it wouldn't have been a real victory. It would have been a sham victory. I wouldn't want to win the pennant then. We've got to have the guts to face it. Every one of us must try to become as good as the other so that we can all do our best. If we get to be like that and still don't win then I'll chop off my head. Like this!" and she made a gesture of chopping off her head with her hand.

That made everyone laugh and broke the tension.

"I see it too," exclaimed Hai-hua, laughing. "I've a quick tongue and a simple head, but now that you have pointed it out to me, I see the whole thing differently. I admit I did put medals first and I did feel glum about our failure at first, but I feel different now."

Conflicting views were expressed at the discussion. This helped us to reach unanimity but did not mean that the problem troubling our minds was completely solved. It was to crop up again as we went through life. After all, ideological work is not that smooth-going.

To return to the time we were on the same boat as the militia from East Beach — some of the girls were wrestling with their emotions.

I whispered to Yun-hsiang, "Start up a song. Otherwise they'll think we're bad losers."

"But the girls have hardly really got over their dumps. Will they sing if I give a lead?"

"Maybe you're right. You give us a solo."

"All right. Let me think a while."

The militia from the other island began chanting, "Give us a song! Concord! Let's hear Concord!"

Huang Yun-hsiang rose to her feet and began.

> *Sea gulls soar over the choppy sea,*
> *The red flag flies in the breeze,*
> *We perfect our skills to win battles,*
> *Bravely we decimate our enemies,*
> *Forward for the revolution!*
> *Form a steel bastion!*
> *The vanguard thrusts forward swiftly,*
> *The rear hurries up determinedly.*
> *Ai yo hai! Hurry, hurry, hurry!*
> . . . .

There was resounding applause at the end of the song.

The ship's whistle gave a shrill blast and the anchor dropped into the sea with a splash. The launch was going to take the others home to East Beach and we of Concord were getting off to continue the journey home by sampan. Wang Yueh-chiu, the leader of the East Beach women's militia company, caught my hand in hers and said, "We have the pennant but the real winners were your platoon, Hai-hsia."

"Not at all. You're a good sport for saying it but we have a lot to learn from you," I answered.

Hai-hua muttered as she clambered overboard, "You can gloat. Words cost nothing and you have the pennant!"

It was obvious that Hai-hua had not yet got over her moodiness. Besides, she was being most unfair. I knew Wang Yueh-chiu wasn't that kind of a person.

"Where's the pennant, Hai-hsia?" called granddad as he steadied the sampan, smiling in welcome.

"Lost it," I said shortly.

"Never mind," he said. "Find out why you failed. But don't let it get you down. It doesn't matter about losing the pennant but you mustn't lose your revolutionary will."

Dear old granddad, how wonderful he is. "Don't you worry about that, granddad. We'll work hard to catch them up."

"Hey! Hey! Wait! Concord, wait!"

I looked up and saw a white-hulled fishing boat from East Beach heading towards us. Granddad shipped his oar and waited.

"Got a visitor for you," one of the fishermen said when their boat drew up. The men on board all knew granddad and greeted him. "We were about to take him over when we saw your sampan so we're delivering him to you."

The visitor had only one good leg but he needed no help from anyone as he slung himself lightly aboard our sampan. He held a crutch and carried a small bag and barber's box. The girls made room for him and he nodded to us as he took a seat up front. I observed him carefully.

His reddish tanned face showed that he was a man used to the sea. He was tall, very powerfully built and appeared about fifty years of age. His right leg ended at the knee where his trouser-leg was folded up and tied with a bit of string. When he smiled at us his white false teeth contrasted sharply with his tanned face. His nose was large and bulbous and stuck out purple and prominent. He wore a straw sandal on his left foot. He wore no straw hat despite the heat and his shiny pate was beaded with perspiration.

After he had settled himself, he said with a sigh, "This is wonderful! Home at last!"

"Where do you live?"

"I don't rightly know myself," he replied to a curious bank of faces. "I've got to ask the local government to help me find that out."

Hai-hua fired a stream of questions at him. "What? You mean to say you don't know where your home is? How did you lose your leg? You're from Fukien, aren't you? I can tell by that accent of yours."

"Yes. I'm from Fukien," he said after a pause. "I lost my leg in August 1949 when Fukien was liberated. I was a litter-bearer for the Liberation Army and lost it shielding a wounded soldier when the Kuomintang planes attacked."

"How heroic!" exclaimed several of the militia casting a look at his empty trouser-leg.

He smiled, took out a cigarette and lit it. I did not like nor yet dislike this stranger. I merely felt that there was something queer about him, something which I could not place my finger on.

Granddad eyed the stranger for a time and then engaged him in conversation.

"Are you a farmer or a fisherman?" he asked as he plied his scull.

"Fisherman. I've fished since I was twelve."

"Ah, a fisherman. Tell me, how many crew members have you on your big Fukien boats? I've heard they're different from ours."

"Twenty-eight."

"How many on the smaller ones?"

"Five."

I did not understand what granddad was driving at, asking the stranger all those questions. However, he continued to watch the man and ply him with questions.

"You must have worked on a lot of fishing grounds. Which are the better ones?"

"The Choushans are the best. They're the best-known in China," the man with the missing leg answered, laughing.

"What kind of fish are mostly taken there?"

The stranger answered the question affably. "As the old saying goes, 'As the herb-gatherer does not know all the names of herbs so neither does a fisherman know all the names of fish.' There're too many kinds. It's almost impossible to count them. Anyway, in the Choushans the four main fish taken are the big yellow croakers, the little yellow croakers, cuttlefish and hairtails. Then there are shads and pomfrets, but they appear off and on and are not very important."

I saw granddad nod in agreement. I could not help admiring this knowledgeable guest.

"There are croakers from February to August, but the main season is from May 5 to July 7. The croakers like warm water. They collect together in spring when it turns warmer and head for the shallow water, coming in from the southeast to north-west and returning along the same route in autumn. . . ."

"I see you're a learned man," said granddad as he plied his scull steadily. "I'm a simple unlettered fisherman so please don't take offence at my asking silly questions. I've also heard that the Choushans are good, but why is that?"

Funny granddad asking him that question. Was he testing the newcomer? But the stranger merely smiled as he answered, "You don't seem to believe me when I say I'm a fisherman, grandfather." Then he laughed and asked, "Trying to catch me out?"

"Not at all," replied granddad with a smile. "You know the old saying about 'girls talk about embroidery, scholars about scripts, farmers about crops and fishermen about the sea.' Just shop talk, you know. If an old fisherman doesn't talk about fish what else can he talk about? But I don't know much. I haven't any learning at all, that's why I'm asking you."

"Oho! So I'm making a fool of myself before an old salt, eh!" But he went on to talk learnedly about temperatures, salinity, tides, depth of water and the migration of fish, their habits and where and when they bred. I had never heard of these things before and I found myself listening excitedly. I saw that the others too were listening with rapt attention.

The wharf was lined with people to welcome us, although we hadn't brought the pennant home.

Aunt Ta-cheng's attitude towards the militia underwent a big change after her daughter joined us. When Sister Ah-hung had left for the militia meeting she left her three children with Aunt Ta-cheng to look after. She was at the wharf with the children to welcome us back.

"Where's the pennant, mum?" Ah-sha shouted as soon as he caught sight of his mother.

"Go away with you. What're you worrying about the pennant for?" she replied testily.

As soon as I got on to the wharf I gave Uncle Shuang-ho an account of what had happened.

"Why didn't you take part in the test?" he demanded. "You would decide for yourself instead of consulting others!"

"I thought it better if I didn't. I've taken part in every test before."

"Who told you to put in a whole squad? You decided yourself, didn't you?" he said in a tone heavily charged with reproval.

"Yes. I did decide myself. Anyway, I see nothing the matter with that," I said stoutly. "The sub-area commander approved of my decision, and at the summing up after the contest, he said that was how it should be and recommended others to learn from us the way we base our training on the principle of fighting a real battle."

"Well, we won't say anything more about that," Uncle Shuang-ho said weakly, backing down. "It's lost and that's that. Can't be good at everything. We'll work hard and hang on to our pennant for production."

"If we see it merely as a matter of losing or keeping that pennant, then we would be losing our sense of responsibility.

We've got to train as if we are really training to fight battles,"
I argued. "We train to fight battles, not to win pennants."

"And where are we going to get the time for that?" he
demanded.

"We can find the time if we arrange things properly. Whatever must be done must be done. How we do it depends on
how we arrange it. We've got to be flexible."

"You for one are not being flexible. You are as stubborn as
a mule. You should know that in production everything is
linked together. If you neglect one link the whole chain breaks."

So we argued as we walked. Reaching the rise, he stopped,
turned to me and said, "See that patch of shore? All of nine
hundred *mu*. I've worked everything out. If we turn that into
paddy and grow two crops a year on it, we should get at least
eight hundred *jin* of rice from each *mu*. Think how much rice
that is! And if we add three thousand clusters of rock oysters
we'll be able to gather in a huge harvest of those to dry and
sell to the state. We'll all be living in plenty and the island
will become a paradise. . . ." He spoke as if he was already
showing someone around this island paradise.

"All you think about is production, production, production.
What about class struggle, political-ideological work and of being prepared against war? You're in sole charge of the island's
work now that Secretary Fang is working with the district
Party committee. You've got to think of all the other aspects
too. To my way of thinking we should first of all make our
island an impregnable fortress, not some island paradise."

"You're becoming insufferably proud, Hai-hsia. You decide
something without first consulting anyone and when you speak
you're too authoritative. That won't do. You're only a child.
You must do as the leadership instructs."

"Of course we must all obey our superiors, but not blindly,"
I retorted. "We must act as Chairman Mao teaches us. Just
because I speak out doesn't mean I'm not obeying the leadership."

We kept arguing like this until we reached the administration
office.

As soon as we entered the building Uncle Shuang-ho walked up to a map of the county. Then pointing to it he addressed me. "Look at this, Hai-hsia. East Beach Island is on the right of the front and Half Screen covers the left approaches. We were on the front line before they were liberated and we had to pay a lot of attention to the work of the people's militia then. But it's different now. We've got those two islands out in front of us. We're now like the pearl behind the dragon's teeth. With those before us, will the enemy dare attack our island? Don't you see why the People's Liberation Army units which were stationed here have now been moved out to those islands? Why, even Company Six has gone to East Beach."

I disagreed completely and argued, "All the more reason for us to strengthen our militia work. Chairman Mao has called on the whole country to take up arms and for everyone to become a soldier. Even on the mainland the people's militia is being set up and training stepped up. Uncle Shuang-ho, you should seriously study what Chairman Mao has to say about a people's war."

My last remark struck him to the quick and his face was tense with anger, but he spoke as if he was humouring a child. "Is that the way to talk to grown-ups, Hai-hsia? You're getting too cocky. Oh, I haven't the time to explain it all now. Let's drop this for the moment. We'll look into this question of militia training later, eh?"

"When?" I pursued.

"I haven't the time now. Wait another couple or so days."

"Another couple or so days" was all I got for an answer! I felt a dull anger rise within me. He was treating me like a child, brushing aside my views as if they were mere childish prattle. What was I to do? Chairman Mao teaches us: **Opposition and struggle between ideas of different kinds constantly occur within the Party; this is a reflection within the Party of contradictions between classes and between the new and the old in society. If there were no contradictions in the Party and no ideological struggles to resolve them, the Party's life would come to an end.**

Indeed, a Communist must uphold the truth. Truth, reason, gets clearer with debate. I must get to the bottom of this. One of us must be right, but which one? When Uncle Shuang-ho saw that I had nothing more to say he pulled some papers from a drawer and began working on statistics about production.

After a long pause to let tension die down somewhat I said in a voice firm and sincere, "Uncle Shuang-ho, I'm no longer a child, I'm a member of the Party and I'm a militia cadre. And it's my duty to make known my views. I'm not here to squabble with you over something personal. Haven't we done everything that you asked of us and was correct? We even did more than you asked us to do. Remember the time we built that dyke? Didn't we work as hard as anything and get it completed a fortnight ahead of the deadline? You've been in the revolution longer than the rest of us and you have much more experience. I respect and look up to you as a veteran revolutionary, but that does not mean to say we must obey you unconditionally whether you are right or wrong. If you are wrong we have the right not only to disobey but even to criticize you. . . ."

"Very well," he said, and put his papers back into the drawer. He looked at me as if he was just getting to know me. "Let's hear your view," he continued in a grave voice.

"I think you're making a mistake, and a serious mistake, if you go on like this. You will make a political mistake if you go on paying attention only to production and neglect politics. You are getting more and more narrow-minded and shortsighted. I too have consulted a map, a map of the world, which Secretary Fang and Comrade Tieh-chun showed me. They showed me our little island, our motherland and the rest of the world. Today you showed me a map of our county and you would like me to have only our island in my mind's eye. I'm not saying we shouldn't have our island in mind but Chairman Mao's instruction, his strategic concept of a people's war, must be borne in mind. We must guard against not only the sabotage and harassment by a handful of enemies but also an aggressive war launched against us by imperialism. Militia work both along the coast and inland must be done well and only then can we talk about drowning the enemy in the raging sea of people's war. . . ."

"Is this the administration office?" a voice broke in.

I looked up and saw the amputee. "Oh, it's you," I answered a little apologetically, getting up and offering him my seat. "I've been so busy talking that I'd forgotten all about you."

CHAPTER 19

THE ONE-LEGGED VISITOR

THE one-legged visitor sat down gratefully, fumbled in his pocket and took out a crumpled piece of paper which he handed to me. I passed it to Uncle Shuang-ho and introduced the visitor. The man bobbed in response but kept his seat.

"I'm here to look for a missing sister," he explained. "This letter was written by my township administration. Will Comrade Township Head please help me?"

Uncle Shuang-ho finished reading the note and gave it to me. It read:

Comrades of the Concord Township Administration Office,

This is to inform you that Liu Ah-tai of our township is calling on you to look for his sister, missing for the past thirty-five years. We hope you will be able to assist him in this matter. Liu Ah-tai lost his leg in 1949 while protecting a wounded People's Liberation Army man during an enemy bombing. He has rendered meritorious service to the revolution and we trust that he will receive the utmost care and help from you comrades.

Our thanks.

Yours with revolutionary greetings,

Tunglin Township Administration Office
of Huian County, Fukien Province

"Can you and your sister recognize each other?" asked Uncle Shuang-ho.

"Not likely. We haven't seen each other for almost forty years. We were children when we were separated. I don't even know what she looks like," replied the visitor. "About thirty-five years ago our mother and father took us up the coast to fish the Choushans. They ran into a storm and the boat foundered. Luckily we were all saved. Our parents had no money for fares home so they sold my six-year-old sister as a child bride to someone on this island. That's thirty-five years ago and we haven't seen each other since then. Just before ma died she made me promise I would find my sister. My poor, poor sister. . . ."

"He probably means Aunt Ta-cheng," I said to myself. "She's surnamed Liu and so is he. . . ."

"Why start looking for your sister only now?" asked Uncle Shuang-ho.

"Ah, it's like this, you see," he explained. "Before liberation I daren't come by land because of the fighting and confusion and I daren't come by sea because I heard that there were pirates off this part of the coast — your Black Wind gang. I wanted to come here right after liberation but unluckily I lost my leg and couldn't get around easily. . . ."

"You're mighty lucky," cried Uncle Shuang-ho. "The person you're looking for is right here on this island. Very likely Aunt Ta-cheng living over at East Yungchiao is your sister."

"Isn't that a bit of good luck, now!" the one-legged man exclaimed.

"How long will you be staying here?"

"I'm permanently disabled, as you can see, Comrade Township Head. I'm all alone in the world except for this missing sister of mine. I've no other living relative left. I hope the government will assist me. I've got a trade." He pointed to his barber's kit. "I can shave and trim hair."

"Very well," said Uncle Shuang-ho after some thought, "we'll do what we can. After all you have meritorious service to your credit. First let Hai-hsia take you to meet your sister. We'll fix you up with a job later. As a matter of fact we need a barber here."

Aunt Ta-cheng lived only just across the hill from the township administration office. As I showed him the way we exchanged small talk but my mind was on other things. I was both happy and sad for Aunt Ta-cheng. She would no doubt be pleased to find her long lost brother and would also be grieved to see him a crippled man.

"Here just to find your sister?" I asked him as I helped him across a particularly difficult stretch of the path. I was not entirely without doubts about him, and of the way he had suddenly arrived out of the sea.

"That's right," he answered, giving me a sharp look.

"Why come in someone else's boat?"

"Why not? Our Fukien fishermen were coming up north so I hitched a ride. Saved me the fare and I was in good company too. We're all poor fishermen and we all help each other," he answered, unperturbed.

We rounded the hill and took the path past the shop jointly run by the two halves of the settlement. This shop sold kerosene, matches and other daily-use articles, besides tobacco, wine, sweets, twine for nets, shuttles and hooks and hoes. The shop assistant was no other than No. 2 Dog. It had been organized to save the people of Concord time and trouble because there was no shopping centre on the island and people had to go all the way over to East Beach if they wanted to do any shopping. Uncle Shuang-ho had got this shop going. It bought goods in bulk at East Beach. As no one could be found to take over the running of the retail shop, Uncle Shuang-ho had asked Dog to take on the job. Dog wasn't the sort that could do a man's work, having served as steward to the big fish merchant Chen Chan-ao. At first Uncle Shuang-ho did not entirely trust him and frequently checked the accounts and always fixed the selling prices. As nothing was found to be out of order the shop was gradually left entirely in Dog's hands. He was left free to do as he liked with his time. When there were no customers about he would sit outside the shop and sing to the accompaniment of his own *erh hu* violin.

When Liu Ah-tai and I passed by, Dog was outside singing an aria from an old-style Peking opera.

"You've got a shop on the island? I'll get myself a packet of fags."

Dog put away his *erh hu* and went inside to serve Liu Ah-tai while I waited outside holding the barber's kit.

Liu Ah-tai paid for his purchase and said playfully to Dog as he was leaving, "Your hair is long enough to plait into a queue. Heat up some water this afternoon and I'll drop round and give you a hair-cut. Show you how good I am with the clippers."

"You are too kind, altogether too kind," said Dog, bowing from the doorway.

Aunt Ta-cheng was completely taken by surprise. Of course she was. She had been away from her native place for more than thirty years and had never heard a word from her family in all that time. Now out of the blue she had an elder brother!

"Where . . . where are you from?" she asked, eyeing him from head to foot suspiciously.

Liu Ah-tai gave a heavy sigh and said, "We've got the old society to thank for this! Members of one family and yet we do not recognize each other. Remember that year when you were only six and mum and dad had to sell you to someone on this island? I remember hanging on to mum and dad begging them not to sell you. I cried, 'Sell me! Don't sell sister!' But mum and dad could not do anything else. They had to sell you. . . ."

"Those were terrible days," said Aunt Ta-cheng, eyes brimming over with tears as she thought of those awful times. "But later, I didn't want to remember them."

Liu Ah-tai, his voice low and sad, said, "After you were sold and we got back home mother fell ill. Before she passed away she made me promise that when I grew up I would look for you. 'You must go back to Concord Island and find your poor little sister,' she said. Dad died not long afterwards."

"Where's my brother-in-law?" he asked suddenly.

171

Aunt Ta-cheng was too distressed to make any reply. She was weeping. Yu-hsiu walked in just then with a basket of faggots. She stared at the stranger, forgetting in her curiosity to put down her load. She had not expected that the one-legged stranger who had come over on our boat would be sitting here in her home.

"This is your uncle," said Aunt Ta-cheng. "Say hello to your uncle, Yu-hsiu."

Yu-hsiu put her load down but she did not call him uncle. "Mother, why didn't you tell me about him before?" she asked.

"This is my niece, is it?" exclaimed Liu Ah-tai, his face beaming. "Why, what a big girl you are! Mum and dad would be ever so happy if they could be here to see you."

"Who else have you in your family?" I asked.

Liu Ah-tai gave a bitter laugh. "How can a poor man find himself a wife? It is like that fishermen's chanty: 'Work like the devil in and out of the water and only just manage to cover your body. The sky for bedding and the sea for a bed. The lonely moon for a partner. . . .' Aye, I'm just a poor old bachelor."

When Aunt Ta-cheng got control of her emotions again she bustled around, cooking her new-found brother a meal. She sent Yu-hsiu to borrow some eggs from neighbours while she discussed with me where to put her brother up. "If you can't manage, the administration office can help," I suggested. "We've still some empty rooms."

Their house was not very different from ours, with two rooms, one leading off from the other and a thatched shed outside where the cooking stove was kept in summer. In winter the stove was moved into the house to help warm up the place.

"We'll put Yu-hsiu's uncle in the shed," Aunt Ta-cheng said after thinking it over. "It's not warm enough to move the stove out yet. I'll share a bed with Yu-hsiu and give her father's bed to her uncle."

There was nothing more I could do to help so I bade them farewell and left. Liu Ah-tai saw me to the door and thanked me profusely.

I went back to the administration office and suggested that a letter be sent to Fukien to inquire about our new arrival, not that I did not believe in Liu Ah-tai, but ours is an island right out on the frontline; it is best to be sure.

My writing is much like the tracks left on the sand by a crab. So I asked Chen Hsiao-yuan to write the official letter of inquiry and told him to dispatch it by registered post immediately. He promised that right away. "Without fail," he added.

When I got home granddad had cooked the meal and set the table. Over our meal we talked about the day's happenings and about the one-legged Liu Ah-tai.

"What do you think of him, Hai-hsia?"

"I don't rightly know," I answered off-handedly. As a matter of fact I had no clear idea at all of what I really thought about Liu Ah-tai. "I've just met him, but he gives one the impression that he is a very experienced fisherman."

"You think so? Well, I don't," said granddad, shaking his head.

My hand holding the chopsticks stopped in mid-air, "Why do you say that, granddad? On the boat coming over he answered questions which only experienced fishermen could answer, didn't he?"

"Yes. He knows even more about the sea than an old fisherman. Still, I don't think he's what he makes himself out to be."

"Why's that?" I questioned, puzzled and scenting something wrong.

"Oh, his face is weather-beaten and all that, but look at his hands and his foot." Granddad held out his own hands, gnarled, thick and sinewy. "His hands are fat and stubby. They're not the hands of a fisherman! Nor is his foot. Our toes are spread out, fanwise through years of gripping slippery, bucking boards. He wears a sandal and his toes are pinched together. And then again there's a shifty air about him as if he can see out of the back of his head."

CHAPTER 20

THE ACCIDENT

ONE evening I called the three squad leaders to a meeting at Ah-hung's house. The four of us, Sister Ah-hung, Yun-hsiang, Hai-hua and myself, met to sum up the experience of the match, repudiate the tendency towards putting medals first, go over some points in regard to the militia women's ways of thinking and decide on our next tasks in militia work.

Not only had the militia itself been thrown into a furore by the loss of the pennant, the reaction of the non-militia members of the populace was also strong. Some thought that losing it wasn't a bad thing, while others strongly opposed this view. The people were at loggerheads. Earlier criticism and repudiation of the craziness about medals had to some extent raised the consciousness of the masses. But the criticism and repudiation had not been thorough enough nor had it always been to the point, with the result that the idea of competing for the sake of winning had not been rooted out. We began by looking at the problems arising out of the loss of the pennant. We all said that theoretically we knew how to view it in the proper light but emotionally it was another matter. We just could not feel happy about losing it. Now, why? It was a matter of "face." Losing the pennant was losing "face."

We went on to examine this thing called "face." As we probed deeper into this question we saw that "face" was inseparable from self, from egoism. Then we got to the root of the problem. We remembered the old saying that "failure is the mother of success." We turned a negative factor into a positive factor. We lost the pennant but we gained by improving ourselves ideologically. We repudiated self and greatly enhanced our modesty and prudence and the revolutionary spirit of working hard and steadily. Our orientation was clearer and our forward drive was strengthened.

Summing up, I said, "We've had an excellent meeting this evening. The political atmosphere tonight was very much in evidence and our attack against selfishness and egoism was straight to the point with no holds spared. Chairman Mao teaches us, **We should check our complacency and constantly criticize our shortcomings, just as we should wash our faces or sweep the floor every day to remove the dirt and keep them clean.** Selfishness and egoism and things like that are the dirt in our ideology and we must get rid of them. . . .

"Another problem which we militia must pay serious attention to at the moment is curbing the tendency to relax our vigilance. Because we are living right now in a peaceful environment we must be on our guard against being caught unprepared. We are not aware enough of the aggressive nature of the enemy. The root of our tendency towards putting medals first lies in selfish ideas but it also shows that our understanding of being prepared against war is not deep enough. We mustn't fix our sights on the pennant and fail to see the enemy. Don't let winning a pennant blind us to the enemy sharpening his knife. That's very dangerous. Don't think for one moment that everything under the sun is all right because our island has been liberated. On the contrary, we must heighten our vigilance a hundredfold. We must be on our toes all the time. In addition to continuing rifle practice I think we should also hold night manoeuvres."

Before the sound of my voice had died away, Hai-hua was on her feet, saying, "I'm all for it. Let's start tonight!"

I said, "But Township Head Shuang-ho has been dragging his feet about this."

"We see less and less of that initiative of yours nowadays, Hai-hsia," interjected Sister Ah-hung. "If you always fear the wolf ahead and the tiger behind, you'll never get anything done. Why wait for him to decide? Can't we decide for ourselves?"

Night manoeuvres are only a part of routine militia training, I reasoned, and do not necessarily require a permit from the township administration. "Very well, then. We will have an emergency muster tonight without warning," I said. "We'll strike while the iron's hot. Tonight's muster will show how we stand. Show how well we're prepared against war. Another thing, a one-legged man named Liu Ah-tai arrived here on our island a few days ago. We're not sure we know enough about him. I'm not saying we should go around suspecting this or that person but neither should we completely trust everyone until we're quite sure. We're an island out in the frontline and we can't afford to lower our guard. We must all show a little caution."

That evening I did not go home but stayed with Sister Ah-hung. Near midnight I went to the big banyan tree and sounded the "muster" on the conch.

The clear night sky was now obscured as a strong wind whipped up sand and dust.

Ten minutes later the whole platoon had assembled. I briefed the ranks, "An enemy squad is expected to put ashore, to attack and carry out acts of sabotage. The probable landing point is Gourd Bay. Squad One is to hold Tide-Watcher's Point and keep Height 203 in our control. Squad Two will proceed via the beach from the left and Squad Three via the beach from the right to close in on the enemy from two sides. All clear? Proceed!"

I followed Squad One up the slope to the Point. The path was narrow and steep but we moved swiftly and with sure feet for we had training in this. Every day we strengthened the muscles of our legs standing sentinel, working in the fields and gathering firewood. We could move swiftly and surely in mist or in the dark without stumbling. Sister Ah-hung led the way at a loping stride, her rifle firmly grasped in her hands. Yu-hsiu dropped behind. I saw her groping for something in the darkness, and chided her, "Hurry up, Yu-hsiu!"

There was the trace of a sob in her voice as she replied, "Curse my luck! I've lost my shoes."

"Here, wear these," I said slipping mine off and handing them to her.

Flustered, she slid into my shoes, picked up her rifle and ran to catch up with the others.

There was a sharp bend ahead, then a bit of a steep ascent. Suddenly I heard a startled scream from up front. Sister Ah-hung had tripped and gone hurtling over the cliff.

We froze where we were. My heart was in my mouth and I felt my limbs grow cold. The cliff was not very high but it was a steep drop and below were bare jagged rocks. I ordered the others to go ahead while I took Yu-hsiu with me to attend to Sister Ah-hung.

I slithered down, calling, "Sister Ah-hung! Sister Ah-hung!" There was no answer and my heart seemed to choke me. I groped about and suddenly found her. She was lying still as death. I picked her up in my arms and gently shook her. "Sister Ah-hung!" I cried.

No sound came from her. Was she still alive? I broke out into a cold sweat. I felt her head and my hand was wet with blood. Her rifle lay broken beside her.

Yu-hsiu stammered, "What'll we do? What'll we do?" She was near to a state of panic.

I put my face close to Sister Ah-hung's mouth and felt her breath. She was alive! I felt a surge of joy. A spark of joy in a sea of disaster.

"Go and tell my grandfather to fetch the boat round and take her to hospital," I told Yu-hsiu. "Hurry!"

She turned and raced off. I picked up Sister Ah-hung and carried her to the quay. Her arm around my neck dangled limply as if held together by a mere thread of skin.

I ground my teeth as I stumbled with my load through wind and darkness. Pain roused Sister Ah-hung and she mumbled, "I won't be crippled, will I, Hai-hsia?" There was a pause and she spoke again, "Even if I do lose my arm I can still use the other to hold a gun, can't I? I'll still be a militia woman!"

Her pluck and determination made my heart swell with admiration.

She clung to me with the other arm. Her sweat felt hot on my neck, but not a sob or sound escaped her. I heard her grind her teeth, fighting down the pain.

The sun was already high next day when I left the hospital at East Beach after seeing Sister Ah-hung taken care of by doctors and nurses. I met Chen Hsiao-yuan as I reached the quay. He had come to call me to a meeting at the administration office. I instinctively knew what the meeting was going to be about.

As I walked down the street I heard people whispering. We'd had some mishaps of one sort or another in the previous few years while carrying out our work, but never anything as grave as this. It was a serious accident!

As I made my way to the administration office, No. 2 Dog sidled up and, feigning solicitude, asked, "Platoon Leader. . . . Ah . . . is she badly hurt? But, then she has always been brash and clumsy. Um . . . she should have been more careful. It was very dark, wasn't it?"

I ignored him. Heaving a sigh and stroking his wisp of a goatee, he scuttled away, but I noticed he moved quicker than usual and his back was straighter too. That slimy thing was actually gloating!

It was a township Party branch meeting, so besides Uncle Shuang-ho there were Party branch committee members from other villages too. Granddad had been newly elected to the branch committee and he had hurried to attend after tying up the boat. After he had declared the meeting open Uncle Shuang-ho asked for a report on Sister Ah-hung's condition.

"It's very serious! Very serious indeed!" he exclaimed when he heard the extent of her injuries. He demanded a self-examination from me.

My head was still spinning, filled with thoughts about Sister Ah-hung's injuries and her three children. I hadn't got round to thinking about self-examination, although I knew that I was responsible for the accident. Uncle Shuang-ho was highly dissatisfied with my attitude.

"As you haven't given it enough thought yet, let me speak first," he continued. "This is a very serious accident and we must send in a thorough self-examination to the district Party committee about it. Comrade Hai-hsia arbitrarily, without permission of the township, decided to hold an emergency muster of the militia at night. This is a breach of discipline and a violation of regulations! And this very serious accident was the direct result of her action. . . ."

I broke in, "I disagree. Night manoeuvres are part of the training and can be decided by the platoon, so there's no question of any violation of discipline and regulations, least of all any grounds to the accusation that the accident was due entirely to my breach of discipline and defiance of regulations. Emergency musters are part of the training programme to boost preparedness against war, a part of regular training. No blame can be attached to that. We mustn't be afraid of eating rice just because there was a grain of sand in one mouthful. Night manoeuvres must not be discontinued."

"What! You'd be continuing with them?" challenged Uncle Shuang-ho, now angrier than ever. "You refuse to listen to what others have to say about it? Why, you're like the person who still insists on sailing after his mast is down and his bow has run on the rocks!"

When others echoed his views, he turned and asked granddad to speak. "Let us hear your opinion, Uncle Teh-shun," he said.

"This is no small matter," said granddad. "Sister Ah-hung's been seriously injured. I think we should first send in a report to District Party Secretary Fang. Hai-hsia should have asked your permission before ordering a night muster. That's something she overlooked. But the blame does not rest entirely on her. You haven't paid much attention to militia work these last two years. It is true that our island has been liberated and that those dogs haven't dared to make trouble, but that doesn't mean we can stop being vigilant. Once we lose our vigilance then we're inviting trouble. You must pay serious attention to militia work. This is something you must not neglect."

"But you know very well how busy production work is," Uncle Shuang-ho retorted. "Where am I to find the time?"

"You can if you really want to," answered granddad, evenly. "Militia activities have not hindered production at all. On the other hand, I think the militia members have been a big help. Without their exemplary role, could production be doing so well?"

Uncle Shuang-ho simmered down and in a calmer voice said, "I have my views and plans about militia activities and I'm partly responsible for Hai-hsia's mistake. I've watched her growing up and I think she has been promoted too rapidly. First she became platoon leader, then a member of the public security committee and then was accepted into the Party. A certain arrogance and air of conceit has appeared and her mistake stems mainly from that."

He summed up, "Hai-hsia has been treated too tolerantly in the past and if this accident is not dealt with severely there's no telling what bigger mistakes she's going to make in the future. Indulgence will only fuel her arrogance. Only strictness can correct her. Besides, she is too young. She's not experienced enough to lead a militia platoon. And another thing, this accident is extremely serious and must be severely dealt with to forestall future accidents. I move that she be removed from her post as leader of the militia platoon! Of course we'll send in a report to the district Party committee for its approval."

I probably had never felt more miserable in my life. The tears welled up but with an effort I quickly fought them back and hung my head.

Uncle Shuang-ho then went on to deal with the second item on the agenda.

"Cover up the sweet potato plants with earth as soon as they've been manured. Don't wait for rain. Water them. . . ."

I interrupted him, "We haven't finished with my business. Who's to take over from me? Who shall I hand my duties over to? The accident is not a trifling matter and I'm prepared to shoulder full responsibility for it. I ask that the cause of the accident be fully looked into and the finding then sent, along with the decision concerning the disciplinary measure against me, to the district Party committee."

"The cause of the accident is quite evident without having to look any further. Emergency muster, pitch black night, high wind blowing, steep, slippery path and one single false step sending her tumbling over the cliff. All very clear. As to your work, we'll wait until we receive an answer to our report." He went back to the second item on the agenda without another word, "We must water them, not wait for rain. The storehouses must be attended to before the rains start. Production on the land must not lag behind production out at sea. We must strive to bring in a double bumper harvest. . . ."

The meeting went on discussing production.

Uncle Shuang-ho had devoted all his time and energy to production and we were getting fine returns. Just before the summer our island had been selected and commended as a model of how to carry out production on an island. Many visitors had called to learn from our experience. But as to class struggle, political-ideological and militia work, well, Uncle Shuang-ho had his own views. When Secretary Fang was with us it had always been "You're a military man, Old Fang, so I'll leave you to look after class struggle, political-ideological and militia work. I'll keep an eye on production, eh?"

In those days the contradiction between Uncle Shuang-ho and myself had not been so apparent. When there was any disagreement, we had only to ask Secretary Fang and he'd make the decision. But Secretary Fang was now no longer with us to resolve the differences between us. And Uncle Shuang-ho was still the same. In the early days following the island's liberation he had believed class struggle had ceased to exist because the landlords and local despots had been knocked down and the bad elements had been placed under surveillance. This way of thinking was clearly evident at the first meeting of poor fishermen and peasants convened to elect representatives. It became more manifest after the islands further away from Concord had been liberated and the P.L.A. garrison had left Concord. Everything is safe and secure, he had reasoned, and enemy in large numbers cannot reach Concord, while small batches of enemy won't dare to attempt it. He was all for "Back to the plough and nets; the fighting is all over." Then again, he was always thinking that he was older, and more experienced than anyone else, and was forever seeing me as a child. He paid little or no heed to what I had to say.

Chairman Mao's teaching echoed in my ears, **The imperialists and domestic reactionaries will certainly not take their defeat lying down and they will struggle to the last ditch. After there is peace and order throughout the country, they will still engage in sabotage and create disturbances in various ways and will try every day and every minute to stage a come-back. This is inevitable and beyond all doubt, and under no circumstances must we relax our vigilance.**

Uncle Shuang-ho, where is your revolutionary vigilance? I thought.

I was miserable and upset, and was the first to leave after the meeting. There were so many things I had wanted to say but where was I to begin? I didn't know!

Granddad fell into step beside me, saying, "You mustn't take it too much to heart, Hai-hsia." How comforting he was!

"Don't you worry about me, granddad," I replied gratefully but firmly, "I'm not the girl I was a couple of years ago."

"You run off home and cook something to eat and then go round and have a good look at the place where the accident happened."

We walked side by side until we reached the crossroads, then I stopped and said, "You go home and eat. I've got to go and see how Sister Ah-hung's three kiddies are doing."

"You're right. Go, quickly. I was so worked up that I completely forgot those three children."

Chapter 21

A STORM IS COMING

GRANDDAD went on home and I hurried over to Sister Ah-hung's house where I found the two younger children in tears. They rushed up to meet me as soon as I entered. The baby was without his pants. Ah-sha, the eldest, could no longer hold back his sobs, and joined his younger brothers.

"Will mother be coming back?" he asked through his tears.

"So you know?" I was astonished. How had he learned about the accident so soon?

"Early this morning I heard someone outside our door shouting that mother had fallen and killed herself."

"Who was it?"

Ah-sha shook his head. "Couldn't make out who it was."

What a rat! Who was it that had come frightening the kids? "Your mother has had an accident but it's not very serious and the doctor at the hospital says she'll soon be well enough to come home," I told him as I helped dress the baby. "I'm telling you the truth, Ah-sha."

Though I spoke calmly, my mind was in a turmoil. Who had told the children? I immediately suspected Smelly had something to do with it and was determined to get to the truth.

Ah-sha, assured by my words, began to play with his brothers.

"You two are the baddies and I'm going to capture you," he told them.

"I'm not! I'm not a baddy!" protested the second child. "I'm a militia man!"

"I'm a mileesh too," lisped the baby. "I's not a baddy."

"Only the strongest can be militia men," Ah-sha announced.

The three began fighting each other. Eventually the baby was captured and tied to a leg of the table, wailing and protesting vigorously.

"Release baby, Ah-sha! Untie him!" I ordered. "Go and fetch me some sticks from outside. I'm going to cook you a meal."

I tidied up the bed and the recent field of battle and lit the stove.

As I fed the fire, in my mind I went over the morning's meeting.

Where had I gone wrong? Uncle Shuang-ho and I held different views on the work of the militia. He was more experienced, but was he wrong, or was it me? Our militia unit held a political study meeting at least once a week and we could almost correctly recite everything Chairman Mao had said about the militia. **After the enemies with guns have been wiped out, there will still be enemies without guns; they are bound to struggle desperately against us, and we must never regard these enemies lightly. If we do not now raise and understand the problem in this way, we shall commit the gravest mistakes.**

Our militia organization is an important instrument of the Chinese people to counter imperialist aggression from without and to exercise the people's democratic dictatorship inside the country. How can we neglect militia work? We should act according to Chairman Mao's instructions and march ahead along the road pointed out by him. I did not think I was wrong. I was pretty sure I was right.

The enemy had kept pretty quiet over the last few years. That was a fact. But was that because we had been making a good job of the militia? Or did it mean that there was little need to go on with militia work? I believed that the proverb "a broken fence lets the dog in" applied in this case. The dog had not entered because the fence was intact, not because the dog did not want to get in. Take No. 2 Dog for example. He had not dared to try anything openly during the past few years but that wife of his had been making mischief, making up and spreading all sorts of rumours and slanders. One could be sure that Dog was behind that. What did he do when he was not serving behind the counter? And what else did he sing besides arias from old-style Peking opera? Did he not also sing "The tiger lurking deep in the mountain waits for a whispering wind; the dragon at low tide waits for the water to rise"? Wasn't that what was in his mind? He was no tiger, merely a dog, a vicious cur. He was no dragon but a venomous snake. He didn't make any overt moves because he could see that we had the rifle pointing in his direction. He was acting meek and mild but that did not mean he was not waiting for a chance to rise up and be his natural self again. That led me to think of the meeting. We should have made a thorough examination into the cause of the accident. Was it an accident or was it a political act of sabotage? We used that particular path every day and nothing had ever happened before. Why did Sister Ah-hung trip last night? Had the dog crept in unnoticed? I shuddered at the thought.

The meal was ready and I called the children.

"Why don't you eat too, aunty?" Ah-sha demanded.

I hadn't had any breakfast, but I did not feel like eating at all. I was too engrossed thinking about the accident to eat.

"I've already eaten," I said. "You kids eat up and behave yourselves while I go out for a few minutes, will you?"

They nodded as they ate and I left them.

I ran up the hill to inspect the scene of last night's accident. Half-way there I ran into granddad, who was coming down.

"I've had a look at that place and I think a stepping stone has been tampered with, Hai-hsia," he said. "Let's go and have another look."

We found one stone step balanced like a seesaw. The other stones which used to support it were missing. Had they worked loose naturally or had they been deliberately removed? Granddad was of the firm opinion that they had been removed by someone.

As I went down the path again, I realized that things were much more complicated than I had suspected. My dismissal from my post had not been confirmed, but it was already known all over the settlement that I had been removed and that to prevent further accidents no more night manoeuvres were to be held. Rumour said this was the township government's official decision. The gossips also said that it was equally dangerous to do sentry work at night. "Someone else could just as easily fall down the cliff as Sister Ah-hung did."

Yu-hsiu came running up breathlessly and offered me a pair of shoes, saying, "Here're your shoes. I've been looking all over the place for you."

Only then did I realize that I had been walking bare-footed since the night before.

"What has your uncle to say about last night's incident?" I asked quietly.

After a pause she answered, "He doesn't seem to be much interested. When someone said there should be no more standing guard, he said, 'Then what's the militia for? Sure there is peace and quiet now but we must still post sentries.'"

In the past, I would have been satisfied and left it at that, but today I knew better. One must not look at things superficially. I analysed Liu Ah-tai's reaction. What did he mean by "peace and quiet, yet post sentries?" Did he really think there was "peace and quiet"? Or did he say that to lull the vigilance of his listeners?

Things seemed more and more complicated. I wanted to talk it over with someone so I hurried over to the administration office. Uncle Shuang-ho was out visiting another village, checking production. Who was there I could talk to? Secretary Fang. But when would he be back?

All the members of the women's militia came to see me at Sister Ah-hung's house, to ask after her and also to express indignation over the proposal to remove me from office. They were concerned for Sister Ah-hung and loud in their indignation about the proposal. Even Ah-sha chimed in to voice his protest. "I say auntie must be platoon leader. She's just got to be platoon leader!"

I made myself heard above the din. "Let's forget that for now and look into some of the rumours which are being spread about the settlement. We mustn't let them confuse the people. We must expose the rumour-mongers!"

But no one paid much heed to me. They kept talking about my being relieved of my post.

"I think we've nothing to worry about," said Yun-hsiang. "Secretary Fang knows Hai-hsia and he knows us. Let's go over what we have heard and send Hai-hsia with a report to the district administration. They'll know how to settle things properly. What's the use of getting all worked up like this?"

This quietened everyone and we began to recall what we had heard. However, no one seemed to remember clearly who had started the rumours. We talked and talked until evening and people began to go home. Before they left I said, "Sister Ah-hung will probably have to stay in hospital a few days so let Yu-hsiu take over Squad One in the meantime. Yun-hsiang, and you Hai-hua, go and call a meeting to discuss this, will you? There must be no slackening in our work, particularly with things as they are. Sentries must be posted."

After they had all left I fixed a meal for the three children and myself.

"Ah-sha," I said after the meal was over, "I'll be staying the night with you. You're not going to be afraid, are you?"

"I'm not afraid!" he replied. "I'm not like baby. He's even scared when he hears a cat miaow. I'm not a tiny bit afraid. I'm going to take mum's place as guard!"

The door was suddenly pushed open and Sister Ah-hung burst into the house, an arm in a sling and her head bandaged.

"Mum's back!" the three children shouted in chorus, and rushed to her.

"Why are you here?" I exclaimed in astonishment. Puzzled but very glad to see her, I supported her to the bed.

Still breathing hard, she replied, "I ran for it as soon as the doctors weren't looking."

"You are a ninny! How do you feel?"

I could see she was exhuasted. I filled a bowl with hot soup and gave it to her. She drank it down and with a sigh of satisfaction said, "There's nothing much the matter with me. A dislocated arm and a few scratches here and there. I'll be all right in a couple of days."

"There'll be a lot of scars, though," I said, peering into her bandaged face.

"Well, what of it? Badges of honour! Glorious wounds sustained in the line of duty."

Her cheerfulness was infectious and I felt a load lift from my mind. "Sure they are, but how will your husband take it? I'll bet you anything you like that he'll tear over and ask me, 'What have you done to my lovely wife!' That'll put me on the spot."

"Where did you learn to make cracks like that? Anyway, we're an old married couple so it doesn't matter. But if you had a few of the scars on your face, you'd have one heck of a time trying to find a husband!"

"Now you're being nasty. I'm going." I pretended I was leaving.

Actually, if she had taken a stick to drive me out I wouldn't have left her, but she really thought I meant it and put out a hand to restrain me. "Stop fooling and be serious," she remonstrated. "I'm worried about that rifle I smashed up. Do you think I can get it fixed?"

"You can have mine."

"And what will you use? A platoon leader cannot be without a weapon."

"I'll use that harpoon of granddad's."

"Mum, auntie's been given the sack. She's not platoon leader any more," wailed little Ah-sha.

"What's this? Quit telling fibs!" And she made a feint to box his ears.

"But it's true! It's true!" protested Ah-sha.

"He's right," I said, hastily. "But it has still to be confirmed."

"What did you say?" Despite her wounds she sat bolt upright. "Don't try kidding me. I won't believe it."

"Then why are you so worked up? Anyway, I've just told you that it's not final. It has to be confirmed."

"Confirm or not, I won't have it! I'm going to see that Shuang-ho and tell him how it happened. It was all my fault. He can't blame you for it. I won't have it, I tell you."

It was very late and the three kids were sleeping soundly.

Suddenly Sister Ah-hung woke and, seeing me still awake, said gently and coaxingly, "Get some sleep, Hai-hsia. You were up all last night and there are bags under your eyes."

"I can't. In a while I've got to go and inspect the sentries. A lot of rumours have been spread today and the girls are a bit upset. I've got to go and see how things are."

"But you're no longer in charge. Why must you go?"

"Chairman Mao calls on everyone to be a soldier and everyone on this island has the duty to defend it. Even if I'm not platoon leader any longer I'm still a militia woman and no one can take that responsibility away from me!"

"If ever you leave our platoon, Hai-hsia. . . ." I felt her hot tears on the back of my hand.

"Don't you worry yourself about that. I'll never leave!"

I rose, picked up my rifle and left the house. The night was dark and black clouds wreathed the Point. A strong breeze tossed my hair and tugged at my clothes. It looked as if a storm was coming. I clutched my rifle and marched firmly to my position at the look-out post.

CHAPTER 22

A TEAR IN THE MESH

TWO days of rain had washed the whole island clean. Everything looked fresh and bright, the crops and trees were glistening green. Even the rocks looked newly polished. The mountain rivulets coursing down the gullies rushed headlong into the sea.

Women were at the stream washing clothes. Their trouser-legs rolled high, clear water swirled about their legs as they pounded clothes on the rocks with heavy sticks.

They chattered as they worked, chiefly of the accident which had happened a few days before. Smelly was there too, in the middle of a group, her high-pitch screeching and squawking plainly heard above the general din. She seemed more excited than usual, as if secretly elated about something. Since our encounter at Yu-hsiu's house she had been fairly subdued, seldom making trouble and acting as if she were on her good behaviour. But today, she was her old raucous self again. Really, as the saying goes, "A whitewashed crow doesn't stay white long." She had perked up and was more lively since she had heard that I had been removed from my post as platoon leader. I went closer to hear what she had to say, but she clammed up as soon as she saw me and looked down at her washing, which she continued silently and intently.

Pointing to the bundle under my arm, Aunt Ta-cheng asked, "Whose laundry have you got, Hai-hsia? Why, you've got children's clothes too!"

"They're Sister Ah-hung and the children's," I answered. "She's hurt herself and can't do any washing."

"I've heard say that the militia won't be holding any more assemblies. Is that true, Hai-hsia?" she asked, almost in a whisper.

"Where did you hear that?" I countered.

"They're all saying it. They're saying the township authorities have decided."

"I was at the meeting and I didn't hear anything like that. Who told you?"

"Oh, I just heard it. Someone in charge probably let it out." It was obvious that she was dodging my question.

I had a suspicion that all the many incidents which had occurred recently had something to do with that one-legged Liu Ah-tai. Something Yu-hsiu told me had given me a clue, but she had not said anything definite, so I decided to see what I could learn from her mother.

"How's Yu-hsiu's uncle?" I asked. "I've been so busy these last few days that I haven't had time to come round and ask. Is everything all right?"

"Everything is just fine," she replied. "Yu-hsiu's uncle is always telling me how well he's been looked after by the township authorities. He's very good to us and gives me all he earns by hair-cutting and with that and what he brought with him we manage quite comfortably."

"Is he worried about Yu-hsiu having to go out at night and stand guard? I mean after what happened the other night."

"Isn't he worried, just! Why, he said it was sheer good luck she got off with a few scratches. He told me that someone in Fukien fell during a militia manoeuvre and was killed. I've been very upset these days worrying about that scatter-brained daughter of mine."

At first there did not seem much wrong with what he had said, but on thinking it over I had my doubts. It could be taken several ways. In any case it was damaging to the fighting morale of the militia. Who was he? I counted the days and reckoned that we should have had a reply from Fukien to our letter. Why hadn't we heard? I must look into it.

I hung the washing on the fence around Ah-hung's house and decided to go to the township office and find Chen Hsiao-yuan. On my way there I saw him coming out of the shop and hailed him.

"Have we had a reply from Fukien yet?"

"No," he answered, casually.

"When did you send that letter? Did you send it registered? Give me the receipt. I want to check up on that letter I asked you to send off by registered post."

"But . . . ," stuttered Chen, his face colouring when he saw I was serious, "I . . . er . . . I gave it . . . er . . . to Dog, er, to post. From . . . from East Beach." He was stammering like a schoolboy trying to recite a lesson he had not learned properly.

I was furious. "You gave it to that person to send? Where's the receipt?"

"What's wrong with sending it by ordinary mail?" he flared.

"It's irresponsible! By ordinary mail, did you say? Then there's no knowing if that letter ever got sent!" My voice was quavering with rage.

"Oh, quit throwing your weight about," he replied, suddenly going onto the offensive. "You're not talking to a member of your platoon now. Remember you are speaking to a clerk of the township administration office. And please also remember that I have been commended by the township head, not like you. . . ." I knew what he was alluding to and was fuming with rage.

"You have been most irresponsible, do you know that? Haven't you one shred of class vigilance left in you? Do you know this is grave negligence in the performance of your duty?"

"Don't give me that guff," he returned. "And now, I want to ask you something. Why have you been trying to break up my engagement to Tsai-chu? If you have anything against me, tell me to my face and don't go slandering people behind their backs!"

Surprised, I asked, "What's that you're saying?"

"You know very well what I mean, so don't try acting the innocent!"

"Are you mad?"

"One of us is," he said, turning on his heel and walking away.

"Hey, come back. We haven't finished yet."

"There's nothing more to be said." He went on without even bothering to look back.

In the past I would have ignored him, but today I knew better. I must have it out with him, but it was no use getting angry.

I walked into the office and found him speaking on the phone. "No, he's not in I tell you. Secretary Fang called him away. . . . What? No! Where am I supposed to find him!" He slammed the phone down.

All this time I was sitting in front of him, waiting. I could see he still had his dander up so I kept a tight grip on myself and said, "Hsiao-yuan, I'm sorry I spoke to you like that just now. I was too hasty. But if you think that business of the letter over coolly you'll agree with me. Have you ever asked yourself what sort of person Dog is?"

He appeared a little mollified as I spoke earnestly and apologetically. He spoke to me more calmly and with a rueful note in his voice.

"I'm not blameless either. I had written that letter and was just going to post it when I found Dog setting out for East Beach to fetch some goods, so I told him to post it for me. . . . Later on, I thought about it again and realized that I shouldn't have. . . ."

"I hope you understand what a big mistake you've made, comrade. As a clerk of the township administration office you should have a better work style. Now I want to ask you, what do you mean by saying that I was trying to break up your engagement to Tsai-chu? Who told you that?"

His face darkened as he curtly replied, "Never you mind who told me. Facts are facts."

"Are you so foolish as to believe everything you hear?"

"You run me down at the militia meetings and that makes Tsai-chu look down on me. She's still giving me the cold shoulder."

"That's something I've been wanting to talk to you about. Frankly, both you and Tsai-chu have serious shortcomings. She's pretty spoilt, headstrong and she cries too much. She shirks work. But she has made a lot of progress recently with help from the others. We've been thinking of making her deputy squad leader. But what have you done? You've not only failed to help her but you have actually been holding her back. You wouldn't let her stand guard at night. Now do you understand why she's been ignoring you? Can you blame her? Comrade, think it over."

"I was afraid there'd be another accident," he answered shamefacedly.

"Afraid of another accident! We can't give up posting sentries and guards just because we're afraid of accidents! The question is how to prevent accidents. I'm asking you again, now, who told you I was trying to break you two up? What proof have you got?"

"Dog told me back at the shop," he said. Then he added, defensively, "Probably he was only joking. I shouldn't have taken him seriously."

"He was in earnest, not joking. You've had a lot of schooling, comrade, but by not using your brain you've been easily taken in. As for you and Tsai-chu, you can rest assured that we all wish you well. It's wrong of her to cold-shoulder you but you should be proud of her for that. She's ignoring you because she doesn't like you holding her back." I tried to break the deadlock by adding, "If you want her to take you seriously, there's always some way of getting her to do it. You could, for example, write out a self-criticism. Try it."

When I saw that he was in a better temper, I asked, "Is it you who's been going round saying that it's been decided not to hold any more emergency assemblies?"

He quickly denied it. "I never said that. I only said that the emergency call-up the other night had not been first approved by the township leadership."

"Ah, so that's it! The enemy has made use of your words to spread ugly rumours to lower our fighting spirit. Comrade, haven't you any notion at all of class vigilance?" He gazed at a spot on the ground and sighed as I continued, "You've seen the nets we make, haven't you? Every mesh is linked. If one of them breaks then the fish escapes. It's the same with catching enemies. Everything is closely interlinked and if a tear occurs somewhere then the enemy slips through and escapes."

"I'll . . . I'll go and ask Dog for the letter, shall I?" he suggested penitently.

"Don't do that. We'll send another letter and inquire if they got it."

"All right. I'll write it myself and send it off by registered post and give you the receipt," he offered eagerly as if to make up for his error.

Secretary Fang and Uncle Shuang-ho walked into the office accompanied by a comrade from the district government in charge of military affairs. The three of them were engaged in a lively conversation when they entered.

"Secretary Fang! I was just going to look for you!" I cried, running up to him like a lost child at the sight of its mother.

"I was going to look you up too," he answered. "Is your grandfather home?"

"He'll be back by noon," I said. "But didn't you come over on his boat?"

"No. We went from East Beach to Half Screen and then came over here. We've got something to discuss first, so you run on home. I'll be around a little later."

He arrived after lunch. I felt like a hurt child and blurted out everything on my mind. I told him about my quarrel with

Uncle Shuang-ho after we had come back from the shooting match, the accident the night I had called for a sudden assembly of the militia, the township Party branch committee meeting, the missing letter, granddad's opinion of the one-legged man and what I thought about them all.

"You're right in some things," Secretary Fang said. "It is very necessary to write and make inquiries about Liu Ah-tai, but you shouldn't place all your hopes on the reply. You should think of using all possible ways and means to find out everything you can about him. If he turns out to be a bad character, don't make any hasty moves and put him on his guard. Find out what he's up to, what he came here for, whom he has contacted, and so on. We want to rope in every one of the enemy in one clean sweep."

He turned and, addressing granddad who was weaving a basket by the door, asked, "Uncle Teh-shun, you say Liu Ah-tai doesn't appear to be a fisherman. What do you think he is?"

"That fellow knows a lot about the sea but he doesn't look like a fisherman. I can't say what he is. All I can say is that he doesn't look like a fisherman."

"Hmm. Knows a lot about the sea but doesn't look like a fisherman," Secretary Fang said to himself pensively. "What is he?"

Turning to me he said, "You're quite right about the cause of Sister Ah-hung's falling over the cliff. We've just visited the scene of the accident and found that that step did not come loose of itself. It was deliberate sabotage!"

"That's strange. If it was deliberate sabotage, how did the enemy know we were going to call the militia out that night?"

"The enemy may have known and then again he may not have known, but that was his handiwork all right. Obviously the enemy had two aims in mind. He wanted to kill some of our militia, and as likely as not he had you in mind when he set that trap. He'd know that you use that path when you go up to check the sentries at night. And another reason was to create trouble and disturb the minds of the people and so sabotage our defensive efforts. Get two birds with one arrow."

I recounted the various reactions and rumours which had followed the accident. "It's had a big effect on our militia and their families, especially on family members of our militia. Even Chen Hsiao-yuan's been trying to drag Tsai-chu back."

"I don't think that people are afraid just because of one incident like that the other night. No. Not at all. I believe some person or persons have been spreading a lot of rumours. You know the old saying about there being 'no smoke without fire.' Let's go over all the things which have happened recently. First there is that Liu Ah-tai. He pops up, then comes an act of political sabotage, followed by rumours. . . . And then there is that Dog in the shop. We must be more vigilant. We leave an opening for the enemy whenever anyone of us drops our guard. That letter you told Chen to write, for instance. If it had been sent, we should have had a reply by now. Very likely that letter is going to cause us some unnecessary difficulties. If everyone of us maintains a high revolutionary vigilance then the enemy will find it extremely hard to make a single move."

Later, we went on to talk about the work of the militia. He asked me what I thought should be done in the future.

"I think we should expand the militia, bring its strength up to at least two platoons. That would allow all the women who are eligible to join. The old militia members are solid and will make a good nucleus. The enemy is trying his best to break up the militia, destroy the militia, so we'll give him tit for tat by building up the militia force and making a better job of our militia work!" I told him.

He endorsed my suggestion and said that he would bring it before the township authorities.

"That's a very good suggestion," he said. "We need that spirit of facing up to difficulties and braving wind and waves if we're to make revolution. As to expanding the militia, as you suggest, that'll need a lot of hard work. People must be persuaded to accept the idea. Likely as not there'll be a pretty stiff fight before that can be brought about."

I knew he was talking about Uncle Shuang-ho. That reminded me about his disciplining me, so I asked, "Does the district Party committee know that I'm to be disciplined? I don't know how I'm going to make a self-examination."

"Nothing has been decided about that yet."

"But everyone already knows that I've been removed from my militia post. With things as they are at present, militia work must be tightened up. I suggest Sister Ah-hung be put in charge as platoon leader. Yun-hsiang could be the deputy. She's very meticulous."

"Don't be in too much of a hurry. At the moment we are considering where to put you. That's enough for the present. Wait and see what the leadership decides for you. Rumours are just rumours, so don't pay any attention to them. Organizational decisions are another thing altogether. Pending the appointment of a new platoon leader you're still in charge. We're holding a Party branch committee meeting after supper to look into some of the things which have occurred. Some ideological problems will have to be thrashed out. You and Uncle Teh-shun must attend. We'll discuss some of the things at the meeting."

He rose and, at the door, turned to say, "Uncle Teh-shun, are you free this afternoon?"

"I've nothing on hand. Anything you want me to do?"

"Yes. As a matter of fact, I want you to row us out to Tiger-Head Isle."

"Right. I'll meet you at the quay." And he went to get his scull.

"We'll see you at the quay," Secretary Fang said as he left. "I'm going to the office for a few minutes and then I'll join you."

"You do that. I'll see you at the quay."

Why were they going out to that uninhabited island? I did not know nor did I ask because I knew Secretary Fang was a careful person and very principled. If I were to have been told he would have done so.

CHAPTER 23

A WIDER VISION

THE Party branch committee meeting started after Secretary
Fang, Uncle Shuang-ho and granddad returned from their
trip to Tiger-Head Isle and had had their supper. The lamp
shone down on the six of us — Secretary Fang, Uncle Shuang-ho,
granddad and myself and two committee members from another
village.

There was a tense atmosphere when Uncle Shuang-ho opened
the meeting. He reported:

"There has been a rash of incidents on the island these last
few days and Secretary Fang has criticized my work style and
the way I look at things. This meeting has been called to hear
what you comrades have to say about me and my work." He
then asked, "Is this the way I should begin, Secretary Fang?"

"Let's try a different approach, shall we? Let's be a little
more relaxed," he suggested instead of directly replying. "This
is a branch committee meeting and also a study meeting. We're
not here solely to criticize this or that person. We want each
one of us to get something out of it and raise our ideology
a bit. Now, Comrade Shuang-ho, I remember you once told me
about the special region Party committee secretary giving you a
Mauser before you left for the island. Would you like to tell
the meeting about it tonight?"

This unexpected request produced a visible change in the atmosphere and we all felt less tense.

But Uncle Shuang-ho appeared not to have understood. After a pause he said, "Right after this island was liberated, the Party committee secretary of the special region said to me, 'Comrade Shuang-ho, we're sending you to Concord to take charge, as you know the island well. Spontaneous struggles have been waged there in the past against the despots, but the Party has no firm base there and conditions on the island are rather complicated. Your knowledge of the island is an advantage, but on the other hand you're rather inexperienced, and no doubt you'll run into many difficulties.'

"When I asked him to consider sending a more experienced comrade, he refused, saying, 'That is out of the question. Cadres are required everywhere. The motherland is being liberated at such a rapid rate, where are we to find enough experienced cadres? Besides, experience comes from practical struggle. I advise you to study Marxism-Leninism-Mao Tsetung Thought well and improve your abilities through taking part in actual struggles. You must temper yourself in the storm and stress of violent class struggles.' "

He had our rapt attention as he continued:

"The Party committee secretary gave me a Mauser along with a dozen or so booklets of Chairman Mao's articles. As he handed me the gun, he said, 'Chairman Mao teaches us, **Every Communist must grasp the truth, "Political power grows out of the barrel of a gun."** Remember those words, comrade. . . .' That was how it was."

"Where's that Mauser now?" asked Secretary Fang. "Let's see it."

He didn't have it on him. It was locked in his trunk. He asked Chen Hsiao-yuan for the key and then opened the metal trunk, took out the Mauser and placed it on the table. It was rusty. Uncle Shuang-ho flushed with shame and I felt pained too when I observed the condition of the gun.

Secretary Fang picked up the rusty pistol and addressed Uncle Shuang-ho in a stern tone. "The enemy is busily sharpening his weapons and you've put yours away, under lock and key! That's very dangerous, comrade! Throw away your gun and you've thrown away political power. Thrown away the revolution and everything the people have. . . ."

Uncle Shuang-ho, torn by self-recrimination and repentance, answered in a low voice, "I was too absorbed with production. I'll clean it."

"Production made you forget about the gun, eh? That's no excuse at all, comrade," Secretary Fang went on. "It's easy enough to remove the rust from the gun, but removing ideological rust is going to be a bit more difficult. Only if you keep yourself ideologically sharp and clean will you have a sharp and clean weapon. Even if you do have a well-looked-after gun in your hands it's useless if your thinking is all rusted over."

Secretary Fang removed the magazine from the pistol and with great difficulty cocked it, for it was so badly rusted. Then he replaced it on the table and in a trembling voice said, "Comrade Shuang-ho, this pistol reminds me of something. I'm from a peasant family and I know from personal experience what oppression and exploitation by landlords means. In my early days I had not much understanding about the significance of guns. When I joined the guerrillas in southern Chekiang, Comrade Li, my platoon leader, gave me a pistol. Here it is," he said taking it out and placing it on the table beside Uncle Shuang-ho's. They were both No. 3 Mausers. Secretary Fang's Mauser gleamed brightly in the lamplight. He then said, "Platoon Leader Li asked me if I knew where it had come from.

"I replied, 'From an arsenal.'

"He shook his head. 'You're wrong there. This reached our hands at the cost of many comrades' lives.'

"This pistol was taken from a landlord's house by a hired farm labourer during an armed uprising. He brought it with him when he joined the guerrillas in southern Chekiang. One day when out on reconnaissance he was surrounded by a platoon of puppet troops. He had fired his last bullet and was badly wounded. The enemy cordoned off the village and started a house-to-house search for him. Meanwhile, an old couple living on the fringe of the village took him in and hid him. They told him, 'When the enemy come here, you're to say you're our son.' 'But some of them know me,' the wounded guerrilla pointed out. 'It's either me or the gun, so take it and hide it well. If you have a chance, pass it on to our guerrillas. Our revolution needs guns. Don't let it fall into enemy hands. I'm going to hide inside that mill over there.' The old man and his wife refused to let him go. 'Do you think we're afraid of being incriminated with you? We're not!' They insisted on hiding the wounded man. 'It's not just that!' protested the guerrilla. 'We'll lose the pistol too.' In the end he made the old couple see his point of view and they reluctantly allowed him to leave the pistol with them. When the enemy entered the mill the wounded guerrilla threw himself at them and killed one of them with his bare hands before he himself was killed.

"Later, some dirty scoundrel tipped off the enemy about the Mauser and they sent men to get the pistol from the old couple. They did their utmost to force the old people to tell where it was, but they refused to divulge their secret and the old peasant died on the execution ground without saying a word. The wife, heavily wounded, managed to crawl away and reached our men. She gave this pistol to Platoon Leader Li."

Secretary Fang picked it up and, weighing it in his hands for a moment, said in a voice charged with emotion, "So, you see why I'll never let a speck of rust foul this pistol, comrades."

Uncle Shuang-ho lowered his eyes. I was greatly moved by this account of how the gun had reached and still remained in revolutionary hands. I knew the importance of guns but I did not realize what a price was paid for them by poor people like ourselves.

Granddad didn't say a word but his face betrayed his feelings. A struggle seemed to be going on in his mind. He suddenly said in a voice hardly above a whisper, "Shuang-ho, do you still remember the night when I ferried you to the mainland after those pirates murdered Elder Brothers Liu and Li?"

"Of course I remember," Uncle Shuang-ho replied, his eyes moist.

"I don't think you do. They haven't been avenged yet. I think you've forgotten it entirely."

"By striking down Chen Chan-ao, their deaths have been avenged," Uncle Shuang-ho argued. "The people of the island have stood up and are living a happy life today. What Elder Brothers Liu and Li wanted has been realized."

"Chen Chan-ao and Black Wind are still holed up in Taiwan," granddad reminded him.

Secretary Fang interrupted, "Even when Chen Chan-ao has been captured it doesn't mean the price has been fully paid. Comrade, we must remember the whole world, remember the millions of people in other parts of the globe still writhing under the lash of the exploiters and oppressors! The enemy won't give up trying to make trouble and Chen Chan-ao is backed by Chiang Kai-shek as well as the reactionaries of various countries!"

Granddad said, "I have a story to tell you too, Shuang-ho. The event happened a long, long time ago and not many people talked about it then, so even less people know about it today. Well, a mason named Huang Jung-ching used to live over there on the far west of our island. One day, sick and hungry, he went up into the hills to quarry stone for a house that the despot was having built. Worn out and his strength completely spent, he suddenly blacked out and tumbled over the cliff to his death. The despot said it had nothing to do with him and even alleged that the dead mason had been passing on his ration of food to his wife and that it was his own fault if he had been working on an empty stomach. 'Serves him right,' the tyrant pronounced.

"As you know, in those days we weren't allowed to carry anyone indoors who died outside. Huang's wife was in a terrible state. She had no one to turn to. There was no firewood in the house, nor a grain of rice. Her husband's body lay outside the house for want of money to bury him. The despot seized this opportunity to force the newly widowed woman to sell herself to him for twenty yuan, so that she could bury her husband. She was then eight months pregnant and begged the despot to let her have her child before entering his house as a bonded servant. The despot agreed, not because he had compassion on her, but because he was superstitiously afraid of some ill luck a poor pregnant widow might bring into his house.

"Huang's widow begged from door to door to keep alive, and finally arrived in Yungchiao. There she found shelter with a couple called Li, and shortly afterwards gave birth to a boy. She nursed him for three months and then was dragged off into the despot's house. He violated her before a month had passed. The poor woman threw herself into the sea without even leaving any word for her child. The couple named Li raised the boy as their own."

"Where's that child now?" asked Uncle Shuang-ho softly, his eyes large and questioning.

"Where? Right there where you're standing!" snorted granddad.

Uncle Shuang-ho gaped and then cried unashamedly, knuckling his eyes with his fists.

There was no other sound in the room. No one spoke, each was occupied with his thoughts. Sorrow weighed our hearts down and stirred up sad memories.

Much later, after we had all spoken of what we felt and thought, Secretary Fang addressed Uncle Shuang-ho. "You have made a good job of production, Comrade Shuang-ho. We have nothing against that. But you must not forget the gun. We must hold a hoe in one hand and grip the gun with the other. You think I'm talking paradoxically? Not at all. There is no contradiction between the two. Take hold of military affairs and you'll promote production. Of course, militia training methods will have to be improved and properly carried out. For instance, militia training should be held during slack periods, when it rains and so on. Cut down massed training and hold training on a smaller scale and wherever it is most convenient, and vary the training so as to make the fullest use of your time. Production and military training must be integrated, not separated. Once this becomes ideologically clear, ways and means of carrying it out will appear. Now, to return to the question of revolutionary vigilance. A comrade fell and got hurt. Was that purely accidental or was it politically inspired?"

Uncle Shuang-ho said, "I did not look at it from the class struggle point of view. As soon as I heard there had been an accident I was so upset that I completely forgot to ask if it could be the work of the enemy. . . ."

"This is what is known as muddle-headed blindness," put in Secretary Fang. "You were ideologically disarmed, so of course you could not see the enemy at work."

"I realize that now," said Uncle Shuang-ho, clenching his fist. "From now on I'll keep the enemy in mind and remember to pay adequate attention to the militia."

We all agreed with him completely and were glad to hear him say it.

Secretary Fang moved that we discuss work connected with the militia.

I said, "I have a proposal to make. As we all know, most of our militia men are out working at sea and the few militia men remaining on the island are left on their own. If fighting suddenly occurs they won't be able to become an effective fighting force quickly. On the other hand, there is only one platoon of militia women, but in the settlement there are one hundred and eighteen women eligible to join the militia. I've counted them. And they all want to join. I suggest setting up another platoon of militia women and organizing the militia men left at home into a separate platoon. On this basis we could set up a militia company operating under a unified command. . . ."

No one objected to my proposal and Secretary Fang said, "Hai-hsia's proposal is a sound one. We must build up our militia organizationally, but more important still, we must strengthen our militia ideologically. I have no clear idea as yet what problems face the militia of this island. We should put the militia through a test, a stiff test. As to the question of expanding the militia, staffing the platoons and company, I'll have to discuss that at district level first. After that we'll hold a special meeting and get everything fixed up."

Just before the meeting ended Secretary Fang asked if anyone had anything more to say. I spoke up. I said, "We've had a good meeting this evening. We were criticizing Uncle Shuangho but in actual fact all of us have had a very profound lesson. Our revolutionary predecessors won state power with guns and it is with guns that we must defend and consolidate our state power. A gun in hand is vital, but even more so we must be ideologically armed. I am referring to political consciousness, the class struggle point of view and loyalty to the revolution, in other words, arming ourselves ideologically with Marxism-Leninism-Mao Tsetung Thought. If we are ideologically well-armed we can use our weapons better in fighting the enemy. If we are not armed ideologically then all the weapons we have will be useless. We'll lose them all very quickly."

The meeting ended, and I walked out into the night with a light heart. The path was barely visible in the dark but my mind's eye could see clearly. It was as if all the cobwebs had been brushed away and the shutters thrown open to the light. I thought, how great is our Party! To how many countless others has the Party pointed out the way forward, and how many have had their eyes opened by it to the vista ahead!

Chapter 24

SURPRISE ATTACK

A S Sister Ah-hung had not fully recovered from her injuries I frequently dropped round to her house to help with the chores. One night, after we had got into bed, she asked me whether I had discussed with Secretary Fang about my dismissal from office.

"We've had a talk about it," I said.

"And what did he say?"

"He said that I'd be given something else to do."

"Oh, will you now!" she exclaimed heatedly, thinking that he had confirmed my dismissal. "I'm going to see him tomorrow and tell him how you've worked to make a good job of the militia work. Remove you, indeed! Hasn't he eyes to see with!"

I didn't know what to say to this and tried to change the subject. "We should have confidence in the leadership," I maintained. "Anyway, it's quite late. Let's get some sleep."

"All right, but be sure to wake me up early tomorrow. I'm going to find him and have a talk with him." She muttered something about "Dismiss her . . . never . . . not on your life. . . ." She fell asleep, probably still arguing with Secretary Fang.

Suddenly the conch sounded. I sat bolt upright and peered out into the inky blackness, straining my eyes and ears.

"Who's sounding the alarm?" asked Sister Ah-hung beside me.

"I don't know, but that's the signal to assemble. I'm going."

"I'm coming too!"

"No, you're not. You stay here. You've still got a bad arm."

"I said I'm coming, and I'm coming!" I could hear her muttering oaths as she struggled into her clothes.

"You stay home," I cried, snatching up my rifle and running out of the house. "You haven't even a rifle!"

When I got to the assembly point I found Secretary Fang blowing the conch. Uncle Shuang-ho and the comrade in charge of military affairs from the district were with him.

"What's up?" I asked.

"Something's up," he answered.

"Why weren't we warned?"

"Is the enemy going to send you a notice when he's coming?"

Then I realized that he was testing the militia. A moment later I saw Sister Ah-hung hurrying up, one sleeve hanging limply by her side.

"What's happened?" she demanded.

"Emergency assembly," I whispered to her.

What a difference there was between tonight's alert and that of the other night. It had taken us only a dozen or so minutes to get everyone assembled then, but tonight there were still many missing. We had to send people out to call them. We finally got everyone out a little after midnight. Tsai-chu, who came up blustering, demanded to know why they were being assembled. "Wasn't it decided that there were to be no more alerts at night?" she questioned.

Suddenly she recognized Secretary Fang, gave a start of surprise and took her place quietly beside me.

Yun-hsiang, Hai-hua and later Yu-hsiu drifted in. When they saw Secretary Fang they all became tense and serious and kept their eyes on the ground. It was the first time our Concord militia dared not look anyone in the eye.

"What on earth has happened to those girls? They're still not here," fretted Sister Ah-hung.

I caught sight of Yu-hsiu with her machine-gun and then noticed that she had come without her ammunition belt.

"Where's your ammunition belt?" I asked in a whisper.

"Oh, I've forgotten it," she answered. Then, as if to console herself, she added, "Luckily this is only a practice and not the real thing."

"But we must treat this as the real thing," I told her. "You hop back and get it."

Too late. Secretary Fang was already addressing us.

"A group of enemy agents are hiding over on Tiger-Head waiting for a chance to launch a surprise attack on us," he announced. "Our task is to ferret them out and annihilate them!" Then turning to me, he commanded, "Take over, Comrade Hai-hsia!"

I was momentarily stunned. All our night manoeuvres had been carried out on Tide-Watcher's Point. We had never been over to Tiger-Head. Now I understood why Secretary Fang and the others had gone over there the other day.

The island was six hundred metres outside the mouth of Gourd Bay and at low tide it extended more than three hundred metres east and west and five hundred north and south. No one lived on this mass of weather-beaten black rock and no ships called. The rocks were covered with oysters, cockles and sea lettuce. When the tide was out the black yawning caverns gouged out by the sea were exposed to view. The mass of rock bottled up the bay. It could also serve as a springboard from which the enemy could launch an attack. Secretary Fang was a military man and could appreciate the strategic significance of this mass of rock. He and some army comrades had made several trips there to inspect the terrain.

I led the platoon to the beach at the double and ordered the three squads to embark on six small sampans and head for Tiger-Head.

This simple action took us almost a quarter-hour of bustling and milling around before we accomplished it. Splitting the three squads into six teams, contrary to our usual practice of splitting into nine, was one of the reasons. Another was that we had little training in tactics.

Secretary Fang stood by, providing situation information but never so much as giving a word of advice or comment. He was calm and collected, like a doctor making a diagnosis, while we were almost in tears.

After the teams had sorted themselves out and embarked, it was discovered that there were no oars or sculls!

Sister Ah-hung danced with vexation and Hai-hua cursed. Yu-hsiu ran around in circles. Things were getting messier by the moment. I shouted, "Detail two from each squad to return to the village and fetch sculls. The rest will check weapons and get ready for battle!"

We managed to make it to Tiger-Head just before the break of day. I didn't know what to do next as I'd never been faced with such a situation. I felt the eyes of the platoon on me, waiting for orders. Six small sampans bobbed in the water in a tight cluster, and I did not know what to do.

Secretary Fang, Uncle Shuang-ho and the district cadre in charge of military affairs appeared with granddad at the scull.

I rowed over to them and asked Secretary Fang for orders. "What next?"

Secretary Fang gave none. Instead he said with a straight face, "You've been briefed and you should act determinedly in the light of enemy deployment. You won't find me beside you as your military advisor in a real battle."

I felt he had a point there. We had always been talking about "in actual battle" in our training, and now a "real engagement" was facing us and we did not know what to do. It showed that it had not really entered my mind that this was the "real thing." If there were real enemies on that island, would I be at a loss what to do? Would I be dithering about like I was doing? If Secretary Fang was not here would I be unable to take action to wipe the enemy out? The enemy was there before me. I could see him now and I had to do something.

"Machine-gun cover! Squad One seize and hold the height on the island!" I snapped. "Search for the enemy, keep an eye out on the sea and give Squads Two and Three fire support in their manoeuvres!"

Suddenly I remembered those caverns. We couldn't flush the enemy out of them from above, so I immediately ordered Squads Two and Three to get them out from their sampans. I could see the importance of having a good grasp of the terrain in a battle. I saw Sister Ah-hung's sampan shooting off towards the highest point on the island and even before it reached the rocks she had jumped down into the sea. With one hand pushing the boat forward, she shouted, "Forward and up! Get a move on!"

I led Squads Two and Three in four sampans round the cliffs to search for the enemy hidden in the caverns. The tide had turned and the caves were half filled with water. I saw that the militia members were only shouting into the caverns and not really searching for the foe.

"Comrades, there are enemies inside those caves. Look out for their fire. Approach the caverns from the side!" I shouted, and leapt into the water, the others following closely.

It was now light and the sun was red in the east. The morning mists had lifted. I found an army water flask inside one cave and on closer inspection saw that it was one of ours. It had been tied to a rock so that it could not be washed away by the tide. I saw that it had been placed there by Secretary Fang to gauge the vigilance and thoroughness of the militia members.

"Found anything?" I asked the others.

Of course they had found nothing, for they had merely shouted into the caverns without entering them.

"You must get inside and collect anything you find unusual," I told them.

As the sampans were turning round to start their search again, we saw Squad One leaving the height and coming to join us. They had been instructed to do so by Secretary Fang. I was puzzled to see all twelve of them packed into one sampan

— dangerous overloading. A wobble to either side and water would pour over the gunwales.

"Where's the other sampan?" I demanded.

"I was busy scaling the height and forgot to tie it up," answered Sister Ah-hung ruefully. "It's floated away."

How exasperating! I told Yu-hsiu to move into Squad Two's boat with her machine-gun. Secretary Fang came over and said, "The remaining enemy are making a getaway in their boats. Blast them out of the water!"

We turned and gazed out to sea where he pointed. I saw a dozen coloured balloons bobbing up and down about two hundred metres from us.

I thought: this is where the fun begins! We'd never hit a one of them. Why, we'd not even practised shooting at a moving target before.

"Good grief!" someone cried. "Put a bullet through one of those?"

I checked myself and gave the command, "Target, balloons out there. Machine-gun to action!" I had completely forgotten that we had not brought any cartridges with us for the machine-gun.

Yu-hsiu cried, "It's my fault!" and, squatting down by her machine-gun, burst into tears.

"This isn't the time for tears!" cried Sister Ah-hung.

"Pick them off with rifles!" I commanded.

The sampans were rocking and rolling and the balloons were bobbing up and down a couple of hundred metres away.

Ordinarily we fired at fixed targets and although in practices we aimed under varying circumstances we weren't very proficient. Besides, we hadn't practised very often with ammunition. Now I was asking my militia girls to shoot from a rocking sampan at moving targets and into the sun at a distance of two hundred or so metres. It was asking a lot of them. Added to all this was the fact that our machine-gun was out of action and our best shot had smashed her rifle and could not take part. It was a real test for the rank and file.

The first volley knocked out four and the second three more. I was very disappointed and said, "Steady! Take good aim!" The third volley eliminated another three but there were still two dancing before our sights as if they were mocking at us. Suddenly Secretary Fang said, "Stop firing!" Then, looking at each of us in turn, he asked, "Is there anyone who would like to take on those two singlehanded?" I saw that he was wanting to gauge the level of our best marksman. Everyone looked despairingly at me.

I was furious, at whom? At myself! I felt ashamed and unhappy for I had let down the Party and the people. We had not yet attained the standard demanded of us.

Eyes flashing with anger, I stared out at the two balloons. Were those just balloons? Weren't they the heads of two evil agents? Chen Chan-ao was there before me! That's his vile face bobbing out there in front of me! Were we going to let him escape because we had been tardy in assembling, because our organization was not up to the mark, because we weren't all crack shots? No! If he got away it would be a slap in the face of us militia women!

He was not to get away! I raised my rifle and fired. A bobbing "head" disappeared. Just as I was about to fire at the remaining one, Secretary Fang ordered, "Hai-hsia, your left arm has been hit. Fire with your right only!"

All the girls looked anxiously at me. But I was not at all shaken, not because I had ever practised shooting with one arm, but because my heart was bursting with hatred for the enemy. I rested my rifle on the gunwale, shoved a cartridge in with one hand, raised the rifle with my right arm, took aim and fired. The shot went true.

The militia gave a shout and, forgetting all the unhappy side of this exercise, clapped loudly.

Chapter 25

GOOD NEWS FROM THE SEA

THE sampans beached and our exercise was over.

The militia, dripping wet, marched up the beach with long faces. I understood how they felt. They were feeling sorry about letting down the motherland and the people by their poor performance.

I looked at Secretary Fang and saw him laughing and chatting with Uncle Shuang-ho and the other cadre as if he had not noticed how down-in-the-mouth we looked, nor the poor showing we had made.

We threw ourselves down on the sand, forgetting our weariness and hunger, and waited gloomily for the criticism to come from Secretary Fang.

"Comrades," he said, his face wreathed in smiles. "I've sprung this surprise on you today and the exercise has given you a good chance of training yourselves for real battle. What do you think?"

He stood there smiling, waiting for our reply.

But there was none. Some of us stared at the shells glistening in the sunlight, others drew pictures in the sand. All were dismally moody.

"Secretary Fang," I spoke up. "Point out our faults. Don't spare us. We can take it."

"What's there to criticize?" he said, smiling. "I'm very pleased with today's performance."

Pleased? The militia women lifted their heads in bewilderment. Was he joking or did he mean what he said?

"Don't give us that, Secretary Fang," said Sister Ah-hung. "We know what sort of a showing we made."

"I mean that, every word of it. You were given a very difficult, a very arduous task to carry out and strict demands were placed on you just as if it were a real battle assignment. Many things were asked of you which you had never met with during normal training and you have carried it all off well. On the whole, I think you haven't done badly."

So, that was it! "On the whole," he had said.

"Of course," he went on, "there were many shortcomings. But the achievements were greater. With a bit more practice you'll do much better. You may ask, 'What's so good about today's showing?' Well, first of all, everyone has been very brave, not afraid of getting into the water, doing everything conscientiously, making strict demands on herself and not being afraid of hardships. This is the first point. Another thing, and it deserves special mention, is that attention has been given to raising the level of marksmanship of the whole platoon. Such training methods are correct and that was what enabled you to knock out all the targets in the water today. As to shortcomings, well, there was some confusion, but then you're not entirely to blame for that. . . ."

Although Secretary Fang spoke with sincerity, we felt he would have done better to have rounded on us and given us a severe dressing-down. What we wanted to hear was "completely battle-worthy," not "haven't done badly on the whole."

And then it came. He began his criticism. He said, "The purpose of this unexpected exercise was to test your ideological, tactical, technical and command preparedness. The reason why there was a bit of a mess-up lies with your command. Everyone of you should discuss each move in the exercise and see if what Hai-hsia did was correct. Let us have some democracy in military affairs. Hai-hsia should make a point of summing up the lessons learned in this exercise and also make a thorough study of the problems existing in militia work. . . ."

"Secretary Fang," Sister Ah-hung interrupted him, "you should have some words of praise for Hai-hsia!" She was not happy at hearing no commendation for me.

"You want me to praise her for her marksmanship, is that it?" The secretary of the district Party committee turned to her with a smile, and then his voice took a sterner note. "As a militia member, Hai-hsia's marksmanship is really not bad, but don't forget that she is also the leader of the platoon. It's her duty to see that the whole platoon are crack shots. Not only must she be constantly on guard but the whole platoon must always be on guard as well. And this latter is the more important. You must all have a high sense of revolutionary vigilance and that is exactly where the main fault of the exercise lies. . . ."

Sister Ah-hung had not expected that her demand for praise for me would call criticism down on my head and she expressed her dissatisfaction with mutterings about "unfair criticisms."

"Standing up for your platoon leader, eh?" Secretary Fang said, still smiling.

"Of course! You're being terribly unjust!" she replied vehemently. "You've wronged her!"

"What is this! Wronged her? Unjust?" Secretary Fang was not smiling now and his voice was serious. "How can you say making a criticism is doing someone an injustice? Without criticism and self-criticism can there be any self-remoulding? How can one continue to make progress?" Then he went on to speak on another problem. "This exercise has also revealed many shortcomings in the leadership at the district and township levels. Many problems stem from my not giving enough thought to things and my instructions not being clear. For example, the women's militia platoon has confined itself to militia women and has not given any thought to the militia men who haven't gone to sea. Should an emergency arise, then co-operation between the two would be difficult. Also, there are many women in East and West Yungchiao who should be in the militia and are not. It is the same in other villages. We should expand and strengthen our militia organization.

"These are problems which should have been attended to and yet they haven't been. Why is that? It looks like a question of method, making the proper arrangements and so on. But actually, it is an ideological question. Sometimes the thinking of the leadership falls behind the reality. After consultations we have now decided to expand the women's militia to two platoons and organize the militia men who stay on land into a separate platoon. The three platoons will combine to form one company. This idea, and it is a very sound idea, was put forward by Comrade Hai-hsia. At the same time this is a criticism of the work of the district and township authorities. It's a well-made criticism; we have been negligent. We welcome such proposals and criticisms. . . ."

Everyone nodded and clapped loudly to express agreement with what Secretary Fang was saying. He looked at his watch and then out to the entrance of the bay. "In another hour we shall hear good tidings. But first of all, let everyone go home for a change of clothes and a meal and then re-assemble here."

We were thrown into a commotion. "What good tidings? Tell us, quickly!" they cried. "Tell us now or else we won't be able to eat a morsel of food!"

"Go home and change first," said Uncle Shuang-ho. "Have your meal and then come back. At least change your wet clothing."

"We're not weaklings. Didn't the leadership ask us to carry out training in the coldest and the hottest parts of the year? People fishing at sea have to put up with the wind and waves all the day so what's damp clothing to us! What sort of militia are we if we can't stand wet clothing!" the militia members protested.

"So no one wants to go home, eh?" said granddad. "Well, since you don't want to go, I'll tell you all a story while we wait for the good news to come."

With cries of "Fine!" "Good!" everyone crowded round him.

Granddad sought out a flat rock and sat down. He stroked his beard and began in a voice charged with seriousness.

"I want to talk about the history of Concord Island. Why is our island called Concord? How did it get its name? Well, it all began some four hundred or so years ago. During the Chia Ching reign of the Ming Dynasty Japanese pirates were harassing our coast and shipping, doing a lot of harm to the fishermen along the coast. At that time there was a garrison force set up to exterminate the pirates, and some local inhabitants were organized to guard this island. There weren't many but everyone fought the Japanese tooth and nail. The pirates had several dozen ships and they laid siege about the island for seven days and seven nights but they could not take it. Finally they gave up and left.

"The soldiers and the people watched the invaders retreating and many said with a sigh of relief, 'Now we'll have a bit of peace and quiet. They've had a taste of what we are capable of. They won't dare stick their heads back here for some time. They're scared of us.'

"With that, they went home to bed and slept. But no sooner had they fallen asleep than someone came running and shouting that two pirate ships had been sighted in the vicinity of Tiger-Head. The soldiers and islanders scrambled into boats to give chase. The pirate ships were intercepted and their crews were either killed or they had jumped overboard. Only two were taken prisoner.

"The victorious soldiers and islanders took the ships back to the island and on examining their holds found that they were full of excellent wine. The soldiers helped themselves and as they drank they questioned the two prisoners. The prisoners said that they had found the soldiers and islanders too formidable and their chieftains had declared that they would henceforth keep well away from this island.

"This made everyone on the island feel very safe and relieved. They broke open the casks of wine and fell to celebrating their victory, playing rowdy drinking games over their cups.

They caroused to their heart's content and were all drunk by midnight, sleeping sprawled out in heaps where they had fallen. Meanwhile, the two prisoners had quietly and unobserved sawn through their bonds against a rock. Then they lit a fire signal."

"The dirty devils!" muttered Sister Ah-hung.

"The Japanese who were hiding out on Tiger-Head saw the signal and stealthily swarmed over to this island. The soldiers and islanders were drunk and did not put up much resistance. Those who were not killed outright escaped into the hills.

"Later, the island was called 'Heartbreak Island' in memory of that disastrous night. Some years later the islanders got together again and chased the Japanese invaders into the sea. Then the island was renamed 'Concord Island' in memory of the way the people had got together and fought in harmony to drive out the invaders."

"The story has a very profound significance, granddad," I said. "Are we supposed to draw the moral from this story, that we shouldn't let down our guard?"

"You could put it that way," said granddad chuckling.

"Don't you worry about that. We'll never be caught unawares!" I assured him.

"But not everyone sees the point of the story," said granddad looking significantly at Uncle Shuang-ho sitting beside him.

"You shouldn't be so prejudiced, Uncle Teh-shun," Uncle Shuang-ho said with a smile. "A man makes progress step by step."

The sound of drums and gongs was heard from the bay and we saw a white-bottomed boat heading for shore with a long red banner stretched between two poles at its bow. The characters on the banner read "Greetings to the Militia of Concord." A red pennant fluttered proudly in the wind.

We were all taken by surprise. What could be the meaning of this?

Men and women, old and young, hurried down to the beach. They had been told by the township administration about this event.

Someone shouted, "Why, isn't that Liu Chi-wu, grandnephew of Granddad Wang-fa, standing there on the bow? Doesn't he look cocky!"

"That's him all right," said Granddad Wang-fa, stroking his beard and grasping his gun tightly. "But why is he coming back like that?"

Liu Chi-wu leapt out of the boat on to the beach and, running up to Uncle Shuang-ho, handed him a letter. "This letter comes from all of us out fishing!" he exclaimed.

"Here's wonderful news. You take this and read it out to the others," Uncle Shuang-ho said to me after he had read the letter.

I took it and read in a loud voice:

To the militia of East and West Yungchiao,

We have had a double good harvest. The planned quota of catch has been overfulfilled by 1,200 piculs of fish and we still have half a month of fishing ahead of us, so we're going to work for an extra big catch to bring home to the island.

Today we had an encounter with a Chiang Kai-shek bandit gang gunboat and drove it away after we had damaged it. We have captured eight of the enemy (five of them wounded) together with five submachine-guns.

During the encounter Platoon Leader Ah-hung fought bravely and well. He used his head and put up a good fight — played a big part in making this victory possible. We are writing a detailed report to the district Party committee recommending him for a citation.

We hope all militia members on the island will work harder at production, train vigorously, raise higher your revolutionary vigilance and strive for yet another double good harvest. . . .

Hardly had I finished reading than Hai-hua led the shouting of slogans.

"Learn from the militia out at sea! Salute the militia out at sea!"

"Be vigilant! Defend the coast! Resolutely wipe out all enemy who dare to invade us!"

When the last echo of the slogans had died away, Secretary Fang was seen holding in his hands the citation from the district Party committee, which was to be presented to Ah-hung.

"Sister Ah-hung," I said, giving her a nudge, "quick, go up and accept the citation. You have a share in it too."

221

The applause was deafening.

But suddenly this woman who was always so outspoken and forthright turned timid. She blushed a bright red and refused to budge. "If I want any citation I'll earn it myself. What's his is his," she said stubbornly. Then she rose to her feet and ran away.

So it fell to me to accept it on Ah-hung's behalf.

When the reverberations of gongs and drums died away Uncle Shuang-ho declared the meeting open. He made a few preliminary remarks, saying that the township Party branch committee had held a meeting with Secretary Fang's guidance the other night in which he was criticized for his benumbing "all's peace and quiet" concept, his neglect of militia work and his concentration only on production to the detriment of political work and so on, and then he asked Secretary Fang to say a few words.

Secretary Fang first praised the bravery of the militia men at sea and then went on to speak about militia work. "We must never drop our guard. We must make a good job of our militia work. When production and preparedness against war are well integrated, militia activity will not interfere with production; on the contrary it promotes production. The reason why the two have not been handled well is due in part to method and in part to ideology. But in the final analysis it's an ideological problem. Once this problem is resolved then the contradiction is solved. . . ." He then read out the decision to enlarge the militia organization and strengthen it by forming a militia company, calling on those eligible to hurry up and join.

As soon as volunteers were called for, Liu Chi-wu walked out of the crowd and strode up to the table to where I was. "Sister Hai-hsia," he said in a loud voice, "I am sixteen today. Put my name on the list, will you?" He stood there before the table, big and solid, looking as if he was determined not to budge an inch until he had seen his name written down.

Granddad Wang-fa stalked up to the table, gun in hand, and casting a level look at the lad, said, "Chi-wu, what's a boy like you doing here!" Then he edged Chi-wu to one side and said, "Put my name on it, Hai-hsia. I'll be the first."

"Hey, you can't do that!" exclaimed the boy. "I was here first. Besides, no one over thirty-five is accepted as a core member of the militia, and you're well over-age!"

"A fat lot you know!" retorted Granddad Wang-fa, glaring furiously at Chi-wu.

I could see they were going to keep this up for some time, so with a sweet smile I said, "You two stop bickering. I've put both your names down. But whether you'll be accepted is another thing. This is just a list of applicants."

After the meeting was over Secretary Fang took me aside and said, "I've discussed it with the township authorities and it's been decided to make Sister Ah-hung leader of Women's Platoon One and Hai-hua her deputy. Huang Yun-hsiang and Yu-hsiu will be leader and deputy leader of Platoon Two. Have you anything to say?"

"I agree, but it would be better if the two deputy platoon leaders swopped platoons for the sake of balancing the temperaments of the leaders."

"And what about yourself?"

"I promise I'll be a good militia member."

"Who'll be company commander?"

"It's for the leadership to decide."

"Want the leadership to send one down?"

I did not at first catch what he was driving at and I merely answered, "Of course it's better if it's someone from the company itself."

"Well, the district Party committee and the township Party branch have decided to let you fill that post."

I was quite unprepared for this. This was something I had not even dreamed of. "I couldn't," I blurted.

"You are afraid of the responsibility?"

"You know very well what my capabilities are. I can only carry fifty kilogrammes but you are trying to make me carry a hundred. How can I manage it?"

"Those who are dedicated to the revolution and have courage are never bowed down by sheer weight of responsibility. The heavier the responsibilities the stronger one becomes in shouldering them."

"I know the spread of my wings and I know I can't fly so high!" Although I said this, I was already thinking over his words, especially the words "who are dedicated to the revolution." They had a telling effect on me.

"The sea gull's wings did not become hardened and powerful by sitting inside the nest, but by fighting wind and rain," he said, looking steadily and kindly at me the while. "Comrade Hai-hsia, this is what the Party demands of you. And remember, nothing is done well at the first stroke. There are no training classes for turning out commanders for militia companies and probably there never will be. . . . You must be good at learning in actual work and struggle. Chairman Mao has said, **It** [revolutionary war] **is often not a matter of first learning and then doing, but of doing and then learning, for doing is itself learning.** Do you understand that?"

"Since the Party demands this of me then I will do everything in my power to do it well. I will never let the Party down."

CHAPTER 26

TWO GENERATIONS

WHO was the honoured guest? None other than young Liu, Liu Chi-wu, who had brought back the good news. The lad had just turned sixteen and looked like any other boy of his age, but he had the tough resilience of a fisherman and in his walk and speech there was that quality of upright straight-forwardness. Being under-age had barred him from becoming a full member of the militia so he called himself an alternate member. There was a bit of a strain between old Granddad Wang-fa and young Liu Chi-wu because the lad was forever trying to separate the old man from his "baby," the rifle. Sometimes young Liu even went as far as presenting an ultimatum to him to "hand over" the gun.

Tonight the lad was revelling in his glory, for he had been received with all the honour befitting a hero from the front. He had been an eye-witness of the sea battle and it was he who had been sent back to spread the good tidings. In the eyes of the militia at home he was no longer just a kid but a hero who had been through the flames of battle.

He was very pleased to regale us with news about the encounter at sea.

"Day had just broken and the fishermen were busy putting out the nets when they suddenly heard the throb of a motor.

"Some said that it was a motorized junk.

"Others said, no. A motorized junk did not make that much noise and why couldn't they see the mast yet?

"They all peered into the distance from which the sound of the motor came. The sun had just climbed above the horizon, when suddenly a fisherman gave a loud cry. 'It's a gunboat belonging to the Chiang Kai-shek bandit gang! It's coming this way!'

"Everyone looked in the direction he indicated and sure enough, there was a gunboat ploughing a white swathe through the sea close by Shark's Reef. It was coming towards the fishing boats.

"There was a stir among the fishermen.

"Ah-hung gave the instructions: 'Don't kick up a racket. Draw in the nets, unfurl the sails and scatter. All militia members get on to my boat.'

"The dozen militia men from East Yungchiao clambered into his boat and pretended to be hauling in the net while they waited for the approaching enemy gunboat.

"'Will we be able to tackle them?' asked one of the men.

"'The Liberation Army can tackle enemy warships with wooden boats, why can't we take on this little gunboat!' said Ah-hung, glaring at the man. 'Get down below deck and have your grenades ready. Wait for orders. The enemy won't expect a fight as they can see we're only a fishing boat. We'll spring a surprise on them. We'll strike and catch them off their guard.'

"The militia men disappeared below, and grenade cords were attached to fingers ready for instant use. The rifles were covered with tarpaulins, out of sight. The rest of the men pretended to be hauling in the net. As the motor-vessel raced towards them a Kuomintang officer was seen scanning the deck through binoculars. He could only see an ordinary fishing smack. There were no militia men or People's Liberation Army soldiers on board. He felt easier. The bandits crowded on deck and shouted as they drew closer, 'Hey! What boat are you?'

226

" 'You've got eyes, haven't you? A fishing boat!' Ah-hung shouted back.

"The bandits had their guns slung over their backs and did not look as if they were expecting a fight. The vessel throttled down and slowly drew up. They seemed to be deciding what to do with such a huge boat. They saw it was too big to tow away and finally decided to send a boarding crew to take over.

"When the two vessels were only ten metres apart, Ah-hung shouted, 'Let them have it!' and hurled a bundle of three grenades at the enemy vessel.

"The militia men sprang out and a flight of grenades straddled the armed motor-boat. A clutch of grenades exploded, throwing the enemy into confusion and panic. Their vessel was enveloped in acrid black smoke.

"Then the militia opened fire with the rifles swiftly retrieved from under the tarpaulins.

"Some bandits were wounded. Some were panic-stricken and leapt into the sea. Their officer in command was killed and there was disorder on board. Like a wounded beast the enemy howled and turned tail, almost knocking the fishing boat over in its hurried turn-about.

"Ah-hung raked the enemy vessel with automatic fire. The enemy seemed to pull themselves together a bit, and some of them tried to reach their gun which was mounted on the bow. Before they could get to the gun they were mowed down by Ah-hung's gunfire.

" 'Unfurl! Let the sails out! Don't let them get away!' cried the militia men when they saw the enemy vessel trying to make a run for it.

"But before they could do that the enemy had put quite a distance between their boat and ours.

" 'To hell with them!' cursed the militia men after the receding enemy. 'Gunboat! Sure, it's a gunboat, gunning their own motor for all it's worth!'

" 'Let them go,' cried Ah-hung. 'We'll skim the scum out of the water.'

"With that they began to pick the enemy out of the water. The other fishing boats came round and helped. Eight captives were hauled aboard, and five guns. The enemy vessel fired a few rounds at the fishing boats but continued to make off as quickly as their motor-boat could take them."

Liu Chi-wu's vivid account of the victorious sea battle was greeted with loud applause.

When the applause died down, Liu Chi-wu spoke again. "Do you know when my birthday is?" he demanded in a loud voice.

"How should we know?" countered Sister Ah-hung. "We're not your mum and dad! Too much applause has addled your head!"

This brought a roar of laughter.

"Who's addled?" demanded Liu Chi-wu, his face beet-scarlet. "Today's my birthday! Do you hear? My sixteenth birthday, today. And I've got back just in time to attend the inauguration of the militia company. How about making me a full militia member?"

"Of course we will," I answered. "Everyone joins up first and then takes part in fighting but you have fought first and joined afterwards! You're going to get top priority consideration! However, we've no rifles to issue."

"Don't you worry about a little thing like that," he assured us. "I know where I can get one. I've had my eyes on it for a long, long time!"

The night following the mass meeting a conference on the reorganization of the militia was called by the township administration. The meeting continued until well past midnight and when I woke the next morning, the sun already high in the sky was sending its rays streaming through my window. I hurriedly dressed and washed, afraid of being late for the inauguration ceremony of the militia company due to start right after breakfast.

As it was high tide early this morning, granddad had risen and left home before dawn. He had left my breakfast on the stove. A handful of brushwood and my breakfast was ready.

"I've got a big problem for you to help me solve, Hai-hsia," announced a gruff voice quickly followed by the appearance of Granddad Wang-fa himself. He stalked into the house, clutching his "old faithful," and plunked himself firmly down on a bamboo chair by the door.

His weather-beaten, lined face the colour of mahogany was set firm and severe. His thick bristly beard and the vertical lines between his bushy brows lent a martial air to his honest mien.

He had put in his application to join the militia at the mass meeting and we had discussed his joining at the militia meeting the previous night. Everyone agreed that he could not be accepted as a full member because of the age limit set by our superiors and because the militia core members were given the more difficult and trying tasks to carry out and this would be too much to ask from a man of his age. It would also be very inconvenient for the others if he was accepted.

I told him of the decision.

He reacted strongly. "Do you remember who it was who taught you that fishermen's ballad the year when you said, 'Uncle Liu told me not to tell'? You were just a little fluff of a girl then. Now that you're a company commander, you've forgotten! You look down on me now!"

I thought this very amusing, and I spoke kindly to him in a roundabout way. "How can you say that, Granddad Wang-fa? You, who have watched me grow up, too! Your age makes it difficult for you to keep up with militia core members who are all young people. It's nothing to be ashamed of. Leave all that standing guard and doing sentry duty to us youngsters. The girls and boys of our village have shot up like those young saplings on the slopes, haven't they? Sturdy saplings become a solid stand of trees within a few summers. Why, even your grandnephew Chi-wu is now old enough to become a full militia member."

He sat there in gloomy silence, unconvinced. Just then Chi-wu came blundering in, a shiny fishing harpoon slung across his back.

"I've been looking everywhere for you, granddad," he said. "I've been accepted by the militia and they're going to announce the list of the new members right after breakfast. You don't want me to stand on parade with a fishing spear, do you? Give me that gun of yours, will you, so that I can look like a real militia man!"

This was not the time to make such a request of the old man. He was already fuming inside and you could imagine that if he spoke the sparks would fly. "You've been after my gun all the time! But I'm not going to give it to a kid who's still wet behind the ears and wants to show off! Do you know that I captured this gun from a bandit of the Chiang gang with my own hands and that I was given permission by the district authorities to keep it? Do you know that a gun is not a toy to show off with?"

"Who's showing off?" Chi-wu retorted. "You tote that rifle around with you but you're not even a militia man. You don't do guard duty either, yet you won't hand that rifle over! Who's toying around with a gun, eh? Do you want me to fight with a fishing spear?"

"Haven't you the least respect left for your elders, you little monkey! How can you say that about me? And what do you know about guns!" His voice was loud normally, but by now it was louder than usual.

But the lad was not a whit chastened. He gave as good as he got. "Why are you always looking down on us young people? I've been through a fight with the enemy at sea and you think I don't know how to use a rifle!"

"You've been through a fight! You!" shouted Granddad Wang-fa. "All you probably did was stand there and watch, and you say you've taken part in a battle! Of course I have no high opinion of you. How do you know what it's like to suffer? You don't even know what a despot or pirate looks like! What do you know about the cruelty and heartlessness of those blackguards? I've swallowed down more tears than you've drunk water in all your life!" He was so worked up that words were failing him.

If the lad said another word then a box on the ears would be promptly forthcoming. I made desperate signs to Chi-wu to keep quiet. He finally saw me and reluctantly went away muttering under his breath.

Granddad Wang-fa remained perched on the chair, his brows closely knit. His rifle was still clutched tightly to his bosom as if he were afraid someone was going to snatch it from him.

I fed the fire and waited for the food to heat up.

After a long silence he demanded challengingly, "What counts in being a militia member, age or strength?"

"You know the saying, 'The years tell' and to ask you to do guard duties and take part in training exercises would be asking too much of a person of your age. We've taken all these things into consideration and that's why we haven't put you in with the militia core."

He was not a bit mollified, and blustered, "No thanks for your considerations! You should consider my application!" Then he shouted, "You have your reasons for not accepting me but I have my reasons for applying! Who hates the enemy more? Me or those youngsters? Tell me that! And tell me who is the stronger, me or those young fellows? And didn't Chairman Mao himself call on the whole people to become fighters? I think everyone, men and women, young and old, everyone who can pick up a gun should be in the militia!"

I was not in the least angered by the way he ranted at me. In fact, I loved him the more for it. Still I could not let him join the militia core. Not only because he was over-age but there were quite a number of others like him. They hadn't been as persistent as Granddad Wang-fa but it took some persuading to get them to agree to our refusal. Take the case of Hai-hua's father. He hobbled up to apply and when we tried to talk him out of it, he said, "When I was backward you made up a play and songs about me. Now that I have made progress, you shut me out! You may say I am old and that I am a cripple but let me tell you this: if you accept that Wang-fa and not me, I'll never forgive you for it! I'm twenty years younger than he is!" So, we couldn't accept Granddad Wang-fa.

I finished my breakfast but he still remained there. The meeting was due to start in another few minutes and he was standing there adamant. What should I do? I had to think about what I was going to say at the meeting and at the same time think of something to bring this "siege" to an end. Suddenly I hit upon an idea. "You know, we're setting up a militia company and that means there'll be a lot of newcomers to our enlarged organization, some of whom don't know much about the significance of having a gun. Nor do they have very much love for the gun. How about you coming in as an instructor? Teach us why it is so important for us to have guns and why we must love our guns. I'll bring up your application at the meeting and let's hear what the others have to say. Let's have some democracy, eh?"

"All right! I've got a bellyful of things I want to talk about." He agreed without a moment's hesitation and was off with his gun almost before he had finished speaking.

The meeting to inaugurate the inception of the militia company was held beneath the big banyan tree. No special arrangements had been made. The stand had several red banners with slogans, quotations of Chairman Mao on people's war, a square table and two plain benches. Shuang-ho spoke of the great significance of setting up a militia company and read out the names of those who had been accepted and the platoons they were assigned to and the cadres who were to lead them. Then it was my turn to address the meeting. Towards the end of my speech I raised the question of Granddad Wang-fa joining the militia, but before I had finished what I was saying he came over and, standing before the table, said in a voice charged with emotion:

"What's wrong with me? When have I ever been backward? I have seen a lot of years but I don't feel the least bit old. I've just spent a few short years of getting to know what it is like to be alive. I've lived like a man should for only a few short years. . . ."

The militia members held their breath, watching him with wide-open eyes.

"In the old days there were four in our family and now there is only me left. Thirty years ago I had to sell my five-year-old daughter Feng-lien for one hundred and fifty *jin* of dried sweet potatoes in order to keep alive. And that very year my three-year-old son Ah-pao died because we had nothing to feed him on. Chen Feng-shih, that despot, that dog that begot Chen Chan-ao, forced my young wife to hang herself while I was out at sea. I could go on till next year with my list of sorrows and sufferings! And every time I think of them it makes me burn, it makes me feel as if a knife was twisted inside me. . . ."

Then he tore off his black jacket and flung it over a bench, exposing powerful bronzed arms. He pointed to a big scar on his right arm and went on:

"I got this scar at the hands of the Japanese aggressors! That's all of a dozen years ago, but I can still remember that day as clearly as anything. We had just cast out nets when those Japanese came straight for us in their motor-boat and knocked our boat over. It sent all of us into the water. Then, as we struggled in the sea they fired at us. That's when I got this wound, those sons-of-bitches! They roared with laughter and clapped their hands when they saw the sea dyed red with our blood. . . ."

He then pointed to a scar in his side. "This I got from one of the bayonets of the Chiang bandits. In those days the Chiang gangsters had check points all over the island. If you wanted to buy something and went to North Hollow to get it you had to pay at least thirty cents as road tax! One day I got fifteen dollars' worth of rice coupons from the fish merchant to draw rice from the rice merchant. I put the road tax receipt and the rice coupon together. When I got to the check point I mistook the rice coupon for the road tax receipt and handed it over. At the rice merchant's I took out the road tax receipt. The merchant thumped me on the head, cursing, 'What oafs you beggars are! You want to draw a ration of rice with a road tax receipt!'

You could have knocked me down with a feather! Ordinarily I would have returned the curses measure for measure but this time I was too stunned to do anything. That fifteen dollars' worth of rice was to feed the whole crew. Without that we'd all starve! So I tore back to the check point where I found the bandit still there. I begged and implored him to give me back the coupon but all he did was sneer. Then he said, 'I'll give you . . . this!' and smashed his fist into my face. I spat blood and saw red. I seized hold of him and gave him back what I had got. That bandit took a step back and ran his bayonet at me. I twisted around but I wasn't fast enough. His bayonet caught me here in the ribs. . . . I'm fit to burst when I think of it even now. If I'd had a bayonet then I'd have run him through!

"And here. . . ." He pointed to another scar. It was on the right side of the abdomen. "This I got from an operation at the No. 1 Municipal Hospital. Last autumn when I was attending a meeting of the district people's congress I suddenly had an attack of appendicitis. The hospital at East Beach couldn't cope and the last ferry over to the mainland had already left. The district Party committee secretary was worried sick. He rang up the army and the soldiers sent a boat right away and took me over to the Municipal Hospital. The doctor who operated on me said I was lucky to get there in time, otherwise I'd be in real trouble. A couple of hours more and I would have had it! . . . All my expenses were paid by the government."

His voice dropped to a mere whisper. "At nights in bed I feel these three scars and think, recalling what I had got from the old society. What did that society give me? Poverty, sorrow and hatred for the reactionaries. I began to know good days only after liberation, in this new society. All the good things the Communist Party has heaped on me! I couldn't count them all if I tried. I think to myself, if I can stand guard, hold a rifle and do sentry duty to guard the motherland, then I shall be happy. Come wind, come rain, I don't care. Give me the most difficult jobs. Wear myself out, I don't mind. I love it! When I think of today, I feel young and full of vigour. When I think of the past I am filled with hatred, and how I wish I could wipe out all those pests! Kill them! Every one of them! That despot Chen Chan-ao, Black Wind and his bandits over in Taiwan. If I don't kill some of them with my own hands I'll not die content!

"The reason I didn't want to give you my gun was because I was afraid you young people wouldn't know how important it is to have a gun. But now I've thought better of it. The elder generation must have faith in the young people. We must hand over to worthy successors!

"Why am I raking up old hurts and wounds?" His eyes grew moist and his voice shook. "I want you young people to remember the misery and sufferings of the past and know what a gun is for! The gun is our source of life! Today, I'm passing the gun on. Giving it to you! When you young people take up my gun, take my heart with it!" Tears rolled down his leathery cheeks and splashed on the gun in his hands.

Mixed emotions stirred the meeting — grief, hatred, anger. No one made a sound but all gripped their rifles firmer. Everyone was breathing heavily. One could sense the pounding of their hearts and the hot blood coursing through their veins. No one could bring himself to accept Granddad Wang-fa's proffered gun. I glanced at Chi-wu, who had coveted that gun even in his sleep, and saw him sitting still as if the two streams of shining tears on his cheeks held him in check like a harness.

Not a sound was heard.

Suddenly Liu Chi-wu stood up, waving his spear as he said, "Keep your gun, granddad. I'll use the spear to kill the enemy!"

The old man gave Chi-wu a queer look and asked, "Why don't you want it?"

"You keep it," Chi-wu repeated. "You know what it is far better than I do and you love it more than I do," he said. "Before, I wanted it because . . . not because I wanted it to kill our enemies but so that the militia women couldn't laugh at me with my spear!" He blushed and hung his head.

A smile lit up the old man's face. "Chi-wu," he said, "take the gun. You now know it's not just for display so I trust you with it. Take it and give me your spear. I know how to use that spear better than you do."

Liu Chi-wu made no move.

Granddad Wang-fa walked over to where Chi-wu stood and pressed the gun into his hand. Then in an authoritative tone cried, "Hand me your spear!"

He held the spear in his hands and glancing at the people he said, "I want to see if there's still any strength left in these old arms of mine." He dropped into a fighting stance and with his right arm hurled the spear whistling through the air to embed its point deep in the big banyan tree forty metres away. Two militia men ran to get it and only by straining every muscle did they finally manage to pull it free.

The militia all looked with admiration at Granddad Wang-fa, and were loud in their praise of his strength. The elderly man looked about him triumphantly as if to say, "Now, what do you think? Old, am I?" When he heard someone audibly marvelling at his prowess with a spear, he said proudly, "If any enemy wishes to die, he can come and get a taste of my spear!"

After the meeting broke up I walked home with Granddad Wang-fa, he in front and I behind. The sun's rays flashed bright and blue on the barbed head of the spear. I hurried to catch up with him, and began in an apologetic voice, "You're not angry about my not accepting your application, are you?"

"Not at all," he answered with a smile that came straight from his heart. "I can trust those youngsters with my gun. We must have faith in our young people, you know."

I was happy to hear him say that and dared to tease him, "People say you're very obstinate, but I think you're not nearly as obstinate as they say you are."

"Ah, you mean the way I gave up my 'old faithful,' do you? And you're also wondering at how meekly I've accepted not being taken into the hard core of the militia? Well, I'll be frank with you. I'm a member of the militia whether you accept me or not. You see, I've set my heart on being one and in my heart I'll always be with you militia members. Understand? I'm very obstinate, aren't I?"

"Very obstinate indeed!"

And we both had a good laugh.

CHAPTER 27

RIDING ON THE CREST OF THE WAVES

WITH the setting up of the militia company we were organizationally much stronger, but ideologically and in practical training much work had still to be done and done rapidly to keep up with the development. Uncle Shuang-ho said to me, "The militia company has been set up and we've got a lot of newcomers on our hands so we're giving you the job of training them and improving them ideologically. We've arranged things to provide time to solve thoroughly all those shortcomings shown up during the recent exercise."

I answered, "I shall fight against the faults and shortcomings as if they were enemies. I'll wipe them out ruthlessly!"

After a hurried breakfast I went to call the platoon and squad cadres together for a meeting to discuss our work. As soon as I stepped out of the door I saw young Chi-wu coming down the street, hopping, jumping and singing, and obviously very happy. He had Granddad Wang-fa's gun across his shoulder and looked as though he would have soared to the sky if only he could have sprouted wings.

> *Armed with sword and rifle,*
> *I feel a surge of power.*
> *A militia man's job is to fight,*
> *I'm ready whatever the hour.*
> *Come one, I kill one,*

Come two, I kill a pair,
Surrender if you would live. . . .

"You are happy, Chi-wu! Where're you going?"

"I came to find you, Sister Hai-hsia. I've got something to ask of you."

"What do you want?"

"Let me fire one shot!"

He stared at me through such pleading eager eyes that I hadn't the heart to refuse him, but I did not agree to his demand immediately. "You should practise aiming first. You only got your gun the other day and you're itching to use it. Don't you remember that we mustn't waste bullets?"

"I've aimed thousands of times already!"

"When did you find time to do that?"

"I practised with granddad's rifle when he was asleep. Once I was so busy practising that when I got back he was awake already, and didn't he give me a telling-off! When we're at sea Ah-hung lets me practise aiming with his gun. He also teaches me how to handle it."

I said doubtfully, "Let me see you take aim." I pointed to the lamp on the fishing smack out in the bay. "Aim for that lamp on the mast."

He shouldered his gun like a veteran and aimed. Yes, the stance, the way the cheek was pressed to the butt, the butt tight against his shoulder, his breathing and the way he squeezed the trigger, they were all correctly done as advised in the manuals. "Good! I see you've put in a lot of practice so I'll let you have a bullet."

"You are stingy, Sister Hai-hsia!" he said in an unhappy voice. "Why, you militia women got at least five rounds! And you give me just one bullet!"

"Comrade, when it's your turn for live firing you'll get five rounds too. This one I'm giving you as a favour." He was still sulky and wanted to argue, so to frighten him I said, "If you're going to haggle with me, I won't even give you that one bullet!"

"All right, all right," he said, fearing that I really meant it. I handed him the bullet and with a smile he turned and scampered off as quick and lightly as the breeze. He'll fire that off in a minute, I thought.

Although the militia company had not yet had time to discuss and make any arrangements, the beach rang with commands such as "Attention! Dress by the right!" and "Forward!" The squads and platoons, all eager to train, had organized themselves. This was fine, just the sort of initiative needed in real combat.

I convened a meeting of cadres of the company right there. I told them, "The enthusiasm for training shown by everyone is indeed very high, but we must see to it that ideological work is not neglected, for ideology takes precedence over everything else."

"How are we going to do that?" demanded Hai-hua.

I pointed to the junks out in the bay, their sails speeding them steadily out to sea. Then I said, "See how swiftly those junks are moving out there! We must be like them. We must fill our minds with Mao Tsetung Thought and, with our heads armed ideologically, we can meet and overcome all difficulties in our forward advance. Listen to what Chairman Mao says: **We should always use our brains and think everything over carefully. A common saying goes, 'Knit your brows and you will hit upon a stratagem.' In other words, much thinking yields wisdom. In order to get rid of the blindness which exists to a serious extent in our Party, we must encourage our comrades to think, to learn the method of analysis and to cultivate the habit of analysis.** Why was there such confusion in the exercise we had a few days back? Because of poor organization! And why was organization poor? We should use our brains and think it over carefully. What were the actual roots of the trouble?"

Everyone was deep in thought and no one answered. I continued, "The reason lies in us not having in mind the idea of preparedness against war. Take for example the way we divided into combat teams. We split the platoon up with the idea of land fighting in mind and did not remember that we must also be prepared to fight on the sea. We forgot we're on an island and we must be expected to fight on the water as well. We should organize the militia in terms of fighting groups per sampan. We must be prepared to fight both on land and on sea."

Sister Ah-hung said, "I know what you're driving at, now that you put it that way. When Secretary Fang told us that night to go over to Tiger-Head we should have immediately remembered to take sculls with us instead of assembling on the beach and then having to run home for them!"

"What's that to do with ideology?" asked Hai-hua. "That was only because we were in such a hurry and overlooked them."

"Not at all," I interposed. "That was not because we were in a hurry. A fisherman never forgets his nets no matter how much of a hurry he may be in. It was because ordinarily we pay little attention to such details. We were ideologically unprepared."

"I've been doing a lot of thinking too since that exercise," said Yun-hsiang. "We generally scored good marks at practice but that night we didn't shoot at all well and that was because we hadn't much practice at shooting from a boat. I suggest that in future we practise aiming at moving targets on the water and also practise shooting from different angles and positions in the hills. Shooting from a slope is different from shooting from a flat piece of ground. . . ."

"Yun-hsiang has made a good point," I said. "We've not trained with a view to fighting a real battle."

We spoke and debated and used our brains. Much thinking on our part helped us to put our finger on the causes and eventually led us to methods of solving our problems.

At the end of the cadres' meeting I pointed out that during the evening's study session we ought to assign those members who were literate to help with the study in the different squads. "Tonight's study material will be Chairman Mao's articles on class struggle and people's war," I told the meeting.

"We haven't enough books!" cried someone.

241

"We'll have enough by this evening," I answered. "Uncle Shuang-ho has sent someone over to East Beach for them and the books will be distributed to each squad this afternoon."

That day marked the beginning of the militia members' serious study of Chairman Mao's works and our diligent participation in military training. Military training was alternated by study sessions, when we sat down together and studied Chairman Mao's works. Our morale was high and our determination firm-set. The cliff was emblazoned with our slogan, "The enemy shall pay with blood for all the sweat we shed during training!"

One day I saw Hai-hua leading a squad on a practice manoeuvre on the hillside. Half of the squad were new members. I suddenly remembered how Secretary Fang had tested us and I decided to do the same with these newcomers. "Hai-hua!" I shouted, "the enemy has been discovered on the beach. Your orders are to lead your squad in a charge on them."

Shouting "Charge!" Hai-hua led her squad down with rifles levelled. I followed close behind.

I was about to give the order to halt when they reached the water's edge. Before I could do so, Hai-hua, with the older militia women hot on her heels, charged into the water. Their swift-moving feet churned white foam under and behind them. The newcomers hesitated slightly, then plunged in after their leader. On and on they pressed until the water was up to their chests, but still shouting "Charge!" they fought their way forward. It was not a very spectacular sight but it was a very moving one. They stopped only after I had given the order to halt. Some of the militia women's actions were not exactly what the manuals called for, but that did not matter. After all what was important was their spirit of daring to do, of being afraid of neither hardships nor difficulties. They had courage and the will to fight and with these qualities, given the necessary training, they would soon become highly proficient.

Tsai-chu was making rapid progress both in her study of Chairman Mao's works and in her practical training. She studied conscientiously and trained diligently. Her elbows were rubbed raw by the sand and rocks but she was not a bit deterred. She bound up her injuries with a handkerchief and continued to press forward.

"You've got yourself as brown as a berry, Tsai-chu," I teased.

She smiled and said simply, "The browner I get, the more hardened I am."

"And your thinking has turned a deeper red, too," cried Hai-hua who came running up, water dripping off her clothing in puddles.

Chairman Mao! Your brilliant thinking lights the way forward for us!

After our evening meal we all returned to the beach for night shooting. We took aim at the lamp on the fishing vessel about two hundred metres out. The boat rocked with the tide and the lamp swayed and danced as it shed its red rays.

"Pow!" There was the sound of a shot and the tinkle of glass as the light went out.

"Who did that?" I shouted springing to my feet and looking about me. Young Chi-wu stood up and casually ejected a cartridge case from his rifle.

I heard shouts of praise from the militia. When word got round that it was Chi-wu who had shot the light out, people could be heard expressing loud comments of admiration. "Not bad at all for someone who's just been given his rifle!" Then Chi-wu was surrounded by a circle of admirers clamouring to be told how to shoot so straight.

I said sternly, "That was a breach of discipline, Liu Chi-wu!"

He was not a bit put out, and said, "I'll make the damage good. I've got a spare lamp at home."

"You'll do that and make a self-criticism as well!"

It was Chang Chin-fu's lamp and I prepared myself to meet an angry outburst from him. I was thinking out an apology on behalf of the militia when Chang Chin-fu himself came running up.

"Who shot out my lamp?" he cried, panting for breath.

243

"Please don't be angry, Uncle Chang," I said. "We'll pay you for the lamp. It was that little devil Chi-wu who smashed your lamp."

Chang Chin-fu looked ready to explode when he heard me. "Who asked you to pay? Do you think that you militia members are the only people who have studied Chairman Mao's works? I've listened in to your study sessions and I know there's someone surnamed Chang in Chairman Mao's books. Chang . . . what's his name?"

"Chang Szu-teh,*" I answered.

"That's it. That's the name. We're of the same family, see! He served the revolution faithfully. I can't compare with him but at least there's nothing to stop me from trying to be a little like him, is there? What's an old lamp to me as long as you people learn to shoot good and straight! Why, if the enemy dares to come, I'll give up my own life! That's what I'll do." Then he turned to look for Chi-wu among the others in the evening light. "Where's that scamp, eh? Afraid to meet me, eh?"

"Uncle Chang," said Chi-wu, stepping forward. "I was only trying out my rifle, but you can box my ears if you like."

Uncle Chang raised his brawny arm and for a moment I was afraid he would, but instead of that I saw him tap Chi-wu's head in a friendly way. "Well done, lad. Keep it up and smash the enemy's heads just like you did now."

Chi-wu was totally unprepared for this. He had been expecting anything but praise, and for a moment was dumbstruck. Then he blurted out, "I promise I. . . ." What he was promising that moment he did not make clear. In all probability he did not rightly know himself.

"Get on with your practice. I'm going to put up another lamp," he said as he left us.

A few minutes later we saw another lamp run up the mast to replace the one Chi-wu had shot down. How red and bright the lamp shone for us!

---

* A communist fighter to whom Chairman Mao paid high tribute in his brilliant work *Serve the People*.

CHAPTER 28

THE ENCOUNTER

THERE was no answer from Fukien in respect to our inquiry about the one-legged Liu Ah-tai. Fortunately we had not placed all our expectation on getting a prompt reply. Our militia was detailed off to keep a weather eye out for him. I gave particular instructions to Yu-hsiu on this. I jotted down in my notebook every suspicious move he made, but up to now there was precious little I had on him.

He sometimes called in to buy tobacco and wine at the shop but seldom talked to Dog. He had aroused my suspicions when he first met Dog and proposed, without being asked, to give that rogue a hair-cut. It made me wonder, was he trying to make contact and establish a liaison with Dog?

My suspicions faded after a few days, especially after Yu-hsiu reported that Liu Ah-tai had expressed regret for his action. He had said, "If I'd known what sort of fellow he was I wouldn't have given him a hair-cut on any account. I serve the people, not any steward of the despot!"

He had also encouraged Yu-hsiu to take an active part in the militia, urging her to "avenge him for his missing leg."

Did he mean what he said? Was I being too suspicious? Or was he saying these things knowing they would be repeated to me by Yu-hsiu?

I heard from Aunt Ta-cheng that the long lost brother treated her and his niece quite decently, giving her all he earned from his barbering as well as the whole of the five hundred yuan he had got from selling all his possessions in Fukien. He only kept enough to keep himself in tobacco and a little wine and never shot off his mouth.

Whatever he did he had done openly and he had never tried to do anything behind the backs of the militia. For instance, he came to the island on the same boat as the militia platoon, and when he offered to give Dog a hair-cut he had done so in my presence. If he went to East Beach he asked us militia if there was anything we wanted him to do or wanted brought back. . . .

At one stage I had even suspected that he was responsible for what happened to Sister Ah-hung, but on thinking it over later I decided otherwise. It would be extremely difficult if not quite impossible for a one-legged person like him to scale that path up the cliff and tamper with that stone slab. I kept turning this question over and over in my mind and the more I thought the more I felt befogged. Dimly, I sensed something wrong, but exactly what I could not tell.

Secretary Fang had repeatedly warned us that the enemy was extremely cruel and at the same time extremely crafty. I had no experience in dealing with hidden enemies so I must heighten my vigilance and learn to use my brains better.

The militia had reported that Liu Ah-tai who went over to East Beach the day before to get his clippers repaired had not returned in the afternoon. I decided to visit East Beach and see if I could find out anything about his movements there and at the same time deliver a report to the district committee. Luckily the tide was in early and I reached East Beach by breakfast time.

The wide road winding up the hill from the quay provided a clear view of the army barracks, training grounds and gun emplacements.

There was a freshness in the early summer morning air and the salty brightness in the atmosphere blended with the fragrance of flowering rice. As I made my way along the road, the fine clean sand gave off a crisp crunch at each step I took.

Two tall banyan trees stood seventy metres apart on a slope by the beach, their branches spread as if clasping hands to provide shelter from the sun for the girls mending and making nets below. The girls were laughing and chattering like a flock of magpies in spring, as their nimble fingers sent the polished bamboo shuttles flashing forwards and backwards. Their smiling faces seemed to express a shared and happy secret.

As I reached them they broke into song, a fishermen's song.

> *On the beach, by the sea,*
> *Beneath the banyan in the breeze,*
> *The fishergirls are weaving,*
> *Weaving nets so fine, oh so fine.*
>
> *On the beach, by the sea,*
> *Rollers break into thundering surf,*
> *The fishergirls are training*
> *With bayonets and rifles,*
> >   *bayonets and rifles.*

I saw their rifles with bayonets fixed stacked under the trees.

The girls looked familiar although I could not recognize any one of them. I had met them before but not at the military sub-area contest. There was not one I could call by name. When they looked up and saw me they fired a string of questions at me.

"Are you from Concord?" one of them asked.

"I am."

"Are you a member of the militia?"

"Of course."

"Are you a member of Hai-hsia's company?"

"Why a member of Hai-hsia's company?" I countered. "You should have asked, 'Is Hai-hsia a member of your company?'"

"Is Hai-hsia in your company?" asked a girl bigger even than our Hai-hua. "We haven't met Hai-hsia, but we know she's really wonderful."

"What's so wonderful about her?" I demanded, blushing at this unexpected and undeserved praise. "Anyway, it was you people who won the pennant."

"That's why she's so wonderful!" exclaimed the girl. "It was she who let us have the pennant!"

I was taken aback by this. Why had she said that? "I don't understand," I said. "If it was she who let you have the pennant then she's a darn fool is all I can say!"

Anger mounted in her cheeks and I could see I was in for a fine argument. "Our company commander Yueh-chiu told us when she came back from the competitions. We were very happy to see them come back with the prized pennant and then Yueh-chiu said to us, 'Don't get smug and conceited. We can't hold a match to those militia girls of Concord. There's a lot we've to learn from them!'

"At first we didn't believe a word of what she said and indignantly demanded, 'If they're so good then why has the pennant fallen into our hands?'

"The company commander then said to us, 'We sent a picked team to take part in the competitions but the Concord militia just detailed a squad. They didn't select their best sharpshooters. One of their competitors brought their score down by getting a mere seventeen points with three shots. If she had bagged twenty-seven instead of seventeen points, then where would that leave us?' And then we understood what she had meant and were convinced."

"What do you mean by 'bagged twenty-seven instead of seventeen?'"

"Well, if their Hai-hsia had taken part they'd have been sure to get twenty-seven points. Most likely twenty-nine points at that." The plump girl spoke as if stating an undisputed fact.

I shook my head in disagreement. "That's not the way to put it. You should have said Hai-hsia's responsibility was to help that girl score twenty-nine points instead of seventeen. That's what Hai-hsia should have done!"

But the plump girl would have none of that. "Stop being so catty," she retorted. "Our company commander said that the competition was not only a test of our shooting skills but was also a test, a much more important test, of ideology, of our style of doing things. We don't strive for any award, we've to strive for a noble style of behaviour. That's why we must learn from Concord Island's militia. Learn from their fine style of plain, honest, down-to-earth way of thinking and acting, and placing the greatest demands on themselves."

I left these good-hearted chatterboxes, thinking as I continued my walk: Yueh-chiu really knows how to do ideological work! She can even find good points in a "defeated" side to learn from, and find faults in themselves by comparing themselves with others. She pays great attention to the ideological job with her company. She's much the better person of us. To be frank, we are much the same when it comes to shooting. Probably they are a bit behind us in this respect, but they were set up much later than we were and what they have done isn't at all bad going. This is another point that puts them ahead of us. They have made much more rapid progress than we have.

A gentle familiar voice broke into my reveries, "Aren't you Hai-hsia?" I looked up and saw Wang Yueh-chiu, the company commander of the East Beach militia company, standing before me.

"Ah, it's you!" I hurried to seize her hand.

"What wind blew you over here?" she asked.

"A force twelve typhoon!"

"But seriously, where are you going?" she asked, smiling.

"To the district committee."

"If you're not in too much of a hurry I would like you to come and see us go through our exercise. We would like to have your opinion. This is our first time, so it won't be much of a show."

"My, my, why have you gone all polite and modest so suddenly, eh?" I teased. "With that prize of yours shining before me, where am I to find the courage to express any opinion?"

"Won't admit you've been beaten, eh?"

"Never!"

249

"All right, try and win it back!"

"Just you watch out." I was stopped from further bantering by the arrival of the girls who came running to meet us. They were puzzled by the way we two were behaving.

Yueh-chiu pointed to the girls and said, "We are going to put this squad through its paces first." Turning to the girls she said, "Let me introduce you all to Comrade Li Hai-hsia, commander of the Concord militia company."

"Aiyah!" exclaimed the plump girl in astonishment. "So you're Hai-hsia herself! Thank heavens I didn't say anything bad about you just then!"

"Oh, didn't you just! Who called me catty back there a while ago?" I teased.

"You'll just have to excuse her," laughed Yueh-chiu. "She's got the quickest tongue in our company. Now, let's begin. Point out any fault you see, will you?"

I said, "I'm here to watch and to learn. I doubt very much if I'd be able to find any fault at all."

To which she replied, "If you don't point out our mistakes then we will not let you go."

The exercise began with a blast from the conch. The girls scrambled to assemble under the big banyan tree, each with her rifle, in neat formation. Wang Yueh-chiu stood before them and gave the order. "Today's lesson is defensive warfare! . . . To your positions!"

Rifles in hand they turned to run up the steep slope behind them. Their dark tanned faces were soon shining with sweat. Mud stuck to their saturated clothes. Some stumbled over hidden rocks, quickly bandaged up their cuts with handkerchiefs and continued upwards.

Yueh-chiu gave another order.

"To your positions! Hsiu-chin, hurry up there! Keep down!"

"Take up shooting positions! Ah-ngo! You're filling your rifle with dirt that way! Keep the muzzle off the ground!"

"Take aim! Chin-lan! Under and up!"

"Commence firing!"

"Forward! Make good use of everything for cover!"

As the squad moved rapidly forward, the girl who had tried to argue with me a little earlier fell behind. She blushed scarlet under her tan when I recognized her.

Even that little aside did not escape the sharp eyes of her company commander. "Tsui-lien! What are you admiring now! Keep your eyes on the enemy! Forward!"

The plump girl now flustered, tripped and fell heavily.

I ran to help her but before I could cover a few paces she hurriedly scrambled to her feet and was again racing madly forward.

Yueh-chiu was like our Huang Yun-hsiang, even and sweet-tempered and soft-spoken. But Yueh-chiu on the training ground was altogether another person. Her commands were given crisply, clearly and firmly. Her eyes saw everything each member of the squad did and any mistakes were quickly and accurately pointed out. The militia girls went through their paces as seriously as if it were a real battlefield movement. They carried out their actions precisely, swiftly and conscientiously. I could see they had much we could learn from.

During the rest break Yueh-chiu summed up, "Let each think over what she has done rightly or wrongly. What is the aim of taking cover, making use of the ground and of obstacles? For the purpose of getting into a good position to make your firing effective, concealing yourselves and eliminating the enemy. I think many of us haven't quite grasped this yet, at least as far as making use of the ground and of obstacles is concerned. I don't know how many times I've told you to remember the 'below-and-up.' But I'll repeat the instruction again. Occupy positions from below up, look from below up, and bring your rifles from below up."

"What if we're behind a window, a tree, or at a corner?"

"Then it is from inside to outside," Yueh-chiu answered. Then continuing, she said, "And then there is the 'three-good-fors.' Good for making observations and developing firepower, good for taking cover and fighting at close quarters, and good for forward movement. Let each of us think over what we have done. Have we done as required?"

I saw this was a good method. What Yueh-chiu was doing was to first ask the militia to think it over and decide for themselves whether they had done as the manuals demanded and then fill in the gaps and correct the errors.

The girls were shy because I was present and they did not speak freely.

Later, Yueh-chiu asked me to say a few words of criticism; otherwise, she threatened, she would not let me go. There was no way out so I stated my views. I said that the most outstanding points in this exercise were that the militia members were brave, conscientious and not afraid of difficulties. However, they had the same fault as our Concord militia, we did not have the enemy in mind when we engaged in training exercises. This had the detrimental effect of holding up our progress. For instance, concealment and concentration of firepower were not fully exploited because we could not visualize the enemy in front of us. And we also forgot that the enemy in front could shoot back at us! Many of the girls had an eye on the visitor while carrying out their movements and were trying to avoid making blunders. So as soon as a hitch occurred, they were thrown into confusion. . . .

After a hurried farewell to Yueh-chiu and the girls I took the path towards the district committee's office at the town of North Hollow. The visit to Yueh-chiu had taken me off the main road and as I had lost some time, I decided to take a short cut along a small path. Just as I rounded a bend after climbing over the foothills I suddenly came upon Liu Ah-tai. He was carrying his barber's kit and was coming towards me. I involuntarily stopped. He appeared to be as surprised as I was at this unexpected meeting, but he quickly recovered himself and was the first to speak.

"What are you doing here, Company Commander Hai-hsia? Why are you on this path?"

"Now isn't that strange! Fancy meeting you on this path!"

"I'd been over to North Hollow to get my clippers fixed," he replied. "It took longer than I expected and I wasn't able to catch the tide so I had to spend the night in town. Luckily the township head had provided me a letter of introduction, otherwise I'd still be waiting." It was obvious that he was saying one thing while his mind was far away on something else.

"How come you're on this path if you came from North Hollow?" I persisted.

A look of anger darkened his face. "A boy told me this path was a short cut! The rascal! He must have been playing a joke on me. Now I'm a long way off my route!"

"So, you've been taken in by a child, eh!" I laughed.

He could see that I did not believe him. The sweat that broke out on his brows betrayed him.

I asked myself, who is he? He's been in Concord for over a fortnight and I've only now taken him on in a face-to-face encounter! I said, "It must be terribly difficult and tiring for a man like you to come by such steep paths. Why, you're bathed in sweat. Come and sit down and rest a while."

I seated myself on a stone and indicated another one for him to sit on.

He had now fully recovered himself and said calmly, "Yes, I think I will have a rest before I go on." He put down his stick and sat down opposite me.

I could feel he wanted to probe into my thoughts. He was probably thinking he could take good care of himself and easily cope with a simple girl like me.

I waited for him to begin, and he did. "Company Commander Hai-hsia, are you going to North Hollow? You must be very busy."

"Well, I won't say I'm not busy. I have been busy and that was why I had no time to look after you better." I was purposely drawing him on.

"Oh, don't say that. I've been well looked after and I'm extremely grateful. You trusted me and even found me a job. No, the township authorities have looked after me extremely well."

"No. Not at all. We haven't paid nearly enough attention to you, especially not giving you enough ideological attention."

He threw me an inquiring look. "How can you say that?"

"Well, let's take this example of your having to come all this way to have the clippers fixed. A handicapped man like you shouldn't have done that. Many of our people come over every day, and if we had thought about it we could have asked any one of them to get the job done for you. That would have saved you a lot of trouble, wouldn't it?" I added, "And then you wouldn't have been taken in by any rascally boy!"

"Well, now, that. . . ." He spoke slowly, groping for words, and was obviously thrown out of his stride by my remarks. His right hand beat a tattoo on his stump. "That . . . er . . . that's nothing at all. Anyway, it's no trouble at all for me to come. No need to bother the township authorities at all."

"As for the matter of politics, now," I went on, looking straight at him, "we should have briefed you about the local situation. If we had, then you'd not have given the despot's steward a hair-cut on your first day here. Of course, giving him a hair-cut doesn't matter much, but we should have told you who are the good people and who are the bad ones as soon as you arrived and then you'd not get taken in by bad people."

He was taken aback that our conversation had turned to the subject of politics so soon, but he tried to make use of this opportunity to sound me out. "I'm to blame for being so impetuous," he said. "But, tell me, while we are on the subject, what sort of person is this No. 2 Dog?"

I wanted to get him off his guard. "Dog's behaviour over the last few years hasn't been too bad. He did his part in exposing Chen Chan-ao and is set on reforming himself." I said this as if I meant it and then asked, "What do you think of him?"

He adopted the tone I had set. "People like Dog are like that. They don't know where they stand. There is no way out for the likes of him if they don't accept remoulding. As you said, he seems to have made up his mind to remould himself. He once told me that he was a new man altogether. . . ."

I interrupted him to break up his train of thought, "And you really think that?"

He perceived the sharpness of my tone and was baffled, realizing that I had changed tack. He did not quite know what to say and replied vaguely, "But I really don't know. Can't make him out. I was talking through my hat just now."

I decided to give him a shaking. "Frankly, I don't trust types like Dog a bit. You said types like him don't know where they stand. You're absolutely wrong there! They do have a stand — a reactionary stand. Those people are wolves in sheep's clothing." I watched him intently as I spoke, as if I could see right through him. He squirmed uneasily, and focussed his attention on a section of the cliff.

He had not expected my abrupt change, and knew he had let something slip. His face turned pale, and he tried to appear as if nothing had happened. "Company Commander Hai-hsia doesn't mince words," he said.

"I speak whatever is in my mind," I answered with a laugh.

"And what do you think of me?" he challenged.

This put me in a spot for I had not expected such a question. What was I to say?

I thought quickly. It was obvious that he knew we suspected him and were keeping an eye on him. He might very well have read the first letter of inquiry we had sent to Fukien. Why not give him a start and watch his reaction?

"I'll give it to you straight. We don't easily trust or distrust anyone without good cause. We do not do anyone an injustice, neither do we let one rotten egg escape us no matter how slippery and crafty he may be. A fox is a fox and his brush betrays him. We're part of the coastal defence here, and you know as well as I do. . . ."

"Sure, sure," he answered, and his hand again began drumming the stump of his leg.

"We've written to Fukien to make inquiries and until we get a reply from them we cannot blindly trust you," I said, making out that I was being quite frank with him.

A ghost of a smile flitted across his face and with relief in his voice he said, "That is very proper. Everyone should be investigated. After all we're on the frontline here."

As though I had given him a tranquillizer, he flashed me a look of relief and said, "Can't sit here all day. Must be getting along."

Now I asked myself, why does he look so relieved all of a sudden? The obvious reason was that the letter Chen Hsiao-yuan had asked Dog to post had got into his hands! He had known we did not trust him and were watching his movements but had not known what steps we had actually taken concerning him. He now thought that he knew. He figured we were waiting for a reply from Fukien and that was just what he had wanted to know. He thought he had learnt that from what I had unconsciously let slip in my naivete and childishness. In all probability he had counted on us waiting for a reply before doing anything. If we waited and, failing to receive a reply, despatched another letter then he would have time enough to accomplish whatever he intended to do. More than a fortnight had passed since we sent that letter.

However, our feet do not tread along paths mapped out by our enemies!

CHAPTER 29

STRANGE SIGNALS

T HE encounter with the one-legged Liu Ah-tai left me feeling more confident that he was an enemy, although there was no tangible evidence, yet. There was, however, enough for me to regard him as one. Lost in thought I suddenly realized that I had reached North Hollow.

North Hollow is a biggish market town on East Beach Island, easy of access and having a thriving economy. It is a centre where goods from the three islands of Concord, East Beach and Half Screen are bought and sold. North Hollow has fishing, handicrafts, farming and commerce, with fishing as its main pursuit. All the others are secondary pursuits complementing or serving the main one. All sorts of fish and processed fish goods are handled here in bulk, and then exported. Imports are mainly rice, cloth, sugar, kerosene, hemp, timber, bamboo, metal goods and various assorted goods needed in production, as well as daily consumer goods. North Hollow is where people came from all over the three islands, and Dog came here frequently to buy goods.

I threaded my way through the bustling streets and, pushing open the door to enter the office of the district government, saw Secretary Fang, the director of the district security department and an army security officer in conference. I hesitated, not knowing whether to go in or retreat.

Secretary Fang looked up, saw me and called out, "You've come at the right moment, Hai-hsia! We've got a tricky problem on our hands."

"I was just coming to give a report on some security matters on Concord," I said. "I didn't know you were having a meeting. I'll wait if you like."

"Don't go away," said Secretary Fang. "Let's hear what you have to say. It might even have some bearing on what we are working on."

I took a seat by the table and the meeting resumed.

When I got to the part about Liu Ah-tai coming to East Beach to get his clippers repaired and my running into him a short time before, Secretary Fang spoke in an excited tone, "These are very important." He then turned to the security officer and said, "Let us analyse what Hai-hsia has just told us. I think what she has said gives us a clue and provides evidence substantiating our little theory."

He then briefed me about recent events on East Beach. New army dispositions had been made on East Beach and two mortar companies had been added. Radar reports showed that the enemy had also been very active of late at sea. The evening before, strange radio signals in code had been intercepted in the vicinity of North Hollow. Obviously someone was sending coded messages to the enemy at sea. The army and militia had been instantly called out and a close search made without results. It appeared that the transmitter had been moved on immediately following the transmission. The same thing had happened a few days before.

I knew nothing at all about such matters but I wondered if this had anything to do with Liu Ah-tai. "When was the first transmission?" I asked.

"At three in the afternoon seven days ago," replied the security officer.

This was the day following the setting up of our militia company. I took out my notebook and found an entry which said that one-legged Liu Ah-tai had visited East Beach that same day. His excuse was that he wanted to buy clippers. Was that visit merely a coincidence? Then why had both transmissions taken place when this stranger was present on East Beach? I pointed this out to the others.

"The times fit," nodded Secretary Fang. "But can we assume that he is the operator of the transmitter?"

The others agreed that the events coincided and we made a specific analysis of the circumstances.

Liu Ah-tai's two visits to East Beach were made after the setting up of the militia company and the new troop dispositions there. His excuses on both occasions appeared legitimate enough — to buy clippers, and the second time to get them repaired. But on closer scrutiny they did not seem very plausible. Why did he have to have the clippers repaired which he bought only a few days previously? Besides, he could have asked anyone coming on an errand to East Beach to get it done for him. It was a lot of trouble for a one-legged man to come here, for it involved climbing the three hills between the wharf and the town itself. But why must he transmit from East Beach? An answer had to be found for this last question. After a lot of discussion we thought we had it. He came to East Beach to collect information, but more important to conceal his true location. No one would have thought of searching Concord Island for the person who was sending coded messages from East Beach. This indicated that we were dealing with a very crafty enemy.

When it came to the part about transmitters, I thought the answer lay in the barber's kit he carried. We were now unanimous in our views and we began to work out a plan. Secretary Fang asked me to get a peep into that barber's kit carried about by the one-legged man but I protested to do that would give the whole game away. We'd be putting him on his guard.

"That's the very idea," said Secretary Fang. "Give him a bit of a shock, like you did a short time ago. See what his reactions are. He's more likely to give himself away when he's flustered. Where I come from there is a saying, 'The hare is easier to shoot on the run and the pheasant on the wing.' "

Secretary Fang accompanied me back to Concord to be in closer contact with the case.

Liu's temporary barber shop was a bamboo and reed affair set up near the entrance to the village. It was the shed we used during the oyster season, and was empty now. When Yu-hsiu and I entered, Liu was shaving an elderly man.

"My rifle strap snapped, uncle," said Yu-hsiu. "I want to borrow your scissors a moment, may I?" This was the excuse we had arranged.

He gave us a furtive glance and then said, "Help yourselves. They're in the box," and went on with his barbering.

Yu-hsiu "accidentally" let the box slip from her hands and it crashed to the ground.

The barber exclaimed, "Why are you so clumsy, Yu-hsiu!" But he didn't stop doing his work.

I rushed over to "help" Yu-hsiu pick the tools up. There was nothing at all out of the ordinary, just combs, clippers, a mirror, brushes and a bar of soap. I thumped and tapped the box, but there was not a suspicion of a radio.

We left the shed disappointed.

Where did he have his transmitter? I couldn't sleep for worrying about it. I thought and thought. I went over everything that had taken place since he arrived, over what he said and what expressions showed on his face. My mind swiftly darted back and forth like the shuttle I used to make nets with. I strung all the impressions together, trying to make a net to catch the enemy.

Suddenly I remembered his stump of a leg. I remembered how he tapped it every time he grew tense. Was that a reflex which had grown out of a habit?

A novel idea formed in my mind. Was the transmitter hidden in the stump of that leg? Was it possible? I knew nothing about things like that but if it were possible to conceal a transmitter there, then that would be most convenient for him. He would be able to transmit wherever he happened to be and without fear of being found out. Who at the check points would think of inspecting that stump of his?

I got up and went to find Secretary Fang, who was at the township office that night. I found him still up, discussing some work with Uncle Shuang-ho.

After I had told them what was on my mind, Uncle Shuang-ho asked, "Is that possible?"

"Absolutely!" exclaimed Secretary Fang. "For all we know his leg may not even be amputated at the knee but at the hip. The enemy is cunning. Have you heard how some agents have even replaced a dog's eye with a camera? Fitting a transmitter into a false leg would be a simple matter!"

"Shall we grab him and search him now?" I asked.

"No!" said Secretary Fang after what seemed a long pause. "I don't think we should be in such a hurry. You ran across him over at East Beach and then you searched his barber's kit. He's sure to wonder if he's given himself away. In such circumstances he is sure to try something else and won't be just sitting there waiting for us to make the first move. We must keep a close watch on him and try to find out what he's up to, who and what he is. He seems very familiar with conditions locally and knows everything to be known about Aunt Ta-cheng. Now, where did he get all his information? His origins are devious and mysterious. He claims he is an invalided fisherman who has performed meritorious work for the people, so he gets himself settled into a poor fisherman's family. It's an ideal cover. But what is he after on this island? And who is working with him? We've got to get all these things straightened out first."

"Will he try to run away or sabotage something?" asked Uncle Shuang-ho.

"Not him," answered Secretary Fang. "Now that we've uncovered him we can think of ways of fixing him. Hidden bombs are only dangerous when you don't know where they are."

CHAPTER 30

AT CLOSE QUARTERS

A S one-legged Liu was staying in Yu-hsiu's house she was our best source of information, for she could watch his every move. We arranged that if anything happened in the night she was to come and report to us at militia headquarters, giving as her pretext that she had to go on duty.

Yu-hsiu told us that Liu Ah-tai had done nothing suspicious. That night he went to bed as usual and quickly fell into a deep sleep. He could be heard snoring his head off. The following morning he left for work with his barber's kit as usual and appeared relaxed and happy as he hummed some nondescript tune.

Were we mistaken? Or was he putting on an act and managing to take in our inexperienced Yu-hsiu? I decided to take a look around.

He put down his barber's kit inside the shed, picked up an empty wine bottle, then made his way to Dog's shop. There was nothing suspicious about this because, after all, the shop did redeem "empties." But I tracked him all the same. He entered the shop by the front door and I kept him under observation through a crack in the back door. This rear door could be reached through Granddad Wang-fa's house. I saw Liu put the bottle on the counter and heard him say, "Give me another bottle of wine, I've brought back the empty."

Without saying a word Dog gave him some change and the bottle of wine and went back to arranging his shelves. Liu carried the bottle of wine back to his shed.

The exchange was suspiciously brief. I wondered, was there anything inside that bottle when Liu returned it? After Liu left I walked into the shop. Dog was trying to remove the cork from the empty bottle. He gave an involuntary start and retreated several steps when he saw me.

"What . . . what do you want?" he stammered, forgetting his "um . . . um" in his fright.

"I want to buy that empty bottle!" I said snatching it from him. His face suddenly drained of all colour till it looked like dirty whitewash. His lips contorted. He was unable to utter a word as his glassy eyes stared at me in fright. His whole frame shook with fear. This lasted only a few seconds. Behind him was a stack of metal goods — iron pots, ladles, shark harpoons and oyster knives. He suddenly ducked and grabbed a shovel. His former fear was replaced by a demoniacal cruelty. He was no longer a human being but a cornered wild beast.

"Put that bottle down!" he screamed, his eyes blazing with exasperation and anger.

I held the bottle tight and stood there calmly watching him. The wall behind me was not a dead end. Behind me was our militia company and the entire Chinese people. I felt the immense power of their solid support surge through me, filling me with immovable might. I had my conviction, and I knew who I loved and who I hated and I didn't feel a twinge of danger. What was he? A cur in his death throes! How could he stand up to me, he who had nothing to live for but to preserve his own cowardly life?

"Put that shovel down!" I ordered, unwavering eyes watching his every movement.

He raised the shovel. His face was like a death mask. He might bring the shovel down any second, but I stood my ground and firmly repeated, "Put that down!"

I did not raise my voice but there was no mistaking the steady firmness of my voice. He collapsed before me, dropping his arms as if he had been shot, as if a knife had severed their ligaments. The shovel fell to the ground with a clatter and he threw himself on to the ground grovelling and pleading, "I'm . . . I'll make a clean breast of everything! Spare my miserable life! Um . . . um . . . I was forced into it. I. . . ." He began snivelling and cringing for his life.

I took Dog to the township office. According to his confession this was what had happened:

One-legged Liu had cut his hair the very evening he arrived on our island.

The "barber" had playfully seized Dog's shaggy hair and said, "Aren't you afraid they'll grab you by this mop? I've heard that you are the former steward of Chen Chan-ao. I see you haven't been doing badly for yourself lately!"

Dog was not sure who the speaker was and replied cautiously, "Um . . . I am making earnest and diligent efforts to remould myself. And . . . um . . . um . . . I'm a completely new man. No one is going to grab me by the hair."

"But you were once the pillar of the Chen household!"

"Um . . . what are you bringing that up for?" demanded Dog, losing his poise. "And um . . . um . . . I've nothing to do with Chen Chan-ao."

"But Chen and his whole family will never forget that it was you who saved their lives. They're eternally grateful to you!"

"What?" He leapt out of his seat as if a bomb had exploded under him. The razor nicked his ear. "Who . . . who are you?" he asked the "barber."

"Do you mean you don't recognize me? Wasn't it you who sent me a note that night to save the Chen family?"

"You're Black Wind?"

"Can't you see for yourself?"

"But . . . your leg . . .?"

"A bullet smashed my leg that night."

"But . . . um . . . you've got gold-filled teeth?"

"As you just said of yourself, 'I'm a completely new man!' Why, even you didn't recognize me. That's a good one. I feel really safe."

264

"Heavens! What a time for you to come! There's no escape. No one can get away from here and yet you come walking right into the trap!"

"You didn't believe we'd come back and take over the mainland?"

"I . . . um . . . I've prayed day and night for that but I didn't really believe it was possible. If you can make a comeback then why did you have to leave in the first place? It is going to be harder for you to recover the mainland than to climb up into the sky. I put all my hopes on a third world war but . . . um . . . those Yanks got a whipping in Korea. I felt lost, devastated. I was like a widow whose only son had died. Um . . . ah . . . at first I tried to fight them, but what was the use? Uh? I was only hanging on to the ledge of the well by my ears, and what could I do? Of course, I hate them but I love my life more. I know what's good for me. Of all the stratagems, acquiescence is the best. . . ."

"Have you forgotten that you're the time-bomb planted at the Communists' gateway?"

"Um . . . but the time-bomb probably won't explode," said Dog in despair. "I'm afraid, you see. I want to do something but I'm scared."

"Won't explode, eh? Got wet, eh? You've made plenty of calculations, Mr. Steward, but don't you forget that it was you who sent me that note to help the Chen family escape! What if the Communists find that out, eh?" Black Wind held his razor menacingly before Dog.

"I . . . I beg you. . . ."

"You're not getting off that easily! Now listen, I have an assignment for you."

"What . . . um . . . what do you want me to do?"

"Chen Chan-ao is in Taiwan. He's a commander of an advance column for the recovery of the mainland and he's itching to get back here to Concord!"

"Will he be able to hold the island?"

"Why hold the island? We're only concerned with making a surprise attack, burning their houses and wiping out all the people. We'll be making a contribution towards the free world that will boost the morale of our forces and lower the prestige of the Communists in the eyes of the world. We'll be showing the world that we can come and go as we please and that the mainland is not invulnerable. Now's the time for it! There are no troops on Concord and the militia men are away fishing, leaving only those damnable militia women. Your job is to scatter and destroy the women militia. You won't be left here. Chen is going to take you back with him. He wants you as his chief of staff. Cheer up and take hold of yourself, Mr. Steward. Don't get disheartened. A good paying position is waiting for you!"

Just as a leopard will never change its spots, so it was with Dog. He pricked up his ears and demanded, "All right. No good doing things by halves. I'll go the whole hog. Um . . . um . . . what do you want me to do?"

"Catch a snake by the head is good advice, and you had better think of a way of getting rid of Li Hai-hsia. See that it's done quietly and cleanly and don't get yourself in trouble."

"Um . . . now that you mention it, I've an idea. Li Hai-hsia goes every night to check on the sentries posted at Tide-Watcher's Point. Uh . . . ha! She'll never even know what hit her! Oh, how I hate her guts!"

And that was the cause of the accident on the night we held our exercise. Sister Ah-hung was the one who got hurt instead of me, but the enemy had almost accomplished their aim. Rumours had been spread far and fast and caused some confusion among the militia, but the enemy did not reckon on us seizing the bull by the horns. We had forestalled them by immediately enlarging our militia organization and setting up a militia company. That forced the enemy to abandon their original plan, to content themselves by gathering information and passing it on to their masters, the agents onboard U.S. warships stationed just off the coast.

Secretary Fang unrolled the note-paper plugging the empty bottle and read:

We've been discovered and the situation is desperate. We have to act immediately if we're to get out of this with our whole skin. We must act before their militia men return. I order you to take action as pre-arranged. Time: 23:00 hours tonight. Your obedience is a life-and-death matter.

"What were your arrangements?" I demanded.

"As soon as he arrived, Black Wind worked out a plan to co-ordinate with Chen Chan-ao's surprise attack on the island," said Dog. "Um . . . when that time came I was to set fire to the warehouses. All the militia would rush to fight the fire and Chen could land unopposed."

This information could have been communicated by word of mouth instead of in writing but Liu thought it risky as people were coming and going in the shop and its walls were thin. So they used the empty bottle ruse to communicate with each other.

Secretary Fang asked, "What signal were you to use to contact them out at sea?"

"Set fire to the warehouses."

"Trying to pull a fast one on us, eh?" I cried. Then I demanded, "Where's your transmitter?"

Dog looked at us anxiously and appeared to be very upset. "Um . . . I . . . I don't know anything about a transmitter. I've told you all I know. I ask heaven to bear witness."

Secretary Fang looked at his watch. It was exactly ten a.m. "We have time enough," he said. Turning to Dog, he commanded, "Go back to your shop and behave as if nothing had happened!"

"Back to the shop?" asked Dog in surprise, and then added ingratiatingly, "You'll catch Black Wind quickly and lock him up, won't you?"

"That's no concern of yours," said Secretary Fang brusquely. "If you want to redeem yourself you had better do as I say. Get back there quickly and remember how many guns we have trained on that head of yours. You don't want to lose it, do you?"

After Dog had left, Secretary Fang said to me, "I'm giving this Black Wind to you to handle, Hai-hsia. You take a couple of militia members with you but don't take him into custody before eleven tonight unless you have no alternative. I'll look after the deployment of the militia and the rest of the arrangements. Well, it looks as if we shall have to waste some cords of firewood tonight."

"No bait, no fish," I said. "But I still think we should pull Black Wind in early."

"If you're going to do that, how will you hook Chen Chanao? And we've got to give that one-legged character a chance to use his transmitter."

"What if he finds out that we're prepared and he tells Chen to keep clear of the hook?" I asked with some anxiety.

"All the better if he does. If he knows, he will try his best to get his gang involved. Look at it this way, rats like them don't care a squeak for each other's lives. They're after money and saving their own skins. They'll even sell their own mothers to save themselves. They'll want to drag others in to share their fate. Of course they'll try and get their men involved so as to make good their escape in the ensuing confusion. From what he wrote in the note to Dog you can see he's desperate. He had not dared to strike before, but only attempts now because he knows he's been found out! He's in desperate need of help and that's why he has decided to take action."

CHAPTER 31

THE END OF BLACK WIND

DAY faded and a mist rose out of the sea. I stationed several militia members around the house and Yu-hsiu hid herself in her room to watch the outer room through the tattered door curtain for Black Wind's return. His bed was in the outer room, where he had placed it several days before when violent rains caved in the roof of his thatched shed. Aunt Ta-cheng had moved in to her daughter's room, leaving the outer one vacant for Liu. In order to forestall any suspicion I had left Yu-hsiu's rifle standing by Black Wind's bed. Yu-hsiu was our machine-gunner but as she also did sentry duty she had been issued a rifle too. We did not tell Aunt Ta-cheng what we intended to do, for her quick temper might lead her to betray our secret. I slipped in when she went out to fetch water so she didn't know I was in the house.

When Black Wind did not return, Yu-hsiu said to her mother, "Will you please mend the sleeve of my blouse in the outer room, mother? I'm fagged and I'm going to bed."

She did as Yu-hsiu asked and began mending the sleeve by the light of the lamp in the outer room. All of a sudden she caught sight of the rifle and asked, "Your gun is here. Do you want me to put it in your room?"

"Don't touch it, mother. It's loaded," she said to stop her bringing the rifle in.

Aunt Ta-cheng began to fumble in her work-box to find a piece of cloth to patch the sleeve. She pulled out her dead husband's old jacket and was about to tear a piece off it when she suddenly stopped and hugged it lovingly, then tears sparkled in the lamplight as they rolled down her wrinkled cheeks.

The door opened suddenly and Black Wind entered. He looked very agitated. As soon as he was inside he asked, "Yu-hsiu home?" He paced round and round the room.

"She's asleep," answered Aunt Ta-cheng softly, swiftly wiping away a tear.

Quick as lightning, Black Wind saw her wet face and sensed something was the matter. "Why are you crying? What's the matter?" he asked.

"I was looking for a patch to mend Yu-hsiu's blouse when I came across this jacket of her father's. I was wondering if he could still be alive." And with that she burst into loud lamentation.

The "brother" sat down opposite to her, glanced at the rifle and solicitously asked, "I haven't treated you badly, have I? We haven't had a heart-to-heart talk since the day I arrived, have we, sister?"

"What are you driving at?" asked the bewildered Aunt Ta-cheng.

"We're born of the same father and mother, flesh of the same flesh and blood of the same blood. If I'm in trouble I can count on you, can't I?"

"What are you talking about? I don't follow you. What's the matter with you?" asked the mystified woman, showing genuine concern for her "brother."

"There's nothing the matter with me, but I am worried about you and Yu-hsiu."

"What is all this? We're both well. What reason is there for you to worry about us? If you have anything to say, speak plainly so I can understand. There's nothing to worry or get upset about. We've got the People's Government. What's there to be afraid of?"

"Oh, you are dense, sister. Ta-cheng is still alive!"

Aunt Ta-cheng stopped sewing. "Is that true?" demanded the "sister" in an incredulous tone. Yu-hsiu gripped my hand.

The impostor said, "Now, don't get excited. I'll tell you everything. I was taken at sea with Ta-cheng by the Kuomintang. You know Ta-cheng's temper. He refused to go along with the Kuomintang and they were going to shoot him. I ran to protect Ta-cheng and that's how I lost this leg." The impostor was speaking as if it had really happened.

Aunt Ta-cheng stared in disbelief at this self-styled brother of hers. Why was he lying to her? "But didn't you tell me that you lost that leg during an enemy bombing, when you tried to save a wounded P.L.A. soldier?"

"My dear sister, how stupid you can be at times. Of course I couldn't tell the truth publicly. You listen to me. When Ta-cheng got to Taiwan, he ran into Chen Chan-ao."

"Oh, heavens! Of all the people to meet! How do you know?" asked Aunt Ta-cheng anxiously.

Liu brushed Aunt Ta-cheng's question aside and continued with his tale. "Chen Chan-ao is a big official but when he saw Ta-cheng he let bygones be bygones, and do you know what he did? They had never been close, as you know, but as they both came from the same district and the same ancestral line, he made Ta-cheng his adjutant."

"I don't believe it! My husband wouldn't have agreed. You're making it all up," cried Aunt Ta-cheng.

"Making it all up, you say? Then see if you can recognize this."

Black Wind walked over to his bed and took out a small black bundle from under the pillow. I could not make out what it was because of the dim light in the outer room. Yu-hsiu gave a start and gripped my hands tighter. Aunt Ta-cheng was momentarily dazed. Then she seized the bundle and pressed it to her bosom. Then I saw it was the tobacco pouch that Uncle Ta-cheng had used.

"He's really alive? You've seen him?" she asked, breathing quickly in her excitement.

"Of course he is. He told me to tell you and Yu-hsiu. . . ."

Before he could finish, Aunt Ta-cheng jumped up and, dropping the pouch on the floor, said, "Come. We're going to report this right now."

Taken completely by surprise, Black Wind exclaimed, "Are you mad? If the Communists know that Ta-cheng is an officer with the Kuomintang then you're going to be branded as enemy dependents, you and your daughter! That means jail for you both."

"So, that's the sort of fellow you are! If I hide this from the People's Government then I'm an ingrate! Come with me. Quickly. We'll tell the township government everything."

"But, sister, surely you must consider Ta-cheng! You're man and wife, for better or for worse. Aren't you going to think of him? Don't you want to see him?" The scoundrel saw that Aunt Ta-cheng meant what she said and, sensing what lay ahead for him, tried a final ploy. "If you don't care about your husband, at least think of your own brother and your daughter!"

"If what you say is true then he's no husband of mine. Yu-hsiu would disown him too! If he ever dares to come back with Chen Chan-ao then I'll tell Yu-hsiu to shoot him! That's what I'll do!" Pointing accusingly at him, she demanded, "What sort of brother are you, anyway? Likely as not you're an agent from Taiwan! And I wouldn't put it past you to have killed Ta-cheng!" She hurled the words at him in a loud, fearless voice. This was quite unexpected, for ordinarily she was a woolly-headed woman. She was clear-headed now and could see right through Liu's lies.

Black Wind realized that he had miscalculated. He had thought he could count on her because of her husband and because he posed as her brother and because she would fear being recognized as a dependent of a Kuomintang officer. Then there was her daughter's future. . . . He had been sure she would side with him. Now that his expectations lay dashed before him, he abandoned all pretence and revealed himself for what he was. He seized Yu-hsiu's rifle and, barring the

272

door, threatened her, "So you want to report on me, eh? Too late! The Kuomintang's advance units are about to land on this island!"

I gripped Yu-hsiu's hands and cautioned her to keep quiet, but she tore herself from me and, brushing aside the door curtain, burst into the outer room. . . .

The one-legged Liu, taken unawares, uttered a loud cry and collapsed on the floor by the door. Levelling my pistol at him, I ordered him to put his hands up and surrender. Yu-hsiu recovered her rifle and her mother armed herself with the big brush-cutter. He was covered by two guns, and a sharp knife was ready for him.

This Black Wind, this pirate who once lorded it over people, was cowering by the door like a whipped cur. I ordered him on to the bed and to expose his stump of a leg.

He saw there was no escape and that resistance was useless, but he was still looking for ways to bolt. However, with two guns and a knife pointing at him, and three pairs of hate-filled eyes focussed on him, he decided he had better give up.

He was in a quandary. He had no alternative but to meekly do as I commanded. Like someone painfully skinning himself, he slowly rolled up the leg of his trousers and revealed a transmitter fitted into his stump.

"Your assignment has ended, Black Wind, so hand over that transmitter!"

He suddenly raised his head and looked out the window. The night sky was lit up by the glow of a fire in the direction of the warehouses. A flicker of hope crossed his face and he yelled, "Fire! The warehouses are on fire! Hurry! Put the fire out!"

I replied with a smile, "It's very good of you to be so concerned. The fish has taken the bait and the firewood will not burn for nothing."

Huge beads of sweat stood on his brow as he moaned, "Then this is the end!"

CHAPTER 32

CAUGHT IN THE NET

THE last-quarter moon slid down behind the hills, and as the night took on a deeper hue the fire by the warehouses seemed to leap higher and light up a greater expanse of the sky.

I handed Black Wind over to a couple of our militia members and hurried over to Gourd Bay. I found our militia positioned high up among the rocks on both sides of the bay as instructed by Secretary Fang and Uncle Shuang-ho. They wore dark clothing and had small white towels tied round their left arms. Their rifles were trained on the sinister black shapes, the shoals, out in the bay. They were ready to greet our "visitors." A dozen sampans had been alerted to cut off the enemy's retreat.

Numerous people, armed with sculls, fishing harpoons, brush-cutters and various other sharp weapons were deployed near the mouth of the cove behind the militia. Hai-hua's crippled father was there with a hank of stout rope. He waved it as I came up. "I'm going to truss up some of those sons-of-bitches!" he vowed, his face flaming with hatred.

"Hey, what're you doing here?" exclaimed Liu Chi-wu when Granddad Wang-fa flopped down beside him, a spear in his hand. "Get back, granddad. Let us handle this."

"Quiet, you! I'm not going to be left out of this event! Tell me, where's your commander? I want to speak to Hai-hsia."

"Keep your voices down!" cautioned a militia man. "Do you want to give away our positions?"

I went up to the elderly man and said, "You must move back out of here, granddad. You're not supposed to be here. Get back."

He protested, "I'm not going to the rear."

"I'm not asking you to go to the rear. I'm only asking you to move back a bit."

"Well, I'm not budging. I'm not moving back one step. I'm going to run this spear through a few of those sneak attackers!"

Secretary Fang came and overhearing his last remark said, "Good for you, uncle! Here's something important I want you to do for me. Will you go and man one of those sampans? I want you to help cut off the enemy's retreat."

The old man sprang to his feet and ran to where the sampans were tied up.

The time passed very very slowly, and I grew impatient, wondering, will the enemy make his appearance tonight? Has Black Wind played another of his tricks on us?

As if he had read my thoughts, Secretary Fang said, "Intelligence reports that the enemy has left the American warships and is heading in this direction aboard a local boat."

"Army intelligence? Does the P.L.A. know that?" My relief was reflected in my voice.

"Yes. The P.L.A. knows all right. I've just had a call from regimental headquarters to say they've taken steps to cut off the enemy's retreat. The P.L.A. asked if there was anything they could do to help us. I thanked them and told them that it was essential for them to close the trap out at sea, and that was all the help we would require in this operation. The Concord militia is quite capable of dealing with these 'visitors.' We don't shoot sparrows with artillery!"

"How many of the enemy are coming?"

"Thirty at the most. That's all their motorized junk will hold."

I laughed and said, "Not even enough for a decent mouthful!"

"Now, don't go forgetting Chairman Mao's teaching, Hai-hsia. We slight the enemy strategically, but tactically we must pay them the utmost attention," Secretary Fang advised, knowing that I hadn't lost my head but believing a word of caution is never wasted. "We must treat a weak enemy as if he were a powerful one. These are a desperate bunch we're dealing with. They've all been through U.S.-Chiang schools and are trained agents in subversion. They're a thoroughly hardened reactionary lot. We could come a mighty cropper if we are the least bit careless."

The fire by the warehouses was dying down and I could sense the rising impatience of the militia members. Suddenly the dark moving shape of a man was seen rising out of the foaming white billows. Hai-hua covered him and challenged, "Hands up! I've got you covered! Who are you?"

The dark wet shadow hesitated a second, then quickly dived under water. Liu Chi-wu plunged in right after him. There was a brief struggle before Chi-wu emerged from the water grasping a man tightly.

The drenched stranger fell to his knees when he saw our guns levelled on him. He grovelled in the sand pleading, "Spare me! Spare me! I was forced into this. I'm one of the fishermen they kidnapped!"

"How many of you are there? And where are the rest?" Secretary Fang demanded curtly.

"I'll tell you everything, officer. Everything. I don't want to work for them. I want to go home."

Briefly, this was his story. After Chen Chan-ao was put in charge of the detachment, he led his men, twenty-seven all told, aboard an American warship moored off Concord. There they waited for Agent 301's signal to attack, Agent 301 being Black Wind's code name. Concord had been selected because they learned that there was no P.L.A. unit stationed on the island and thought it would be a push-over. Black Wind's message had been received that afternoon, and the attack was planned to take place after dark.

Their American advisors wined and dined them. At sunset they were transferred to a local motorized junk and made their way to Tiger-Head Isle. The crafty Chen Chan-ao had decided to make doubly sure and sent a swimmer to scout out the situation. Men asked to do this job made excuses one after the other, pleading they were unfamiliar with the terrain. At last Chen Chan-ao decided to send Chang Ah-ping, a former resident at Half Screen. This fellow had been kidnapped with Chen Ta-cheng, and Chen Chan-ao had spent a lot of time working on him, wheedling, coaxing, bribing, threatening and fooling him into joining their gang.

The problem now was what to do with him. Send him back or lock him up? Secretary Fang was not decided. If he did not return, then Chen Chan-ao would realize something was wrong and not try a landing. If we let him go back he might blow the gaff and they'd all escape.

Finally Secretary Fang made up his mind to take a chance and let the fellow go. "You tell me that you used to be a fisherman. If that's so then you know who exploited and oppressed you in the past. Those despots, pirates and Kuomintang bandits! You ought to know why you should not do their dirty work for them. If you want to go home to your family, you can. That's up to you. You'll get lenient treatment if you repent your evil ways and prove it by your deeds. You can make a start right now by returning to Chen Chan-ao and telling him that everyone is away fighting the fire and there's not one militia man left guarding the bay. Tell him also that his former steward is waiting for him at the beach."

"Yes, yes. I'll do that," Chang Ah-ping complied with much bowing and nodding.

"Don't try to pull any tricks! You're trapped and none of you can get out of it. Either you'll get shot or you surrender, there's no third choice. Get me? If you really want to rejoin your family then you had better do as we say. The govern-

277

ment will be lenient with you if you carry out our instructions. Understand?"

"I promise to do everything you have said. Just remember my name's Chang Ah-ping." He dived back into the water and was gone.

"Hai-hsia," said Secretary Fang as soon as the man was out of sight, "we've got to make a slight change in our plan. We can't wait for Chen Chan-ao here. That dog is cunning. He won't land even if Chang Ah-ping does all that we asked, not unless he sees agent 301 for himself. He could have sent people to follow Chang to check his movements. If that's what he's done then he'll know we're waiting for him and he'd leave. We've got to be prepared for that eventuality, so you take two platoons in sampans and go behind Tiger-Head. I'll stay here with Platoon Two to guard the island. We're not going to let them get off the hook if we can help it."

It took us less than five minutes to get ready.

Before we shoved off, Secretary Fang gave us a parting word of advice. This veteran of many battles said, "Take good care. Be extra careful, for this is a night operation. They're well hidden and you're out in the open. They've got the elevation while you're out exposed on the open sea. Don't try anything rash. Don't be afraid to wait for your opportunity. Wait for the chance and then seize it. Once you start to close the trap they won't get away. Start shooting whenever it suits you but make sure you've picked the right moment. Attack when and where it suits us."

Our little flotilla of twelve sampans moved silently. Yu-hsiu had mounted her machine-gun on the prow of the sampan I was in. Granddads Wang-fa and Teh-shun sculled for two other sampans. The training exercise we had carried out previously now stood us in good stead. As we converged on the little cluster of rocks I passed word down the line to look out for places to steady themselves and provide cover, and for everyone to keep her eyes peeled for any sign of the enemy.

My plan was to wait for daybreak and then attack if the enemy had not descended the crest. That would minimize the number of our casualties. If they tried to get back on their boat that would make it all the better. We'd have them all bottled up ready to pick off from the sea.

Our sampan, the nearest to the little island, came to rest in a shallow, and Yu-hsiu steadied her machine-gun. We could make out a cluster of dark shadows in a hollow. It was the enemy about to leave for their boat. The wind was blowing in our direction, and we heard them quite distinctly.

"Shall I give them a burst?" asked Yu-hsiu.

"No. Wait. Let them get aboard first."

"You dog! Trying to put a fast one over me, eh?" came a strange voice. "You thought there was no one on your tail? I had someone following you!" It was Chen Chan-ao bawling out Chang Ah-ping. Secretary Fang was right.

"It's the truth, so take it or leave it," Chang flung back at Chen.

"Take us out to sea and I'll forget everything." Chen Chan-ao was trying to slip off the hook he found himself on.

"You won't get me to do that," replied Chang.

"If you refuse I'll have you shot!" Chen Chan-ao yelled.

"You can't do that, chief," interceded one of Chen Chan-ao's men. "He's the only one who knows these waters. We can't get out of here without him. The whole damned place is ragged with rocks."

Chang Ah-ping was suddenly heard to say: "All right. All right. I'll take you out of here."

Chen Chan-ao shouted to his men, "Brothers, we've been spotted and the militia has been put on the alert. We've got to get back on board and make a run for it."

They all made a headlong rush for the boat and then we heard the motor rev up.

"Hold your fire until they come a bit closer," I instructed Yu-hsiu.

We then saw the junk suddenly veer to one side and heard loud noises of the rending apart of timbers and of men shouting. The boat had run onto submerged rocks. We saw the bandits leaping into the water.

Before I had a chance to give the order, Yu-hsiu opened up with a withering fire. Tracer bullet trails zipped through the air and the other sampans opened fire on the bandits. The sound of crackling rifle shots merged with the rattle of automatic gunfire into a thundering hammering roar.

We saw a black mass floating towards our little boat. I was about to take a shot at it when I heard someone yell: "It's me! Don't shoot. It's me, Chang Ah-ping! I surrender. I'll make up for the crimes I've committed."

We brought our sampan closer to the struggling mass in the water. It was hard to distinguish what was what, for Chang was locked in struggle with one of the bandits. We dragged the two aboard. Chang lay prostrate at the bottom of the boat, badly cut up by the bandit. We heard him say in a weak voice: "I . . . I want to atone for my crimes. I want to go home."

The bandit we had fished out of the water was retching badly, spewing out sea-water and pretending to be worse off than he actually was. From the wounds inflicted on Chang it was easy to surmise that this was a desperate character, fierce and stubborn, so we bound him up securely. Why should we worry how much sea-water he had swallowed!

With the dawn light came and the battle was over.

Sister Ah-hung was disappointed. "You mean everything is over? Just like that? And they call themselves special agents trained and armed by the U.S. and Chiang! Why, they're just a bunch of softies!"

Tsai-chu chimed in, "Short and sweet, I call it."

"Call this fighting? Why, it's no more than just raking up some mucky scum! I didn't even use up my second belt!" said Yu-hsiu as she checked and cleaned her machine-gun.

I called all the boats together to check on the captives. Twenty-four were accounted for, alive, wounded or dead. This tallied with what Chang and others had told us. So apart from Chen Chan-ao, the chieftain, there were still two unaccounted for. A further check showed that the second in command and the chief of staff had not been taken prisoner. This was strange. Three were missing and all three were heads or petty-heads of the gang. It was unlikely that they had escaped out to sea and there were no bodies floating around.

Then I realized what had happened. They had not boarded the junk with the others. Chen Chan-ao had learned from the agent who had tailed Chang and returned with him that the militia had been alerted. The brigands had realized that it was impossible for them to escape by sea and had stayed behind, abandoning the junk to effect their own escape, much as a lizard discards its tail to distract its enemy. No wonder they had shouted and bullied the others to scramble aboard! But where had they disappeared to?

By this time the sun was up in the sky. A light mist still hung over the sea and the air smelt of gun-powder. I issued instructions for the next move. Platoon Three, the men's platoon, was ordered to search every nook and cranny above the water line because they were the better swimmers. I took Platoon One to scour the crest. I was about to send the prisoners away with one squad when Secretary Fang and Uncle Shuang-ho and Platoon Two turned up accompanied by a horde of people aboard assorted craft. I handed the prisoners over to them and led Platoons One and Two on a search-and-find operation. We were to comb Tiger-Head Hill for the missing enemies. Everyone's morale was very high, so I cautioned, "Let no one drop his guard. There are only three of them but they are the wiliest and the most stubborn. Casualties are unavoidable in fighting to win a battle but I don't want casualties caused by carelessness! Start operations by the combat team!"

A militia man asked, "You want them dead or alive?"

"Alive if you can manage it."

"What if they won't surrender?"

"Then wipe them out!" I shouted, bringing my fist down with a thump. "Make the best use of the terrain! Let's get going!"

The morning mist was now lifting and the top of the hill could be seen glowing rosily. The hill was not a big one but climbing it was a highly hazardous venture. Strangely shaped rocks jutted out of the earth, or lay sprawled in tangles, and spears of barbed wild grass flourished abundantly in the cracks and spaces between them. There was no path and every step had to be taken with caution. Our hands and the soles of our feet were soon bleeding, gashed by the spiked grass which was everywhere. However, no one paid much attention to such details, for all our thoughts were concentrated on wiping out the enemy.

The grass was trampled down in several places close to the hill-top and I knew that the enemy had been there. I took cover behind a largish rock and carefully surveyed the scene. It was an ideal spot for a sniper.

Sister Ah-hung was climbing for the crest, gun in hand, when she shouted, "I've discovered a cave, Hai-hsia!"

I shouted, "Keep away from the opening!" and rapidly clambered towards her. I could hear our militia girls searching a little lower down.

I got closer to Sister Ah-hung. She had positioned herself to the left of the mouth of the cave where the grass lay flattened. I was positive that the enemy had gone to earth inside the cave.

I calmly announced, "We've got you surrounded, Chen Chan-ao, so come on out with your hands above your head! If you don't come out, we'll blow you to bits inside!"

There was no reply. Not the slightest movement could be heard.

"Don't waste your breath on those sneaky curs. Let me lob one in and finish them off," offered Sister Ah-hung, raising a grenade aloft. The very moment she exposed herself there was a burst of automatic fire from the cave. The bullets splintered pieces of rock near where she stood. I fired twice in rapid succession as Sister Ah-hung fell. I thought she was wounded and as I was about to rush over I saw her lob a grenade arcing through the air towards the mouth of the cave. She had feinted injury in order to get the enemy to expose himself. The impetuous hothead was using her brain! The grenade landed near the mouth of the cave and exploded.

A stream of bullets poured out from the cave. We were dealing with a very stubborn enemy. I saw red and hurled a grenade plumb inside the cave. The enemy was silenced. Sister Ah-hung tossed a couple more grenades inside through the acrid, dense smoke issuing from the cave.

Suddenly one of the enemy came hurtling out, like a torch aflame. Sister Ah-hung ran over to trap him. He pointed his pistol at her. I lunged with my bayonet and sent his pistol flying.

Quick as lightning Sister Ah-hung clubbed him with her rifle butt and was about to bring it down again when there were cries of "Spare me! Spare me! I give up!" He rolled over and fell on his knees. It was Chen Chan-ao!

"Tell them to surrender!" I ordered.

"No . . . no need. No need to," the bloodied burnt bundle stammered. "They're all dead!"

"That's what all their like deserve!" said I.

Sister Ah-hung wasn't taking any risks. Her grenades all gone, she took one of mine and pitched it into the cave. In the silence that followed the explosion we searched and found two battered bodies.

I ordered our prisoner to move on. My bayonet directed at him, I said, "Agent 301 is waiting for you over at Concord!"

Head hanging low, Chen Chan-ao stumbled ahead.

The sun hung red in the sky surrounded by fiery pennants of clouds, like the multi-coloured bunting of victory. The waters lapping the shore seemed to sing and ripple with laughter.

We marched our bag of running-dogs reared by the U.S.-Chiang reactionaries up the beach. There the despot was reunited with Black Wind and Mr. Steward to await sentencing and punishment by a people's court.

The angry crowd surged up to Chen and shouted curses.

"We've been looking for you for a mighty long time, Chen Chan-ao!"

"And today he's delivered himself to us!"

"You've had your day of dirty deeds! Not even Black Wind can save you now!"

Chen Chan-ao, the vaunted chief of the "advance column," stood shaking from head to foot before the people, his bloated head hung low above his big paunch, his jowls quivering like those of an overstuffed sow's. His clothes hung in scorched tatters.

Black Wind followed behind, hobbling along with the aid of his crutch. His hideous face was the colour of wood ash. After him shuffled the other desperadoes reared by the U.S.-Chiang reactionaries.

On both sides of the line of prisoners were the militia with rifles at the ready and many of them weighed down with captured weapons. They were wreathed in smiles and marched firmly and triumphantly.

As he marched Secretary Fang quoted Chairman Mao, saying, "**All reactionaries are paper tigers.** These fellows came to dash their heads against the people's wall of bronze, or were they merely mayflies trying to topple the giant tree?"

After the battle Uncle Shuang-ho said to Secretary Fang, "It's been like waking up after a dream. I've been with the revolution for years and to think that I've been acting as a shelter for these enemies through being woolly-headed and lowering my guard. I am real sorry."

"If you realize that, then it's all right," answered Secretary Fang solemnly. "In peace-time we are liable to let our ideological defences get somewhat slack and forget about the class enemy. We've got to pay attention to production, but it's more important that we pay attention to revolution and class struggle." He glanced at the silent Uncle Shuang-ho and went on, "We've wiped out this bunch of class enemies but the enemy won't give up. Who knows, one day they may make another try. There'll be other Chen Chan-aos. . . ."

I drank in his words, for although it was a conversation between the two of them, it was something which I felt I must pay attention to and learn well.

We saw Chen Hsiao-yuan hurrying towards us almost breathless. "Here is the reply from Huian Township in Fukien. . . ."

I read aloud, "As to your inquiry about a one-legged man named Liu Ah-tai, we have no knowledge of such a person in our township. . . ."

Chen Hsiao-yuan shifted uneasily when he heard this and was torn between wanting to run away and staying with us.

I said to him, "Comrade Hsiao-yuan, let this be a lesson to you. The consequences of your action could have been very serious, but luckily we've come off without anyone getting hurt badly." I saw that he was terribly upset but I pressed ahead. "We must be strict and conscientious in revolutionary work. We cannot afford any loopholes which the enemy can make use of."

"I won't forget it, ever," he said, lowering his gaze. "I know I've been a big help to the enemy and proved unworthy of the Party that taught and brought me up. I'll write out a self-criticism tomorrow asking the leadership to decide my punishment."

Secretary Fang and Uncle Shuang-ho watched the whole incident without a word. Uncle Shuang-ho's brows bunched up but he made no move. Then Secretary Fang said, "Comrade Hsiao-yuan, meting out punishment is easy but to really understand your error will be more difficult. Leave the question of punishment for the time being and think over what Chairman Mao has taught us. Your first step is to get down to the root cause, the ideological roots of your error!"

CHAPTER 33

READY IN BATTLE ARRAY

THE day we wiped out the armed bandits Aunt Ta-cheng and Yu-hsiu came to seek news of Ta-cheng. Was Ta-cheng still alive? And what had he to do with Black Wind? How did Black Wind come to know so much about Aunt Ta-cheng and her family? And how did Ta-cheng's tobacco pouch get into his hands?

On interrogating Chen Chan-ao and Black Wind, we found out everything. It happened as follows.

After Concord was liberated, Chen Chan-ao stayed on the island and worked out a scheme with Dog for the latter to worm his way into the confidence of the government and people and carry out sabotage. If Chen Chan-ao was arrested, then Dog was to pretend that he had turned on Chen Chan-ao and make Chen take all the blame for their crimes. This was why Dog got up at the big accusation meeting and "exposed" Chen Chan-ao. Actually, what he told the meeting were things everybody already knew — such as the store under the rockery and so on. In this way Dog earned himself a new cover and he wasn't arrested but left free to move around.

Black Wind was hiding out at Tiger-Head Isle at that time and it was Dog who had sneaked out on a stormy night to lead Black Wind in and take Chen Chan-ao and his family away. Dog had wanted to go away with them but Chen Chan-ao ordered him to stay behind as he had already lulled the suspicions of the people and misled them into thinking that he had turned over a new leaf. He was instructed to stay under cover, like a hidden deferred-action bomb, and wait for a chance to "explode." The night they came and effected Chen Chan-ao's escape our soldiers had rushed down to the beach to try and stop them. They got there a little late and all they could do was fire at the fleeing gang. A few bandits were killed and Black Wind was wounded in the leg. Later, the leg was amputated.

With the support of the U.S. imperialists the Chiang bandit gang holed up in our Taiwan Province and rounded up some runaway landlords, despots, pirates and other scum and started a training centre for agents to harass the mainland. Black Wind was specially singled out by them for his past. He was no ordinary thug, but a hardened criminal, cruel, fierce, wily, as slippery as an eel and with a good knowledge of the sea. True, he was an amputee, but what would have put many out of the running as an armed bandit proved useful to him. His stump provided an ideal place to conceal a radio transmitter. After training he was sent to Concord Island under the guise of a fisherman.

The enemy knew that this would not be easy to accomplish, so they first had to provide him with a new identity and a safe base of operation. The cunning bandit decided to search among the fishermen they had seized for an identity which he could safely assume.

Black Wind was planted among the fishermen as one of themselves and it was spread about that he had lost his leg to the Chiang bandits. This, of course, aroused the sympathy of the kidnapped fishermen. He later told them that the Chiang bandits were going to let him go back to the mainland as he was of no use to them as a soldier. He asked his "fellow victims" if they had any messages he could pass on when he got back home, presumably doing them a great kindness. The fishermen told him everything about themselves and he promised that he would be sure to look up their families and pass on

287

their messages. Chen Ta-cheng had survived the incident at sea and had been captured and taken to Taiwan along with the other fishermen.

After Black Wind had learned all he required from the fishermen he decided that Chen Ta-cheng would best serve his purpose and concentrated on him. Chen Ta-cheng was an honest bluff fisherman without a trace of wile in him so he was easily taken in. He told his new "friend" everything about his home and family. Black Wind asked him for a written message to take back and, as he could not write, Chen Ta-cheng gave Black Wind the precious tobacco pouch which his wife had sewn for him.

When Black Wind had everything prepared he dropped his guise and together with Chen Chan-ao tried with threats and enticement to persuade Chen Ta-cheng to join their gang. Ta-cheng flew into a rage when he saw he had been deceived and tried to get his tobacco pouch back. Black Wind plunged his knife into Chen Ta-cheng's chest, yelling, "You're of no more use to us! Take that!"

Black Wind forged identity papers for the role he had created for himself in accordance with the information he had wormed out of Chen Ta-cheng. Then slipping aboard a fishing boat heading north to the fishing grounds, he transferred onto one from East Beach. He thus finally made his way to Concord where he immediately got in touch with Dog. The first letter we sent to Fukien fell into Dog's hands and he turned it over to Black Wind. They were not very much upset by its content. They reckoned that by the time we sent off a second letter and got a reply at least a fortnight would have passed, and that was all the time they needed to accomplish their nefarious scheme.

They had thought of making use of the opportunity afforded when Sister Ah-hung fell and hurt herself to launch an attack on the island. We foiled that scheme when we reinforced our militia work and did not let the "accident" and the confusion slacken our efforts. When their scheme to attack the island was unexpectedly frustrated, Black Wind was ordered by his chief to gather military intelligence and bide his time to escape.

My chance encounter with Black Wind on East Beach put him on his guard, and when we searched his barber's kit the following day he was very shaken and decided to make his getaway. He knew we now had him under close observation and it would be impossible for him to escape. So he hatched a scheme to get away by calling the bandits to attack from the sea and in the ensuing chaos hoped to slip away. He ordered Dog to set the warehouses on fire that night while he radioed Chen Chan-ao to attack.

Even after he had despatched his message he was still not at ease. He was afraid Chen Chan-ao might not make it in time or even get ashore or, in case his friends did manage to land, he still might not be able to get away. So he worked out yet another plan. He would try to blackmail Aunt Ta-cheng and her daughter to side with him and help him under threats of informing the government that Chen Ta-cheng had collaborated with him.

There was a huge victory celebration the third day after the battle. The air was filled with the sound of bursting firecrackers and the din of clashing gongs and cymbals. The islanders came dressed in their very best as on a festival.

Granddad Wang-fa sat in the front row with all those who had taken part in the fighting. A huge red flower was pinned on the chest of each one of them to the loud applause of all. Secretary Fang addressed the meeting. He urged the militia to continue to maintain their high vigilance and strive to win new victories and be sure to wipe out all who dared to invade.

A big red banner with the words "Wall of Bronze" embroidered on it was presented to us by the military sub-area.

Everyone was happy and went about with a smile. The biggest scourge of the island, Chen Chan-ao, was put under lock and key and Black Wind was now just a bad smell. Of course everyone was happy! Their smiling faces and animated, carefree chatter showed this. I saw behind the laughter and relaxed

289

mood a lowering of vigilance against attacks from the Chiang gang ensconced on Taiwan Island and the U.S. imperialists. The enemy before us was receding and soon people would be lulled into a false sense of security and begin to think there were no more enemies around.

At the end of the celebrations I went up to Uncle Shuang-ho and said to him, "I want to call another emergency muster tonight."

"Good for you. I'm all for it," he replied. "Our militia has passed the test of war with flying colours. Let us now see if they will pass the test of peace equally well." Then in a quiet and frank tone he said to me, "You plan much ahead of me and can delve more deeply into things than I can. You've grown up a lot, Hai-hsia. You're much abler than I am although I'm much older than you in years and took part in the revolution earlier than you. I've fallen behind, but I'll try hard to catch up with you."

I was moved by his words and very happy to see that he too had progressed and was much more politically conscious. This led me to think of my own shortcomings. I said, "Don't say that, Uncle Shuang-ho. I've got a lot to learn from you. As long as we follow Chairman Mao's teachings, I'm sure we'll both make continual progress under the Party's guidance."

I rose at midnight and taking the conch made my way to the big banyan tree. The moon was high in the sky. There was still a nip in the air although it was already summer. The beach was white as if covered by frost and the billows washing up the sand shimmered as though of silver. There was a deep nocturnal silence over the island. But our people were on the alert. One blast of the conch and the whole island would leap to life.

The weather at this time of the year is known to be fickle on our island. A sudden wind is liable to spring up and rain lash down from what was a cloudless sky a moment before, and stop just as suddenly. As I neared the banyan tree, a thunderhead rose swiftly from behind the hills to the southeast.

It grew larger and larger until it covered the strait and seemed to be creeping quickly over the waves. Soon the stars were blotted out and the moon was lost behind it. The island was enveloped in darkness. Then there was a bluish flash, followed by a crash of thunder which reverberated over my head. A fierce gust of wind whipped the salt spray into my face. The trees and grass moaned and soughed and the waves mounted the beach like angry animals. Sea, land and sky merged into one. A blinding flash of lightning lit up the village and there was another mighty clap of thunder directly overhead. Big raindrops slashed down, growing larger and larger till they became a pounding, continuous torrent. I raised the conch to my lips and blew with all my strength.

The booming hoot of the conch rose above the noise of the wind and rain, sped through the night into every house on the island, into the hearts of the people.

The militia members came flying through the wind-whipped rain to assemble under the banyan tree. Uncle Shuang-ho was soon there with his old Mauser slung on a strap over his shoulder.

We fell into formation quickly and found that only a few were missing, among them Chen Hsiao-yuan, who only the previous night had written a self-criticism. Scouts went out to round up the missing ones.

One of the late arrivals demanded, "What's the idea of calling a muster tonight? There's no more fighting now, is there?"

He sounded as if he had a real grievance but was quickly silenced by a chorus of "Do you belong to the militia or don't you?"

I was very pleased to hear this response.

The last arrival was none other than Chen Hsiao-yuan. He was challenged by Uncle Shuang-ho's "Why are you late?"

He muttered, "I went to bed late. I had stayed up reading. Didn't hear the conch. Besides, we've wiped out all the enemy so how can you expect anyone to be ready for a muster?"

"What were you reading?" Uncle Shuang-ho asked.

"What you told me to read. Fishing and farming."

"Reading books on production is necessary, but don't forget politics. You should read more of Chairman Mao's writings. Remember that!"

He looked with amazement at Uncle Shuang-ho. "I don't remember you telling me that before!"

"I was wrong before, but I've woken up now," retorted Uncle Shuang-ho. "Now get into line!"

The lad fell into place without another word.

The rain was coming down hard so Uncle Shuang-ho asked me to lead the militia into the oyster shed where Black Wind once plied his trade.

Once inside he asked, "Why have we all been called out on such a night?"

Sister Ah-hung quickly replied, "To test our vigilance and our preparedness!"

"But Chen Chan-ao, Black Wind and their gang have been wiped out! What fighting have we to be prepared for?" I asked.

They looked at each other, puzzled.

"You tell us," asked Chen Hsiao-yuan. "Chen Chan-ao, Black Wind and their gang have been wiped out by us, so who's going to attack us?"

Tsai-chu snapped, "You're wrong there. The guns in our hands are not just to fight a few bandits like them! We've cleaned up that bunch but that's not to say there won't be any more like them. Anyway, don't forget those imperialists!"

The girl had hit the nail right on the head. Good for her! You should have seen Chen Hsiao-yuan's face! We were all surprised, too, at the way she spoke out and contradicted him. She had made a lot of progress in a very short time. I felt I wanted to hug her.

Chen Hsiao-yuan kept his eyes on the ground.

"Tsai-chu is dead right. We must be prepared every minute to fight while imperialism is around."

I dismissed the militia. Chen Hsiao-yuan came up to me and said repentfully and sincerely, "Company Commander Hai-hsia, I've also read Chairman Mao's works, and I've heard those reports about militia work, too, but I never can remember them. . . ."

"That's just the problem," I told him. "Why can't you remember? Comrade, it is not a question of remembering words but a case of having the idea of class struggle always in mind. If you remember class struggle and keep it in mind then every word will be impressed into your heart. If you don't, then it is as you said. You'll never be able to remember. You study to guide your actions, to do as Chairman Mao teaches us. And you can take an example from Tsai-chu's conduct in this respect."

"All right. I won't write out a self-criticism this time, I'll write out a challenge!"

"Who are you going to challenge?" I persisted, although I knew the answer.

"Er . . . one of the militia members, of course!"

"The one who rebuked you a little earlier? The one who said you were wrong?" I asked laughingly.

He saw my point and said, "That's a military secret."

I was delighted to see the change in him. I think that if anyone were to ask me now about our militia on the island, I would answer without any hesitation, "You can depend on us. If we always do things according to Chairman Mao's instructions, then we militia of Concord will pass any test with flying colours!"

CHAPTER 34

THE END OF THE STORY

E XPRESS No. 13 pulled into the station and my account of
our militia came to an end.

Hsiu-chen, the elderly comrade seated opposite to me, said
after a pause, "Hai-hsia, your story of how your militia unit
grew up proves very clearly the wisdom and greatness of Chairman Mao's thinking on people's war. Chairman Mao has taught
us, **What is a true bastion of iron? It is the masses, the millions
upon millions of people who genuinely and sincerely support
the revolution. That is the real iron bastion which it is impossible, and absolutely impossible, for any force on earth to
smash. The counter-revolution cannot smash us; on the contrary, we shall smash it.**"

The other delegates returning home from the militia conference silently thought over Hsiu-chen's words and in their minds
traversed the fighting path our militia had taken.

The guard blew his whistle. There was an answering hoot
from the engine and our train was off again, taking us swiftly
over the spring-awakened vastness of the motherland.

Very soon I'd be getting out of the train and leaving my
companions to go their separate ways home. I shall tell my
militia all that I have seen and all that I have heard, and I
shall also tell them of my impressions, all that passed through
my mind. I shall tell them all about it.

I reached our beloved Concord the third morning after leaving Peking. Flocks of island gulls hovered and swooped in the golden sunlight high above the myriad sails speeding over the water. I saw our militia girls rushing through the morning haze to greet me.

When they had gathered me into their midst they asked with one voice, "Did you see our great leader Chairman Mao?"

"I did! I did! Chairman Mao shook hands with me!" I loudly proclaimed, almost choking with happiness.

A loud "hurrah" went up from them and they thrust their hands towards me. "Quick, shake my hand!" "Shake mine! Mine!"

Chairman Mao! Your hand has brought happiness to us working people! Your hand it is that guides China's revolution to victory! How happy to shake your hand! I shook hands warmly with every one of our militia girls, eager for them to share my happiness and good fortune.

I described my meeting with our great leader Chairman Mao and told them how fit and well Chairman Mao was. This was greeted with loud cheers and shouts of "Long live Chairman Mao!"

Their happy shouts and ringing cheers re-echoed through the air, from the sea and high hills.

"What went through your mind after you had met Chairman Mao?" asked Yun-hsiang.

"Now, how can I put what I felt and thought into a few words? Of course, meeting with Chairman Mao was supreme happiness for me, an event which I'll never forget. I was so excited and so many thoughts crowded through my mind I couldn't sleep for nights afterwards. I remembered the happiness and the misery, the sweet and the bitter. I recalled the grass roots I had eaten, the tattered rags I wore and the slights and hurts and the blows I had suffered when I was small and poor. And today? Today, I am at the pinnacle of happiness. I leapt there from the abyss of suffering and misery.

"I wanted to run to Chairman Mao and tell him, tell him all the thoughts that welled up in my heart.

"This supreme happiness and greatest honour inspired and encouraged me tremendously and at the same time made me very uneasy, for I knew I did not deserve so much. I recalled the day of liberation, the day I stood before the red flag of the Party and with clenched fist swore that I would work hard to serve the Party and the people.

"Today, I see how very little I really have done, far too little. The love and care the Party gave me is vast as the ocean and the little I have done is but a mere drop in the ocean. I am always thinking how to repay all that the Party has done for me.

"Comrades, what should we do in return for what Chairman Mao and the Party have done for us? We should give our answer in our deeds!"

Hand in hand, we militia women march forward, singing as we go:

> *We're the people's militia,*
> *Red of heart and mind.*
> *Defend the motherland!*
> *Build up the motherland!*
> *Hai! Let us show what we can do.*
>
> *We're good at production,*
> *And no laggards at fighting.*
> *As handy with pen as with rifle,*
> *Everyone a soldier!*
> *Hai! We have immense strength.*

Our voices are strong and militant. Our song rising over the land soars to the skies, skims the sea, stirring heaven and earth. . . .

海 岛 女 民 兵

黎汝青 著

蔡荣 插图

*

外文出版社出版（北京）

1975年（28开）第一版

编号：（英）10050—830

00210

10—E—1360p